Mission and Betrayal, 1940–1945

Mission and Betrayal 1940–1945

WORKING WITH FRANKLIN ROOSEVELT TO HELP SAVE BRITAIN AND EUROPE

René de Chambrun

HOOVER INSTITUTION PRESS
Stanford University   Stanford, California

Originally published as *Ma croisade pour l'Angleterre, Juin 1940,*
© 1992 Librairie Académique Perrin
The Hoover Institution would like to acknowledge the generous support of
the Fondation Josée et René de Chambrun in the publication of this English-
language edition.

Hoover Institution Press Publication 414

First printing, 1993
99 98 97 96 95 94 93   9 8 7 6 5 4 3 2 1
Simultaneous first paperback printing, 1993
99 98 97 96 95 94 93   9 8 7 6 5 4 3 2 1

Manufactured in the United States of America
The paper used in this publication meets the minimum requirements of American
National Standard for Information Sciences—Permanence of Paper for Printed
Library Materials, ANSI Z39.48-1984. ⊗

Library of Congress Cataloging-in-Publication Data
Chambrun, René de, 1906–
  [Ma croisade pour l'Angleterre. English]
  Mission and betrayal, 1940–1945 : working with Franklin Roosevelt
to help save Britain and Europe / René de Chambrun.
      p.   cm.
  Includes index.
  ISBN 0-8179-9221-9 (alk. paper). — ISBN 0-8179-9222-7 (pbk.)
  1. Chambrun, René de, 1906–   2. World War, 1939–1945—
Diplomatic history.   3. Europe—Foreign relations—1919–1945.
4. World War, 1939–1945—Personal narratives, French.   5. Diplomats—
France—Biography.   I. Title.
D748.C4713 1993
940.53′2—dc20   92-35463
                                                             CIP

Contents

*My wife, Josée, took no part in the writing of
these recollections, and it is to her,
who never let me down, that I dedicate them.*

Preface

"MY COUNTRY WILL NEVER FORGET." THOSE WERE THE WORDS OF LORD Lothian, the British ambassador in Washington, on June 18, 1940, to express the gratitude of his government to Captain de Chambrun, then aged thirty-four, who could claim to be "the man of June 17," just as de Gaulle was to become known as the man of June 18, the day on which he made his famous call to all Frenchmen on BBC radio to continue the fight against Germany.

Indeed, on the eve of that call, Chambrun's powers of persuasion and his conviction that the war was not lost because Britain would remain invincible in her island had won the support of President Roosevelt and of the American government, which had been prey to a growing pessimism and tempted to revert to their country's traditional isolationism. They decided to lift the embargo imposed on deliveries of tanks, planes, and antiaircraft guns, ordered by France before the collapse of May 10, and, at Chambrun's insistence, to reship them to the beleaguered British Isles.

Thanks, therefore, to René de Chambrun, the first shipments arrived a few weeks ahead of schedule, and the four thousand antiaircraft guns they included played a decisive role in the Battle of Britain: out of 247 heavy German bombers sent over London on that first night of September 7, 1940, forty-two were shot down.

What was the basis of this young officer's conviction? The striking superiority demonstrated over the Luftwaffe by British fighters in an air battle he had witnessed over the Channel during the evacuation of the British Expeditionary Forces from Dunkerque.

It is a strange paradox of history that made the descendant of Lafayette and the son-in-law of Pierre Laval one of the key instruments of this decisive turning point in the genesis of World War II. Thanks to his family connections with President Roosevelt through his American mother and his close links with all the members of the American "establishment," Chambrun had free access to the White House, to all the levels of the administration, and to press and business circles in New York. Those proved invaluable in his "battle of Britain," which he describes in this book of recollections covering the dramatic events of 1940–1945.

In addition to access and connections, he also had the faith that moves mountains. His account of those events surprises the reader by its sincerity and spontaneity, the more so in that it has no literary pretensions. He refrains from passing judgment on people and events and does not try to draw from them any philosophical conclusions. He is content to remain unshakably loyal to convictions that are and remain entirely his own.

It is possible not to wholly share his opinions, notably on the part played by Pierre Laval during the German occupation of France. But his good faith and the solid evidence that he adduces cannot be impugned and should further pave the way to the abatement of the "Franco-French war" of which Valéry Giscard d'Estaing, the former president, has so often spoken—short of regarding this war as everlasting! In a comment on a remark by Aleksandr Solzhenitsyn—that the real crime of the Soviet regime was to deprive the Russian people of their history—a British critic has written that it was not a case of the absence of history but of its abundance, not of its rediscovery but of its mastery and even of its exorcism. The work of René de Chambrun contributes to this exorcism through the wealth and quality of his documents and his unfailing memory for detail, thanks to the habit, even in the very midst of the upheaval of May 1940, of recording his conversations and impressions at the close of each day and of carefully filing every document, important or otherwise.

Thanks to this self-imposed discipline, readers can relive, almost as if they witnessed it, a forgotten episode of the "phony war," the molelike existence Chambrun—and others—led in the bowels of the Maginot Line, which he gave up with a twinge of regret to become a liaison officer with the British Expeditionary Force shortly before the deluge of fire and steel unleashed by the German offensive. This episode of his military career inspired from pages worthy of the *Silences of Colonel Bramble,* André Maurois's classic about World War I. It is not surprising that Maurois remained one of Chambrun's closest friends.

Thanks to Bullitt, the American ambassador in Paris, Chambrun was entrusted by Paul Reynaud, the French premier, and by Weygand, who shortly before had become commander in chief of the French forces, with a vital mission to Washington designed to speed up deliveries of American weapons to France, already at bay. Chambrun learned of the capitulation of the French army on board the president's yacht during a weekend spent with Roosevelt, Harry Hopkins, and Averell Harriman. Through his unshakable faith in Britain's invincibility, this "special envoy" succeeded in convincing those men that military aid had to be sent to England immediately.

But he also had to enlist the support of the American "grass roots" for whom the war in Europe and the collapse of France were light years away and beyond their understanding. So it was that Chambrun, with Roosevelt's blessing, embarked on a crusade that led him deep into the "prairies," where he preached the good word before rarely hostile but frequently skeptical and occasionally even enthusiastic audiences of trade unionists, farmers, and businessmen.

His frequent visits with some of the main actors of the history of those times made it possible for him to produce stunning portraits of men like Roosevelt (who actually told him that if the French Senate had not voted down Leon Blum, the socialist leader, in 1936, defeat would have been averted in 1940), Pershing, Marshall, Weygand (who wanted to believe a miracle was still possible), Hoover, Hopkins, Cordell Hull, Stimson, and Abetz (the German ambassador to Vichy), not to mention others who have faded from our memories. He also describes at length his impressions of Pétain and of Pierre Laval, who welcomed him to his country home at Châteldon in August 1940 with this disenchanted remark: "I have done everything to avoid this . . . and now we must repair the damage."

There is another battle that Chambrun lost (though the odds were strongly against him) trying to get the United States to dispatch food supplies to unoccupied France. Roosevelt agreed and so did Churchill, but de Gaulle opposed his veto, and the president, manipulated by Hopkins, went back on his word. The intimate friend of Franklin Roosevelt, his most influential adviser, had fallen under the spell of Joseph Stalin and become the leading Soviet agent in the United States, at the head of a crew of agents that included Harry Dexter White and Alger Hiss at the State Department and Henry Morgenthau at the Treasury, the author of the monstrous plan for the "pastoralization" of a defeated Germany that was inspired by the Soviet dictator.

Against it, Cordell Hull, already seriously ill, summoned his last remaining strength and succeeded in getting Roosevelt to rescind it. The struggle killed him. Hopkins's complicity explains why, at Yalta, Stalin was given a free rein in Eastern Europe without anything in return for the Allies.

One likes to imagine what the sequence of events of the last half-century could have been if Hopkins had been the agent of Churchill and if the Allied landings had taken place, as he originally wished, not in Normandy (where fate would have it that I should find myself, slightly bewildered, on the morning of D day) but against the "soft underbelly" of Nazi-occupied Europe.

Chambrun knew too much, which is probably why Hopkins tried to have him shoved aside by the French government after the Liberation. He has written this book, which reads like a novel, because he recently gained access to key documents that had been covered by a fifty-year embargo from the National Archives in Washington and the FBI.

People rarely draw lessons from their past, but American, British, and French readers of good faith, once they have closed this book, will take a different view of events that continue to have consequences to this day.

Charles Hargrove,
former correspondent of *The Times*,
corresponding member of the
Institut de France

Mission and Betrayal, 1940–1945

CHAPTER 1

August 1939: Two gendarmes knock at the door

ON AUGUST 22, 1939, I HAD JUST LEFT MY OFFICE ON THE CHAMPS-Elysées to return home on foot, as I did nearly every evening. Paris seemed practically empty, and I had the impression, during this holiday season, that the city, in a way, belonged to me. The law office I had set up was about to celebrate its fourth anniversary.

It was a modest office, made up of clients who always remained loyal. Mademoiselle Chanel was the first. In becoming her counsel, I got to know all her secrets, and she was soon a great friend. This was also the case with the well-known Spanish painter Jose Maria Sert. I had, that spring, fought two legal battles in Washington against the secretary of war to get him to realize that, at long last, the United States should pay the royalties due to Esnault-Pelterie, the inventor in 1916 of the joystick, and to Raymond Saunier, who developed the ejectable seat a few years later. My argument was as follows: "Since you do not dispute the validity of these two patents, the inventors must receive their due. Otherwise, they and others after them will lose confidence in the United States. They will no longer register their patents in Washington and thus your defense capacity in a next war will be weakened!"

How could I possibly imagine on that day that I was crossing the Seine for the last time and would only return to my office two years later. When I reached home, I found my wife busy with arrangements for the following day, which was my birthday. We had decided to celebrate it by spending a few hours in Deauville, on the Normandy coast. The news from Germany and Poland got worse with each passing day. I was then quite ignorant of the pact between Hitler and Stalin, which was to break upon the world two days later, so I went to sleep without too much concern.

The following morning, I was awakened early by a ring at the door. Outside on the landing were two gendarmes. One of them pulled out of his satchel a call-up order requesting me to join my unit immediately. The other added in a tone of disenchantment, "This may be it." As I read the order over again, I suddenly had the feeling that war was inevitable. I packed a few things and put on my uniform, which reeked of mothballs. When I told Josée I would take a taxi alone, to spare her the pangs of leavetaking at the station, she insisted on driving me there in our little two-seater Hispano.

I asked a porter how long it would take to get to Metz (five hours away in normal times). He said the journey could now last anything between ten and twenty hours. In the overcrowded train, I came upon a few officers whom I had not set eyes on since Saint-Cyr, where, like many university students before the war, I had gone on a reserve officer cadet course. As I had been posted to one of the four regiments manning the Maginot Line, I was part of the French army's "advance guard"; general mobilization was not decreed until two weeks later.

My own marching orders stipulated that I go to Amanvillers, a small village north of Metz and some thirty kilometers behind the Maginot Line. There I reported to my unit, the 162d Fortress Infantry Regiment. The forts of the Maginot Line stretched from Luxembourg to the Swiss border. My regiment was known throughout the area as the "Regiment of the Nied" because all its forts, pillboxes, and dugouts were located southwest of a little river called the Nied, which meandered through the rich rolling fields of Lorraine before flowing into the Saar.

All the reserve officers of the regiment, including myself, were Lorrainers, save one, a Gascon, whose name was Saint-Guily. He liked to recite, in a warm stentorian voice, the rhymes of *Cyrano de Bergerac,* Rostand's famous play. It did not take me long to get to know and like the people of Lorraine, in whose midst we were going to live and fight. The Lorrainer is quiet and hardworking. He stays in his province, is attached to his land, and rarely speaks to "foreigners" from the rest of France, in whom he takes little interest.

All the formalities of the call-up, the kit, and the vaccinations were dispatched with an efficiency that surprised me, used as I was to the less disciplined troops of Central France and the Midi. The officers, NCOs [noncommissioned officers], and men made up the crack units of eastern France, whose ancestors had fought in the First World War in such famous regiments as Sambre et Meuse and the Gunners of Metz, part of the Sixth Army Corps, and the Fortieth and Forty-second Divisions de Fer, the "Divisions of Iron."

When our unit was formed, every man, whether regular or reservist, found his appointed place unhesitatingly in his section, his platoon, or his company, as if he had known from the outset what he should do and when. I felt as if I were on a stage, at a dress rehearsal, before the tragedy of

Europe was about to be performed. The men of the Maginot Line had "rehearsed" the play twice, as they had been called up in March 1938, when Hitler invaded Austria, and six months later, in September 1938, just before the Munich Agreement and the grabbing of Czechoslovakia. Twice before, they had had to leave their homes at only a few hours' notice and assemble at Amanvillers. This explained their feelings of exasperation against Germany and their secret longing that this time would be the one.

At dawn the following day, we moved in column of march in the direction of Metz, along the valley of the Moselle. We had hardly been going an hour, when, in all the glory of the rising sun, the spires of the cathedral appeared through the light mist hanging over the river. When we reached its outskirts, we took the road skirting the town and got to the main highway leading northeast, straight to the German frontier. The ramparts built by Vauban in 1678 to protect France against Germany, and partly destroyed by the Germans after the Franco Prussian War, lined our route. Suddenly, we came face to face with the proud Porte des Allemands, an old fortified gateway with twin towers and a drawbridge spanning the Moselle, a true predecessor of that Maginot Line we were about to defend.

My most vivid memories of that first day on active service are linked to my back and my feet. For years, my only exercise had amounted to short walks in Paris. At the end of the twenty-odd kilometers we marched that day, I had the sorry satisfaction of seeing that my feet were not the only ones to be rather the worse for wear. We had reached the little village of Piblange, where we were to remain about a week, until we began our underground existence. It was here that I really got to know the true soul of Lorraine.

The woman in her eighties, whom I saw as I entered the house where I was to be billeted, looked at me for a long time without rising from her armchair. Her gray hair was gathered under a traditional white headdress, and she wore a shiny black gown. She was seated near the fireplace of a large room that was a sitting room, a dining room, and a kitchen all in one. Her name was typically French: she was called Madame Auburtin. Her daughter, no longer young, and unmarried, acted as interpreter, for her mother spoke only the local Germanic dialect and my German was too sketchy to understand or speak to her. "You must forgive my mother," the daughter said. "She was only ten when the Germans occupied Lorraine, and after that we were forbidden to speak French. When France liberated us in 1918, she was too old to revert to it." She added that the previous year, they had already taken in other officers—a captain and a lieutenant—when "they" had invaded Czechoslovakia. Then she asked me whether I thought they would have to abandon their home. I replied that I did not think so, and this seemed to pacify her.

I had barely taken possession of my room when Mademoiselle Auburtin knocked at the door and gave me a huge bottle of colored glass containing at least one or two liters of spirits. "This brandy is very old," she said. "It was made by my father before the last war. Father was killed in 1916, in Russia, where he had to fight in the German army against his will." She went on to add that "there is a room just under yours. With a few bales of straw on the floor, we could put up a handful of men. My mother would very much like to take them in." I immediately went off to have the billeting order made out.

The twenty officers of the Second Battalion of the 162d Fortress Infantry Regiment were billeted all over the little village, and I was to meet them for the first time that very evening at our mess, which was a few houses away from my own billet. Our commander, Major Louis Cuvillier, presided over it with real authority. He had fought in the 1914–1918 War as an infantry sergeant, second lieutenant, and lieutenant and had been wounded four times. In addition to the infantry officers of the battalion, there were also two gunners, a sapper, and a doctor.

After meeting each one of my fellow officers, I noticed, to my shame, that Saint-Guily and I were the only ones who did not wear the blue and white medal ribbon for Voluntary Service. This was a distinction given to those reserve officers who had volunteered for additional training beyond the regular, brief camps we all had to attend. I understood in a flash that while Saint-Guily and I had been enjoying life, he in the South and I in Paris, all these men of Lorraine had given up far more of their time and energy than we in the service of their country.

The next day was Sunday. I still vividly remember our first mass. The village church was too small for the whole battalion. An altar was built in a wide glade with boards set on four logs. The whole enclosure was surrounded by branches of willow gathered from the trees lining a stream nearby. The priest, who came from a suburb of Metz, was one of the sergeants in our battalion—our regiment included more than twenty priests drafted for regular military service.

His sermon was extremely moving. Facing the battalion commander, all his officers, and practically all the troops, he spoke with a voice of calm resolve, "My dear friends, what we have feared for many years has, it seems, come to pass. We are determined to face up to any danger without fear, with our chins up, for France and for Lorraine. Remember this: there are many things more ghastly than war. One of these is bondage and, with the help of God, we will fight to ensure that our soil remains forever French."[1]

---

[1] I reproduce here his exact words as I noted them down at the time. As the reader will realize, I took many notes during the troubled years that followed.

The news got worse each day, and new contingents of the draft were called up one after the other. The better-off inhabitants of the village, who had a car or a cart and also, more often than not, a place of refuge further south, were making ready to leave. But the others, whose sole possessions were a house and a plot of land—often shared with another family—had no option but to remain and hope for better days, with the slender consolation of being close to their husbands or sons serving underground, nearby on the Maginot Line.

On the evening of September 2d, the commanding officer called together all the platoon commanders of the battalion and read out to them the text of Order X, which he had been instructed by telegram to carry out. Order X provided for the complete evacuation, in four hours, of all the villages located in front of the Maginot Line. There were about twenty in our sector, and a lieutenant was put in charge of each. The commanding officer gave me the task of carrying out the order in Gomelange, a hamlet of 318 inhabitants, just south of the Nied.

The first door on which I knocked was the modest home of the mayor. Like practically all the villagers, he was a farmer who had served in the infantry in World War I. He had been wounded several times.

He appeared with a coat thrown over his shoulders and a candle in one hand. "So they are coming; we must leave," he said before I had even apologized for waking him up in the dead of night. "How much time do we have to get ready?" "A little more than three hours," I replied, "Can we take our carts and perhaps some cattle?" "No, I am terribly sorry. The orders are very strict. The inhabitants can only take what they can carry." I added that, within the next two hours, a big cart driven by a gunner with two horses would arrive and take those too old to walk and their belongings as far as Amanvillers. "So be it, we have no time to lose," the mayor concluded. And as he put on his wooden clogs, he added, "We are going to wake up the *garde-champêtre*[2] and ask the curé to ring the church bell."

One of the corporals in the regiment took his bugle and sounded the call to evacuate, while the church bell tolled.

All the inhabitants learned that they were to leave their homes as rapidly as if the whole village were on fire. With the mayor, his assistant, my sergeant, the corporal, and my few men, we were to tell all these poor people that they had only a few hours to gather up their belongings and might take only what they could carry on their shoulders. Very few complained. Some said they had had the feeling that this was bound to happen. Others asked as if I could read in the stars whether they would be able to

---

[2]Village policeman.

return. As I answered hesitatingly, "Soon I believe," I thought my words gave them some solace.

Anxious mothers and fathers, forgetting that there were more than fifteen thousand men on the Maginot Line and that I only knew a few dozen, asked me if I had seen their sons, who had left for the army a few days before. A four- or five-year-old boy, who recognized in the darkness one of the men with me, exclaimed, *"C'est Papa!"* and threw himself into his arms. The old farmer who acted as the mayor's assistant said, "After all, now that our fields are to be flooded, we might as well leave. There's nothing more for us to do here and the sooner we go the better because I don't want to see our fields disappear under water."

As daylight started to appear, the slow march into exile began.

In 1870, Gomelange was partly destroyed during the German advance into Lorraine. From 1870 to 1914, the inhabitants, who had rebuilt their village, lived under German occupation but did not give up the hope of becoming French once again. In 1914, the men had no choice but to serve in the German army, against the cause that was dear to their hearts, or face a firing squad. In 1918, American and French troops, fighting side by side, liberated that part of Lorraine and the old town of Metz, from which Lafayette, at the age of nineteen, had fled from his regiment, the Dragons de Noailles, and volunteered to fight for American independence.

Then came the Versailles Treaty, and the inhabitants of Gomelange were again called upon to make the further sacrifices required for building the Maginot Line. Many had to give up their land, sometimes with little compensation, but they never expressed the slightest recrimination. I could not help but think back on their tragic destiny as I saw them walk off, bent under the weight of their bundles, the oldest among them, who had lived through all these vagaries of fortune, abandoning Gomelange once again without a murmur or a tear.

During the long five years of the war, I saw many atrocities and much suffering, but nothing moved me so deeply as the heartrending sadness of the evacuation of Gomelange.

At dawn that same day, I returned to Piblange and Madame Auburtin's house, where I tried with difficulty to get some sleep, but I kept thinking of all those poor people trudging along the roads in the half-light. A few hours later, Mademoiselle Auburtin knocked at my door and said, *"Mon Lieutenant, c'est encore la guerre."*[3]

---

[3]"It's war again."

CHAPTER 2
Life underground
on the Maginot Line

My ONLY EXPERIENCE OF LIVING LIKE A MOLE HAD BEEN ACQUIRED ON THE New York subway, between Grand Central Station and Wall Street. So September 4 did not find me particularly well prepared for a new life in Rotherberg Fort, where I was to remain for three months 150 feet below ground, under layers of earth, concrete, and steel.

The fortifications of the Maginot Line were divided into six categories to take advantage of the lie of the land. Those of the first category were manned by about one thousand men, their turrets equipped with light and heavy artillery and mortars. Those of the fourth category, like Rotherberg Fort, were manned by a company of infantry equipped with antitank guns, infantry mortars, and double-barreled machine guns. My fort was commanded by Major Cuvillier, who had presided over our mess at Piblange. In addition to two captains, Lieutenants Saint-Guily, Bentz, Billet, myself, and the doctor, he had under his orders about twenty NCOs and 140 men. Saint-Guily and I were the only ones with no experience of this anthill existence, as all our recent military training had been in the sunny camps of the Midi.

The Rotherberg was located underneath a small wood, at a depth of around two hundred feet. I walked down the 140 steps that led to the central gallery, and after wandering for about ten minutes through numerous corridors, I found the small low-ceilinged cubicle that was to be home during my service underground. I was to share it with Lieutenant Bentz. There was just about enough room for two mattresses, which were our beds, and a wardrobe built of steel in order to protect our belongings from the all-pervading dampness. "Just imagine that you are a monk in the Middle Ages," Bentz remarked jokingly on the day of our arrival. And every morning, in the spirit of his remark, he would ask me in a pious tone of voice, "Dear brother, have you slept well?"

The first few days, my reply was decidedly negative. The diesel engines of the air-conditioning machines were only switched on three times a day, for a total of eight hours. During that time, one could breathe almost normally, read, and write. But unfortunately, every night at ten P.M., the shrill blast of the whistle of the engineer officer on duty resounded through the galleries, the huge dynamos ground slowly to a halt, and the lights grew gradually dimmer until we were plunged in complete darkness. The vibration of the walls ceased in turn, and in the stygian darkness, the deadly silence became oppressive. One felt as though one were in a submarine stranded on the bottom of the ocean.

I have never forgotten that first night in our monastic cell and the ghastly feeling of claustrophobia that overwhelmed me after barely an hour of trying to get some rest. Bentz was sound asleep. I lit one match after another to look at the time, which seemed to be standing still. Finally, I decided to get up and, with my torch, groped my way through the galleries and found the stairs leading out of the fort. I slowly climbed the 140 steps, only to find that the heavy steel door of the exit was closed and barred. All I could do was to lie flat on my stomach in my bedroll and put my nose as close as I could to the crack under the door to catch a breath of fresh air.

I had not been there for more than five minutes when I heard the sound of footsteps echoing on the stairs. It was Saint-Guily, the Gascon, who had come up from the depth of his cavern to join me in search of air. We decided that we were not yet seasoned "boys of concrete" and debated the possibility of joining the Foreign Legion, in order to serve out in the open. But at five the next morning, the dynamos began to hum again, the lights came on, and we forgot how sorry for ourselves we had been a few hours earlier. I got back to my friend Bentz, who, for his part, had slept like a log. He had gradually become accustomed to the trials of life underground by graduating from a strongpoint to a pillbox and then to a real fort.

The next day, I was initiated by Bentz into the mysteries of our own fort. It took almost the entire day. Our long expedition of discovery ended in the men's quarters, where the system of watches in use in the French navy had been successfully applied: one-third of the troops was on guard in the gun turrets, while another third slept, and the rest was eating or off duty. That evening, before retiring, Bentz and I went to see our two orderlies who slept in a large dormitory. The bunks were arranged in two tiers on either side of the room. At last I, the newcomer to Lorraine, found that I could teach those "boys of concrete" something they did not know, which was how to put on and take off one's trousers without getting out of an upper bunk. They asked me where I had learned this extraordinary technique. And when I told them it was from innumerable journeys in American Pullman sleepers, they found it hard to believe. The lieutenant, they thought, must be having them on, for everyone knew that the United States was the country of creature comforts par excellence. And yet it was true!

Every evening, before or after dinner, Bentz and I would go and spend half an hour with the men in their quarters. Some would already be dozing off in their bunks; others were writing to their wives and sweethearts; others still were playing cards. One small group usually gathered round a violinist who used to play before the war in a Metz cafe. From time to time, they would join in a sing-along of old Lorraine airs under his direction. Whenever I heard the familiar "Marche Lorraine" I always had a lump in my throat.

Little by little, I began to realize that our fort, which had seemed to me huge at first, was really only one small link in a mighty chain that stretched from Luxembourg to Switzerland. In 1936, when Belgium put an end to her defense agreement with France and chose neutrality, the idea arose of extending this impregnable wall along the Franco-Belgian frontier as far as the channel. But King Leopold III, who reigned at the time, informed the French government that he would regard it as an unfriendly act toward his country. I have asked myself since, when the Belgian ruler decided to capitulate and to lay down arms in Flanders during the German offensive of 1940, whether he did not regret his decision of 1936.

A few months later, when I was seconded to the BEF[1] as liaison officer, I was detailed to take Lord Gort and a group of British generals on a tour of the Maginot Line. We inspected several of its defense works. The British commander in chief made no secret of his amazement, for it was his first visit to the line. He asked me how much it had all cost. I replied that since 1930, the French government had spent about fifty-five billion francs of that time on its construction. The British officers were not greatly impressed by the figure, used as they were to counting in pounds, shillings, and pence.

I wondered how I could bring home to them the hugeness of the sum, and suddenly I thought of the Royal Navy. I realized how much the defense works of the Maginot Line had in common with the units of a great fleet. I began in my head to convert expenditures on the Maginot Line into ships of the line. I reckoned that battleships like the *Dunkerque* and the *Strasbourg* had cost about two billion francs apiece. We had two ships of this class, the British had five, and all the fleets in the world a total of twenty-five. If France had devoted the sums she had sunk into the Maginot defenses to building ships of the line, she would today have a fleet twice as large as all the world's navies put together. Lord Gort then understood the magnitude of the French defense effort and the cost involved. It was not surprising that after such a huge undertaking, France was financially or industrially

---

[1] British Expeditionary Forces.

incapable of producing the necessary tanks and war materials, especially in the conditions created by the forty-hour week introduced in 1936 by the Popular Front government, at a time when the Maginot Line was more or less completed.

The most cheerful spot in the whole fort was undoubtedly the officers' mess, where the doctor had drawn on the walls caricatures of all its members. Perhaps mine is there to this day. The doctor had talent. He had shown me running behind an ambulance, my lawyer's gown billowing in the wind, in the hope of finding a client at last. On the walls, he had also painted a few army sayings. I noted a few in the scrapbook I took to the United States in June 1940:

> Before carrying out an order, always wait for the counterorder.
> Do nothing but do it early.

I also remember a few light-hearted definitions:

> A lazy soldier: a soldier who does not pretend to work.
> Promotion: the fact of being considered incompetent by an ever-increasing number of subordinates.

One could also read on the wall the following maxim:

> Lieutenants are friends
> Captains are comrades
> Majors are colleagues
> Colonels are competitors
> Generals are opponents
> Marshals are enemies.

One of the doctor's favorite quotations was the celebrated epigram of Madame de Staël, doubtless penned with Napoleon, with whom she had a bone to pick, in mind. It ran as follows: "One sometimes succeeds in 'militarizing' a civilian, but never in civilizing a soldier."

Odd as it may seem, news of the great world outside, from which we seemed so far removed, reached us through a small radio set in the mess. I believe the steel structure around us accounted for the fact that the reception was so loud and clear. I often tuned into the American stations, which, outside, would probably have been impossible to get with a set like ours. Saint-Guily, who was a practical joker and our signals officer, dreamed up the idea of transmitting a mock broadcast by the minister of information. He made me privy to his joke and, with the help of two or three signals

NCOs who knew the works, we set out to carry it out. At dinnertime, sensational news, uncensored in part, sometimes even of a scandalous nature, was read out by a voice that seemed to be that of the minister, Jean Giraudoux. In fact, it was a corporal speaking from the cookhouse into an army microphone. The broadcast was a real hit while it lasted.

To break the monotony of those days underground, anything was fair game. I remember the time Bentz and I had been on duty in an outpost in front of the Maginot Line. As we returned through Bouzonville, a small town on the Franco-German border, we noticed in the window of an abandoned fashion shop a life-size dummy, which looked for all the world like a handsome girl with dark hair. We immediately thought that this could turn out to be the first woman to penetrate into the bowels of the Maginot Line. A few minutes later, the dummy, wrapped up in some potato sacking found at the local grocer's, was lying voluptuously on Saint-Guily's mattress, with its flowing black hair spread out on the pillow and the blanket pulled up to its chin.

After the evening meal, we played chess as usual. But as soon as the lights went out, we escorted our friend to his cell and bade him goodnight. We stood outside in the dark without uttering a word and had the pleasure, through the door, of hearing him remark, when he trained his torch on the sleeping form, "Madam, madam, what on earth are you doing here?" He got no answer, of course.

This trick became memorable, for very soon every officer in the fort was keen to play it on his immediate superior. Thus our waxen beauty spent a night in the captain's bed, another in the major's, and left the fort to go to the colonel's headquarters. We never learned whether our heroine ever made it to the army supreme command, but I do know that she became famous, for Cholly Knickerbocker, the celebrated New York columnist, wrote about her in one of his articles on the "phony war."

The lieutenants would go in turn once a week to the outposts ahead of the forts. This gave us a chance of spending a day in the open and of breathing fresh air. Those outposts were to be surrendered in the event of an attack, their only purpose being to act as trip wires and raise the alarm so that the forts could get ready for combat. Luck would have it that I was in one of these outposts on October 15, 1939, when—or so we believed, at least—the German "blitzkrieg" was due to begin. On the previous day, an order signed by General Gamelin, the French commander in chief, called for all-out resistance in all sectors of the front. It was pitch dark, and around eleven, after being warned that the Germans were advancing, we put down an artillery barrage that was to last on and off until daybreak. We were using our machine guns for the first time. At all events, either because the German war machine was not quite ready for an all-out offensive or because the Maginot Line proved too strong for a frontal attack, that night operation led to nothing.

Strange as it may seem, however, during those few days spent aboveground, I regretted the monotony of our daily life underground. The impression of isolation from the rest of the world, which seemed unbearable at the start, had come to seem almost agreeable. Unconsciously, in a way, I increasingly appreciated this simple and intimate life with a few comrades who had become real friends. We no longer took any notice of the passing of the days and were ignorant of dates. Most of the time, we did not even know whether it was a sunny or rainy day outside, light or dark. The daily letters from Josée brought me a distant echo of the world. But apart from this tenuous link with men and events, I felt as though I were becoming an integral part of the soil of Lorraine, indifferent to what was going on above my head.

This was not to last. One evening, in the course of a particularly agreeable dinner, the wireless operator brought a message informing me of a new posting. I was detached to the British Expeditionary Forces and had to report to GHQ (general headquarters) in northern France within thirty-six hours. My new duties were those of a liaison officer. I cannot exactly describe my feelings when I got the news. This posting gave me no pleasure. Life on the Maginot Line had had a strange effect on me. I belonged to Rotherberg Fort, and it belonged to me. I wanted to remain there and suddenly realized that I was not my own master but a pawn on a chessboard, like some five million others, moved by an unknown hand, which had decided to get me out of my familiar niche and cast me out into the great unknown. My friends, I sensed, sympathized. Major Cuvillier ordered a bottle of champagne, and we drank it sadly.

My marching orders had to be complied with immediately. I left at once, and the heavy steel door of the fort closed behind me. For the last time, I heard the dull sound of its weight against the concrete. It was raining slightly, and in the darkness of night, I trudged along the muddy track that led to Piblange. My orderly helped me carry my belongings. Once in the village, we made for the house of Madame Auburtin, where I intended to rest for a while. I pushed the door open, but the house was silent. No one answered my call. The two women had left for a place of greater safety. We went into the kitchen. I sat on my luggage. My orderly moved toward the rocking chair where, a few months earlier, Madame Auburtin sat making lace. A strange feeling made me tell him not to sit in it. The old lady's memory had made me feel sentimental. An hour later, we resumed our march to Metz. On the road, I hailed an army truck driving past, and it put me down at the blacked-out station of the Lorraine capital. It was November 18, 1939.

CHAPTER 3

With the British forces: The "phony war" on the front line

Hundreds of women stood waiting on the platform of the Gare de l'Est, in Paris, as the train drew in. I had sent off a telegram to Josée from Metz, and her piercing black eyes had no trouble finding me in the crowd of men in khaki pouring out of the carriages. We were going to spend a few hours together, and this was some compensation for leaving Lorraine. She told me that, like thousands of other women, she was doing her bit for the war effort. She had closed down my office and now devoted her time to refugees, the sick, and the few wounded from the front.

My transfer to the British forces gave me a free day in Paris, and we decided to celebrate by dining at Maxim's. The war did not seem to have affected the tempo of Parisian life in the slightest. I was shocked by the luxury, the abundance of rich and expensive foods. But for the past three years, the government had never ceased repeating that all was for the best in the best of all worlds and that everything would be all right in the end. Even after war was declared, this policy was pursued. The Ministry of Information led the French population to believe stories about rationing in Germany and the poor morale prevailing beyond the Rhine. As for us, it claimed, thanks to the economic blockade, we would not need to make much of an effort, and the fruits of victory would simply fall into our laps.

The following morning, I boarded the train for Arras. I did not expect, on arrival, to discover that the whereabouts of the British GHQ was shrouded in so much mystery that everyone would refuse to indicate it to a French officer who had to report there. When I got off the train, I went up to a British officer who seemed to be in charge of movement at the station and asked him quite innocently where it was. With an air of suspicion, he asked for my papers, and having ascertained that I was indeed to report to Lord Gort's headquarters, he directed me to the Arras Town

Commandant, Boulevard Vauban, and told me to ask for Captain G. The latter would provide me with all the necessary details.

Having located Captain G., I put the same question to him and got the same reaction. He could not tell me anything. He would put me in the hands of a driver who would take me to GHQ without telling me where it was. I said I simply wanted to know whether we would be going a long way and whether I would need to spend the night at a hotel and leave my luggage there. This question seemed to him indiscreet, and he replied, "I am sorry, but I am not authorized to tell you anything." I tried to get the information out of the driver but with the same lack of success. I therefore flung my bag and parcels into the car and settled into my seat with the curious feeling of being like a gangster whom a rival gang was taking off to an unknown destination.

After driving a few dozen kilometers along roads dotted with military signposts, we arrived in a village called Habarcq. The GHQ was there. I spent the evening at the French liaison officers' mess and had begun to recount my adventures when the German radio, broadcasting in French from Stuttgart, told us that whoever wanted to see Lord Gort need only look for him in a little village of the Somme called Habarcq! This was one of the unexpected paradoxes of the "phony war."

Besides the regular liaison officers attached to British units, there were also a good number of liaison agents—NCOs or other ranks from the reserve—who acted as interpreters. I discovered that, strangely enough, they almost invariably belonged to one of the three following categories: international bankers, managers of French hotels or restaurants in London, and young Frenchmen of the aristocracy brought up by English nannies. This surprising mix produced excellent diplomats and good soldiers.

Only a few days after my arrival at Habarcq, I heard that, a few days before, General Gamelin had remarked, in a talk to the commanders of the BEF, that no British troops had yet been to the front, although the war had been on for three months. Following elaborate diplomatic and military maneuvers, and in an attempt to counter the negative impact of German propaganda claiming that France was fighting a lone battle for Britain, it was decided that a British brigade (about two thousand men) would be sent to the Moselle front and would man the sector of a French regiment for about a week or ten days. The French division to which this British brigade was to be attached was, as usual, relieved every month; but the British brigade, for its part, would be relieved every ten days, in order to ensure the training of the largest possible number of men. So it turned out that in the four months that preceded the German offensive in Belgium, the British defended a sector only three kilometers long, out of nearly a thousand kilo-

meters of the future front between the Straits of Dover and Switzerland—
or a little less than .3 percent.

A more or less permanent liaison officer seemed required in this sector,
not only to maintain contact between the forward troops, the rear, and the
French division but also to serve as a link between the constantly rotating
British units. I jumped at the opportunity of returning to the "boys of
concrete" in Lorraine, and my candidature, which got me a third bar, was
fortunately accepted. I was posted to the Third Infantry Brigade of the
BEF, the first British unit to be sent to the front, and therefore returned to
Lorraine where I remained until the early days of May 1940—just before
all hell broke loose. This gave me a chance of getting to know all the
brigades of the small expeditionary force that were sent up to the frontline.
On May 10, 1940, when the war began in earnest, its total strength was
ten divisions, or about 200,000 men.

The Third British Brigade, the first to be sent to Moselle, entrained at
Douai. Never did I see such a collection of trucks and vehicles, of cooking
utensils, stores and stoves, and teakettles. Several trains were needed to
transport the three battalions!

I found myself in the same compartment as eight British officers. After
an interminable day's journey, punctuated by numerous stops as inexplica-
ble as they were mysterious, I felt a little stiff and was anxiously wondering
how I was going to spend the night. It was then that I discovered how
Britain had built an empire. At the signal of the senior officer in the carriage, all my fellow travelers pulled out of their kit bags the most extraordinary collection of hammocks, carpets, inflatable cushions and mattresses,
as well as thermos flasks. They all began to lay out and blow up these
contraptions with so much gusto that one would have thought they were
inflating a barrage balloon. In a quarter of an hour, these French railway
compartments were turned into a British colony, with all the creature comforts. We were all able to settle down for the night, and I thought, as I
dozed off, of this French quip: "One Englishman, a fool; two Englishmen,
a match; three Englishmen, a colony!"

The following day, we arrived at a little station north of Metz, not far
from the village of Amanvillers. A few hours later, I was accompanying
Brigadier Curtis on a reconnaissance in the sector his troops were to hold.
To my great delight, I discovered that our sector was only a few kilometers
away from my Rotherberg Fort. The brigade was to occupy a line of crests
between two woods. We went up to "Hill 301," the highest ground in the
area. The Germans had certainly earmarked this as a likely enemy observation post, for we had barely been there five minutes when 105-mm shells
began raining down all around us. The artillery fire was accurate, and we
fell flat on our faces.

That evening, the brigadier called me in to work on the order of the day, which would be read the following morning to the troops. It had to be drafted in such a way as to be given out also to the French of the Forty-second Division. Here is the document which, to the best of my knowledge, has never been published.

3RD INFANTRY BRIGADE

ORDER OF THE DAY

29th November, 1939

I wish every Officer, W.O., N.C.O. and private soldier to realize that this moment is an historic occasion. The 3rd Infantry Brigade has been chosen to go into action as the vanguard of the British Army. We shall be in the closest touch with our Allies, who have extended to us the warmest of welcomes. Unless everyone had done his duty since arrival in France, this unique honour would not have been conferred on you. The enemy awaits our arrival with expectancy. The opportunity is yours to maintain and enhance the glorious traditions inscribed on your Colours. Be vigilant, keep cool and fire low. To the last round and the last man and a bit more.

Not only the eyes of Yorkshire, Nottinghamshire, Derbyshire and Shropshire are upon you, but those of our Allies and the whole Empire.

With justice on our side, your proud watchwords will be: "On ne passe pas—We will stop them" and "On les aura—We will win."

H.O. Curtis
Brigadier Commander,
3rd Infantry Brigade.

Thus, for the first time in history, British troops were to "fight" in Lorraine. André Maurois's celebrated book *Les silences du Colonel Bramble* was regarded in both France and Britain as the best psychological study of the British soldier during the First World War. At the beginning of World War II, this became the bible of all liaison officers, and I read it with pleasure a second time as soon as I began working with the BEF. One of Maurois's characters in the book is a Scots captain who, throughout the war, went on repeating to his comrades, "This war is an affair between the Scots and the Germans." I met his counterpart in Lorraine—another Scotsman who almost succeeded in convincing me that it was the same this time, too.

Although the three battalions of the Third Brigade were made up of men from Nottinghamshire, Cambridgeshire, and Shropshire regiments, the major who, along with myself, was responsible for liaison with the French division was a Scot. His name was Malcolm, and his regiment, the celebrated Gordon Highlanders. At our very first meeting, he proved to me that, once again, this was a conflict between the Germans and the Scots or rather between Hitler and the Gordon Highlanders. He even advanced proof to back his point. Had not the only German raids at the time been made on Scapa Flow or the Firth of Forth? Even the hares killed by German bombs were, like the major himself, natives of the Scottish Highlands.

As I was to be responsible for contacts with all British units in the sector, I asked Major Malcolm one evening for a list of the sixty or seventy British regiments normally responsible for the defense of Britain and the empire. I begged him, for my own personal enlightenment, to underline the names of those ten he regarded as the best, from the standpoint both of their past record and of their present valor. After pausing for thought, he gave me his list—nine of them were Scottish and only one English! The Gordon Highlanders came first in his classification, and the Black Watch, tenth. A few weeks later, the Black Watch were to get their own back and give their opinion of the Gordon Highlanders. Major Carthew-Yorstoun, who belonged to the first, had replaced Major Malcolm as liaison officer. I submitted to him the same list of all British regiments and asked him to pick the ten best. He agreed with his predecessor about the indisputable military superiority of the Scots, who, in his selection, also accounted for nine of them. But the Gordon Highlanders brought up the rear of the list, while the Black Watch had moved to the head of it.

Every morning, together with Major Malcolm, I would make the rounds of the outposts. The British sentry on guard on the line of antitank defenses never failed to present arms as smartly as if he had been on duty outside Buckingham Palace. Then we would drive to a little village called Waldweistroff, which I had rechristened Vladivostock, as it seemed to mark the end of the civilized world. Battalion headquarters was in an abandoned grocer's shop. The village was located on the slopes of a hill, about one kilometer back from the outposts on the line of hilltops. It was therefore invisible to the enemy but did not, for all that, escape shelling. Our daily routine involved asking the colonel and the battalion commanders what had happened during the night—killed, wounded, prisoners, etc.—and climbing up the hill to have a look at the outposts.

At either end of the sector held by the British there was a sort of international post. Each of these was manned by twenty to thirty French and British soldiers, one under command of a French lieutenant, the other of a British lieutenant. Although it was contrary to orders, the major and I decided one evening to spend the following night in each of the two posts. As luck would have it that night, I had a foretaste, on a minute scale, of what the real German "blitzkrieg" could be like. I took a few notes on the night's events in case I should be asked any questions. Here they are:

—1800 hrs. Arrival at Post 65—The "international" post on the right in the Hartbuch. Armament of the post: two batteries of artillery. Request for a barrage ahead of the post, one green rocket with three flares. All-out barrage in the event of a major attack, one red rocket with six flares. Post commander Sgt. Monahan, liaison agent. The garrison of the post includes one section of the Duke of Cornwall's Light Infantry and a French combat group from the 102d Infantry Regiment.

—1818 hrs. Three shells fired over the post landed two hundred meters to left, probably 105 mm.

—1900 hrs. Shelling on Grosswald, about two thousand meters to the left.

—2120 hrs. Grenade and machine-gun fire in Grosswald-Wood.

—0010 hrs. Patrol returns.

—Intermittent shelling around us during the rest of the night at a range of thirty to two hundred meters.

—0610 hrs. Just before sunrise, intensive shelling over and around the post. Shrapnel from 105 mm and mortar shells hit trees in vicinity. Two batteries not in position previous day open up from hilltop in front of us at point-blank range. Eight to ten mortars also. For about twelve minutes, impossible to peer over trench parapet. Two men slightly wounded by shrapnel. Then firing over our heads and to our left abates for a few minutes. We fear a sudden attack. Telephone out of operation. Liaison agent Monahan goes, under enemy fire, to right-hand post to ask for artillery support. At the same time, about eighty *Stosstruppen*, German commandos, wearing leather jackets and equipped with automatic weapons, wire cutters, grenades, etc., double up the hill toward post on our left. A few minutes later, they double back with a group of prisoners. The shelling continues.

Our post opens fire on the enemy, which makes its getaway, probably killing one or two and wounding several.

German patrol reaches the village of Zeurange. German guns pulled back.

I run to the neighboring outpost, which has been under attack. Its British commander has been killed, as well as the corporal. Two dead Germans remain trapped in the barbed wire. Sixteen British soldiers are missing. The sole survivor, suffering from shock, cannot speak. I bring him back to our post.

A few hours later, I added to these notes the report made by the survivor, who had recovered in the meantime:

Two men were on guard. The others slept. Suddenly, we were woken by heavy shelling and fell flat on our faces in the trench or the dugout. In a few moments, without realizing how it had come about, we were surrounded by Germans. I got a blow on the head with a rifle butt, which knocked me out, and I believe all the others were taken prisoner.

This attack was a perfect example of the remarkable efficiency of the German war machine—of which our Popular Front government had refused to acknowledge the growing strength.

I remember to this day the statement, at a dinner, by a then foreign minister, who claimed that a large number of the tanks of the Third Reich had broken down. Such were the illusions that some politicians instilled in the minds of Frenchmen. It was a time when, in France, you were accused of being a Fascist if you maintained that Germany had a powerful army and made the most of her people's sense of discipline. You were also a Fascist if you argued that, to prepare for war, to match the German war effort, and to beat the Germans at their own game, you had to work fifty, perhaps even fifty-five hours a week (the forty-hour week had been introduced by the Popular Front).

Like everything the Germans did, this raid appeared to have been carefully prepared for several days by elite troops and carried out by specialists. They had kept the outpost under close observation, as well as the two neighboring ones. They had drawn up and adjusted their fire plan the night before. And they had brought up a company of the elite *Stosstruppen,* which was not part of the normal complement of the regiment facing us. They probably took cover in the village of Zemange during the previous night. Just before sunrise, at a given signal, they called for an artillery barrage. Several batteries of guns demolished the post that was earmarked for attack and isolated the two neighboring outposts that could have lent it support.

During the shelling, the company of *Stosstruppen* assaulted the hill, using the cover, which had been reconnoitered previously, to maximum advantage. Within a few yards of their objective, these troops sent up a flare that brought their own artillery barrage immediately to a halt. The grenades did the rest. They lost two or three of their own, but they took prisoner all the men in the outpost, with the exception of the two killed and the one I found knocked out. . . . This lightning raid was carried out to perfection.

Similar probing raids occurred periodically along the whole length of the front. They enabled the Germans to identify our units and to discover our order of battle. As for our troops stationed in northern France, south of the Belgian frontier, the Germans easily obtained all the information they needed about them through innumerable agents and spies. A great many of these were Belgian citizens. They enjoyed the privileges of residents in the frontier areas and could cross over into France as and when they pleased. It is now obvious that, when the Germans launched their great May 1940 offensive, they knew exactly the strength and dispositions of all our forces.

When I returned to divisional HQ, Major Malcolm gave me to understand how much he deplored the sorry events of the past night. "All this would never have happened had the Gordon Highlanders been there," he added. Perhaps he was right!

CHAPTER 4
A visit by King George VI and Neville Chamberlain

ANDRÉ MAUROIS WROTE THAT ONE OF THE BRITISH OFFICERS SERVING IN HIS brigade defined the First World War in the following terms: "A fascinating game, which occasionally involves real danger." My impression is that my British friends in Lorraine took the same view of the 1939–1940 phase of the war. For them, it was only a matter of the excitement it provided, and this attitude had undoubtedly a great deal to do with their excellent morale. For instance, they spoke of patrols only as pleasant outings, and it must be said that these "patrol parties" were indeed one of the major forms of entertainment in our sector. Young officers would dress as ordinary soldiers in order to be chosen to take part in them. They were brave and sometimes foolhardy.

The starting point of the patrols organized by brigade headquarters was the gendarmerie of a little village called Halstroff. I often went to the early morning rendezvous and had the impression of being at a shooting party in Essex or Somerset.

The Forty-second Division, as well as the British brigade, were at the front when a telegram informed us that an important person was due to visit our sector on December 7th. He was to spend a few moments in the area defended by the British brigade, have lunch in one of the forts, take the parade of a battalion of the Forty-second Division, and return to Paris by train. General Condé, who commanded the Third French Army, called on General de la Porte du Theil, the head of the Forty-second Division, and told him confidentially that the person in question was the king of England.

In France, it is difficult, if not impossible, to keep anything secret for any length of time. I was therefore not unduly surprised when, the following morning, my orderly asked me, as he was polishing my boots, whether I knew King George VI would soon pay us a visit. Naturally, I replied that I had no knowledge of such a rumor. At that very same moment, I was about to reconnoiter the ground and choose a spot to which General de la Porte du Theil could take the king and show him part of the front.

Finding an observation post that provided every guarantee of security for a royal personage was no easy mission. The post had to be close enough to the enemy so that the king might get at least an approximate idea of the layout of his positions. But at the same time, it had to be out of reach of small-arms fire. The general had added, as he gave me my orders, that the chosen spot should be on sufficiently high ground but in no case must the Germans be able to spot the group of fifteen to twenty persons who would be accompanying the king and General Gamelin. It was not an easy task.

I spent the morning in search of the ideal spot and discovered a small orchard at the top of a hill about two miles from the frontline. After reporting to the general, he returned with me to the spot in order to convince himself that it was. He was a picturesque old soldier, who, after the Armistice, was to become the head of the Chantiers de Jeunesse, the youth camps set up by the Vichy government. He had bright, piercing eyes and a long, drooping mustache, which earned him the nickname of Vercingetorix, after the leader of the Gauls against Julius Caesar. After a moment's thought, he approved my choice and added, "I may need you as an interpreter tomorrow, for I shall have to show the king our division's positions and will probably have to reply to his questions."

The following morning, a fleet of cars drove through the two or three villages in the area that had been evacuated at the beginning of hostilities. Naturally, there were no civilians along the road, and the only spectators were French or British soldiers who did not have time to present arms for the king or for their commander in chief. General Gamelin sat at the left of the king, who wore a light-colored gray coat with only the insignia of a field marshal, two crossed batons, on his shoulder straps.

The caravan stopped in the little village of Saint-François-la-Croix, at the foot of the hill we would have to climb in order to reach "my" orchard. The royal party was strung out along a muddy path guarded at intervals by sentries. Halfway up the hill a company of the Black Watch stood rigidly to attention. All the men were absolutely of the same height. When the king appeared, an NCO barked the order, "Present arms!" They remained in that position until our party reached the orchard when, in the distance, we heard the same voice shout, "Stand at ease!" The king moved forward with Colonel Steven, the battalion commander, and stopped under one of the trees at the far edge of the orchard, facing the enemy. General de la Porte du Theil was waiting a few yards back with General Gamelin for the king to finish his talk with Colonel Steven and join them. I was standing behind in case my services should be required. Suddenly, a German battery opened up and fired a few shells. Gamelin, obviously concerned for the king's safety, turned to General de la Porte and asked dryly, "Who chose this position? It is too close to the enemy."

I was trembling in my boots, but then, contrary to the time-honored rule Saint-Guily had taught me, that, in the army, the man responsible is always the next lower in rank to oneself, old Vercingetorix growled, "I chose it."

General de la Porte took over from the colonel of the Black Watch and signaled to me to follow him. Pointing with his stick, he showed the king the positions held by the British troops, in the center of the Forty-second Division sector, flanked on the left by the 151st Infantry Regiment and on the right, by the Ninety-fourth. Then, turning to me, the king said there was no need for me to translate because he understood easily what was said. He merely asked for the explanation of one or two words, then wanted me to show him a light machine gun, which he had noticed nearby in a dugout. As he handled it, he remarked that it must be a convenient weapon on patrol, and he seemed to remember Chicago gangsters used something like it at one time. He asked me for the French equivalent of the word *gangster,* and I told him it was the same word we had imported from the United States.

We came down the hill. As we passed in front of the 150 men of the Black Watch who had presented arms on our way up, we were greeted with the traditional three cheers. The next item on the royal program was lunch at the Mont-des-Welches Fort. After that, along a road nearby, the king inspected a regiment of the Forty-second Division. Then we got into the waiting cars and left at high speed for Pagny-en-Moselle, where the royal train was waiting.

Night was falling, and we were plunged in a thick fog. The band of a light infantry battalion was lined up on the station platform, and as soon as the cars came to a halt, it struck up "God Save the King" and the "Marseillaise." That was moving enough, but what followed was even more so. Two light infantry battalions, just relieved at the front, suddenly emerged from the fog. They wore their traditional dark blue uniforms, covered with mud up to their knees. The sharp staccato notes of their bugles pierced the air, while the regimental march seemed literally to drive each man forward at the traditional quick pace of the French *Chasseurs à pied*.

King George saluted the glorious flag that opened the march. It had been through four wars and was in tatters. A silken net held together the sacred shreds of blue, white, and red still hanging from the pole. Section after section, they marched past, each row of men giving an "eyes right!" in salute to the king, who stood motionless as they came up to him. Finally, far behind the last company, a soldier closed the rear. He was small and stocky and, with a determined look, carried a gun that seemed bigger than himself. The king, who had been on the point of lowering his right arm, resumed his salute for this lone soldier, who looked him straight in the eye as he marched past. It was almost a symbolic salute of a great sovereign to an unknown French soldier. And the little man, in turn, vanished in the fog. For a few more seconds, the king remained motionless. Then he lowered his arm and silently joined his escort. A few old peasant women who had watched the scene had tears in their eyes.

Some time later, we also had to take the British prime minister on a tour of the front. I had expected a similar caravan of cars in the village and was disappointed to see only one large limousine without escort. It stopped near the church, and two men got out: Neville Chamberlain and General Condé.

The British premier seemed very spry in a dark gray overcoat and a black felt hat. He visited every corner of the sector and scampered up and down the muddy hills of Lorraine like a young man. The British brigade commander was a personal friend of his, and as I followed a few steps behind with a small group of officers of his escort, I heard them talk about the *Graf Spee,* which was the main topic of discussion at the front at the time. The German cruiser had just taken refuge in Montevideo, and everyone was asking himself whether it would come out to do battle with the three little British cruisers that had scored hits on it, one of them being badly damaged in the encounter. Chamberlain took the view that the *Graf Spee* would not come out of port, and he added, as though it were a state secret, that Churchill had phoned him that very morning with the news that the *Dunkerque,* the *Renown,* and another battle cruiser had just reached Argentina's territorial waters.

As soon as the prime minister had left, I rushed back to Rotherberg Fort to see my old comrades of the 162d Infantry Regiment and give them this tip about the *Graf Spee.* I had not the slightest idea at the time that it was all a hoax concocted by Churchill, who was then first lord of the Admiralty. He had phoned the "news" of the reinforcements to the prime minister in Paris, before he set out to visit the front, in the hope that the German fifth column would get to hear of it. I have since learned that the message did get through and that the *Graf Spee* scuttled itself rather than face a battle against such unequal odds. That may indeed be true.

CHAPTER 5

My last merry Christmas: A Franco-Scottish occasion

A FEW DAYS BEFORE CHRISTMAS, I GOT TO KNOW MAJOR CARTHEW-Yorstoun of the Black Watch. We saluted each other and introduced ourselves. "I believe you are the officer entrusted with the liaison between the French division and our brigade," he said. "I have been detailed by my battalion to work with you."

It had begun to snow, and never before in living memory had the region experienced such intense cold. The ground was hard as rock, and the sandbags on the parapets of the slit trenches were split open by the frost.

We shook hands, and I asked him, absentmindedly, if he had already seen any snow this year. "Certainly," he replied. "I was on leave in Switzerland when the war broke out and was ordered back to England just as I was about to climb the Jungfrau." I asked him whether he ever suffered from mountain sickness. "Never," he replied. I felt that I had made a faux pas and added; "You must have ancestors who were mountain dwellers." "My ancestors all came from the Scottish highlands," he replied, a little stiffly. "Yes, every one, otherwise I would not be an officer of the Black Watch."

Despite this initial misunderstanding, the major and I became the best of friends. I can even go so far as to say that we were always together, save at night, during the whole of the time he remained in our sector.

Over the long winter evenings at headquarters, he told me the story of his regiment and, with pencil and paper, sketched out the positions of the respective forces in the famous battles the Black Watch had fought in its long history.

One evening, I asked him the meaning of the red feather hackle he wore on the right-hand side of his bonnet. "We are very proud of it," he explained. "You see, it happened in 1813. Our regiment was in Belgium, fighting Napoleon. On our right flank, one of the king's cavalry regiments was in a sticky spot and lost several guns. In an attempt to win them back, it charged repeatedly but without success. Then the Black Watch was called

in to do what the cavalry had been unable to achieve. After this engagement," he went on, "King George III took their hackle away from the
cavalry and gave it to the Black Watch, the heroes of that memorable day.
We still wear it." And Major Carthew-Yorstoun removed his bonnet and
fondly stroked the red feathers.

One evening, I took the major over to the "boys of concrete" for dinner,
in the depths of the Maginot Line. As the rather confined atmosphere of
the fort was not quite the thing for a Highlander who was a mountain
climber as well, I asked the fort commandant, who readily agreed, for the
air-conditioning system to remain in operation during the whole of his
visit. I do not think that even in the happy September days of my own life
underground, full of pleasant memories, our concrete mess was the scene
of a more joyful dinner. After having tasted all the known vintages of
Moselle, Lieutenant Billet showed the major how the "boys of concrete"
went about opening a bottle of champagne. With a sharp circular flick of
his bayonet, he cut off the necks of all the bottles brought to him and filled
our glasses with the foaming liquid.

The atmosphere was so convivial that, after a brief and heartfelt toast,
the major plucked the hackle from his bonnet and did something unheard
of in the Black Watch—he offered it to Major Cuvillier.

As the evening wore on, the bond of friendship between the "boys of
concrete" and Major Carthew-Yorstoun grew stronger. To set the final seal
on it, they decided that, the following day, he would bring the pipes and
drums of the Black Watch over to Piblange by truck. It was to be the first
time they would give a concert on French soil to French troops. Our colonel considered the event so exceptional that he agreed to grant leave to a
third of the men in the forts so that they might attend it.

Leslie Hore-Belisha, the minister of war at the time, had made himself
very unpopular with Scottish regiments by forbidding them to wear their
kilts and play their bagpipes in France. This did not prevent the Black
Watch from disobeying the order and bringing over to France their kilted
pipe and drum band, without which they could not live, love, or fight.

The village of Piblange was snowbound, and the empty houses were all
shuttered up when the big truck stopped a few yards away from Madame Auburtin's home. The men of our fort were drawn up on either side
of the village square. Wide-eyed and open-mouthed, their gaze was riveted
on the drum major, who marched and countermarched in front of them
with his small band of six pipers and six drummers. At every turn, they
changed step, and this coincided with a new tune. The farmer-soldiers of
Lorraine were dumbfounded by these strange Scottish customs, by the kilts
flying in the wind above the bony knees, as they marched proudly up the
main street of this Lorraine village. Then, by degrees, it began to sink in

that these bandsmen were peasants like themselves, from an unknown country, who, in their Scottish highlands, worked the poor soil of their moors, among the thistle and the heather, while they, more fortunate, had worked the fertile lands of Lorraine. The kilt was the only point of difference between them.

I had the impression that these plaintive Scottish airs, so new to them, brought back memories of their own native soil. And Saint-Guily, our Gascon comrade, was as moved as I was. The sound of the bagpipes was to his ears like the fifes, which, three centuries before, at the siege of Arras, had brought the men of Gascony to the brink of tears. And slowly, in a half-whisper, Saint-Guily recited the lines from *Cyrano de Bergerac*:

> Small, demure tunes
> Whose every note is like a little sister,
> Songs heard only in some long silent voice,
> Not quite forgotten—Mountain melodies
> Like thin smoke rising from brown cottages,
> In the still noon, slowly—Quaint lullabies,
> Whose very music has a southern tongue.[1]

Then, like Cyrano, turning to the group of French officers present and pointing to the Highlanders, he went on in ringing tones:

> Listen, you Gascons! Now it is no more,
> The shrill fife—it is the flute, through woodlands far
> Away, calling—no longer the hot battle cry,
> But the cool, quiet pipe our goatherds play!
> Listen—the forest glens, the hills, the downs,
> The green sweetness of night on the Dordogne
> Listen, you Gascons! It is all Gascogne![2]

---

[1]Translated into English verse by Brian Hooker. French text by Edmond Rostand:

> Ces vieux airs du pays, au doux rythme obsesseur,
> Dont chaque note est comme une petite soeur,
> Dans lesquels restent pris des sons de voix aimées,
> Ces airs dont la lenteur est celle des fumées
> Que le hameau natal exhale de ses toits,
> Ces airs dont la musique a l'air d'être en patois!

[2]In French:

> Ecoutez, les Gascons! Ce n'est plus sous ses doigts,
> Le fifre aigu des camps—c'est la flûte des bois!

The next day was Christmas. And for the first time since the outbreak of war, not a shot was fired along the whole front from Luxembourg to Switzerland. The enemy forces had decided to honor the coming of Christ.

The major invited me to spend the evening with the officers of his battalion. At the dessert course, they blew out all the candles, and at the same time fourteen little Christmas puddings, drenched in brandy and set alight, were brought into the room. All those present rose from their seats and, with one voice, sang the national anthem. The puddings were a gift to all the officers and men from the queen, who was honorary colonel of the regiment. There was even a pudding for me, and Colonel Steven, leaning over with a smile and a twinkle in the eye, exclaimed, "You see, the queen even thought of our liaison officer!"

It was my last merry Christmas of a war that had not yet even begun.

Ce n'est plus le sifflet du combat, sous ses lèvres,
C'est le lent galoubet de nos meneurs de chèvres!
Ecoutez—C'est le val, la lande, la forêt,
Le petit pâtre brun sous son rouge béret,
C'est la verte douceur des soirs sur la Dordogne,
Ecoutez, les Gascons: c'est toute la Gascogne.

CHAPTER 6

A handsome American woman visits the Maginot Line

THE LAST GOVERNMENT OF THE THIRD REPUBLIC HAD CREATED A MINISTRY of Leisure but not a Ministry for Women's Affairs, and no woman, not even a cleaning woman, had ever penetrated the bowels of the Maginot Line. Cadets were taught at Saumur, the French cavalry school, to beware of women in front, of horses behind, and of senior officers on all sides. But there was never any need for the "boys of concrete" to beware of women because they had never seen one underground.

At the very beginning of my time in New York as a young lawyer, from 1930 to 1934, I had been struck by the beauty of Clare Boothe. Before she turned thirty, she was the head of one of the leading magazines of the powerful Conde Nast group of publications (*Vogue*, etc.) and her play *The Women* had had a triumphal reception on Broadway.

She quickly won the favors of the man who was then becoming a big magnate of the press, Henry Luce, the publisher of *Life, Time, Fortune, March of Time,* etc. She spoke French fluently and loved France. She also had a great fondness for the Foreign Legion, which my father had commanded when he was head of the French forces in Morocco, and had become the "godmother" of the First Regiment of the Legion based in Fez, of which my mother was an honorary corporal.

At the time of the mobilization in France, she had learned that I was stationed on the Maginot Line and had asked to be allowed to become the "godmother" of one of the forts of the regiment. The Mont-des-Welsches was granted this privilege.

In March 1940, armed with letters of recommendation from President Roosevelt and Senator Robert Taft, the leader of the Republican opposition (she herself was a Republican), she decided to visit France and Britain at war. Her charm worked wonders with General Gamelin, who had decreed that no woman, on any pretext whatsoever, should be allowed to go to the front. But Clare knew how to get what she wanted, and I was given the order, transmitted to me by General Condé, to be on hand on April 9 at 10 A.M. in the village of Metzervisse, near Metz, to meet a captain on the staff of the commander in chief who was detailed to escort a handsome American woman and introduce her two "godsons," the First Regiment of the Legion and the garrison of the Mont-des-Welsches.

Early in the morning, Colonel Robert, who commanded the First Regiment, after being informed by General Condé, himself alerted by GHQ, ordered all his men, whatever their duties, to turn out as neatly as if they had been on a traditional July 14th parade at Fez. The companies were drawn up in impeccable squares, and all the officers and men stared at this handsome woman in a blue two-piece suit who stopped here and there to have a few words with an officer, an NCO, or a soldier.

Luncheon was held in the Officers' Mess under canvas, while the regimental band played traditional marches. In a little speech, the colonel asked Clare Luce to explain to her friends in the United States that the Foreign Legion, which was made up of men from so many different countries, was convinced it was fighting for a just cause; he gave her the regimental badge—and a kiss on both cheeks.

Then I took the visitor to the Mont-des-Welsches, where she was going to donate to the garrison a pennant and, especially, cartons of American cigarettes. Our car drove up to the entrance of the fort where Major Tari was waiting. Then she began to climb up the hill above the fort. At the top, she saw the mushroom-shaped steel domes, barely protruding above ground, which housed the antitank guns and machine-gun posts. For her benefit, the turrets rose a few inches to reveal the muzzles of their weapons.

From the top of the hill, she scanned the neighboring forts. Major Tari, striking the ground with his stick, said, "Madame, here, under our feet, some forty to one hundred yards down, your six hundred 'godsons' live and work, day and night." Whereupon, in her characteristic, persuasive tone of voice, which always drove those who listened to take immediate action, she exclaimed, "Then may I go down and see them?" The major did not hesitate one second. It was the first—and last—time a woman visited this very hush-hush spot!

Our group arrived in one of the steel turrets where the camouflaged guns were mounted on a central shaft that pivoted noiselessly. A sergeant shouted, "Attention," and his loud voice echoed down the steel stairs. Immediately, the twenty-four-strong gun crew took up battle stations, and the two hundred tons of steel of the turret rose with a pivoting motion. A few seconds later, the two guns, which could easily have neutralized the thickest armor, opened fire.

Our car had stopped close to the Mont-des-Welsches, and as we walked side by side, I sensed that she was deeply moved. I escorted her back to Metz, with the staff captain detailed by General Gamelin sitting beside the driver. The day before, a wing commander of the RAF [Royal Air Force] on an inspection told me of the Allied defeat at Narvick, and during the short drive back to Metz, I had a premonition of great impending disaster. I naturally told Clare about it and insisted that her husband act immediately and speak to Roosevelt and Taft, giving her the reasons for my fears.

"Write me a letter," she said, "explaining the grounds for your pessimism. It is the only way of getting America to come to your aid. I am leaving for Britain day after tomorrow," she added, "and from there, I will return to New York as soon as possible." I replied that I would write tomorrow at the latest, in English, in the form of a letter to Josée in which I would indicate that it was to be forwarded to her. Here is the full text, as Clare included it in her book, *Europe in the Spring,* published as early as August 1940 [by Alfred A. Knopf, New York, 1940].

The colonel of the corps (Editor's note: A British corps which was, one presumes, in Norway.) gave me some very precise details about the Norwegian campaign. It can be summed up in this sentence: on sea and on land, the Allied navy and the expeditionary force have been bludgeoned by the German air force.

For the first time since the beginning of the world war, a naval force has been under air attack. On the first day HMS *Rodney* (England's largest battle cruiser) was badly hit in the bows and had to turn back. Churchill had counted on leaving the large units permanently at anchor in the narrows, as the navy did to blockade a port. He changed his mind fast. On land, it was total disaster with bombing of air bases, crossroads, troops on the march, mercilessly and very effectively.

In announcing several weeks ago "the Norwegian victory," the first "mistake of Hitler," Paul Reynaud [then prime minister] declared:

1. The Narvik-Lulea railway is definitely cut.
2. Not a ton of Scandinavian iron can ever be shipped to Germany.
3. Allied divisions are on the way to Norway. (The French ones at that time were between Bouzonville and Metz.[1] Only a brigade of Chasseurs Alpins had landed at Narvik.)

But let us examine the first two points: Before the war, Germany imported six-tenths of the total output of Swedish ore. She has just, as I will prove, secured the whole output.

In fact, by the military occupation of Norway, she places Sweden in a vise between herself and Russia. Thanks to the occupation of Denmark, and to her air force, she seals off both sides of the Baltic-Atlantic channel. Sweden can then only export to Germany, or to Russia—with Germany's

---

[1] It now seems that mountain regiments threatened to mutiny rather than embark for Norway. The defense of their own soil was the only ideology understood by many unquestionably "patriotic" French peasants.

permission. Even if we succeed, which is improbable, in holding Narvik for a long time, we cannot prevent Sweden, a neutral country, from working her own mines. During the six summer months the ore from the north, the production of which can be intensified at this time of year, will use the Lulea-Stettin route—during the winter, the south-bound railway. Thus, by occupying Norway and Denmark, Germany has just obtained absolute control of Sweden. What this all means for Germany is iron, chromium, nickel, and cobalt.

But here is also something very serious: England and France used to control Norwegian cellulose production (which is used in the manufacture of gunpowder of which Norway is one of the principal producers) as well as that of nitrogen and timber. These industries are now in the hands of Germany. Denmark exported to England 40 percent of her total imports of butter, milk, and cheese. All these huge food supplies are now in German hands.

Having taken into account the fact that Sweden (and all her production) falls directly under German domination owing to the occupation of Norway (because of the setbacks of the Allies, the Swedish press has already become very pro-German), you mustn't forget to add that Hitler has further secured, as a result of the war against France and England, control of

The armament industries of Austria and Czechoslovakia (Vienna and Skoda)

The Czech mines

The coal and other raw materials of Poland (and anything else in all or any of these countries of which he chooses to avail himself)

But iron ore, cellulose, nitrogen, timber would have been worth three or four of Churchill's cruisers and destroyers to the Allies!

Let us go back: as soon as Hitler attacked Poland, French propaganda proclaimed: "Hitler makes the same mistake as Kaiser Wilhelm." I answer no, no, and no! While he was building the Siegfried Line, and while conducting the Russian Polish operation, Hitler proved to his own satisfaction that we were mobilizing merely a defensive army on his west front. Meanwhile Hitler had squared his enemy in the east for all time. Wilhelm never did that. And now, with hardly a fight, Hitler has obtained almost everything he needed to wage war against us. Wilhelm never did that. While attacking us Wilhelm had to disperse his forces—and fight Russia, Serbia, etc.

As Hitler, I now believe, intends to attack us this summer on all fronts from Belgium to Tunisia, with the focus on the Maginot Line (Editor's note: This wishful thinking died hard, even for a mind as lucid as de Chambrun's, as Hitler avoided attacking the Maginot Line), he avoided before he began all the mistakes that Wilhelm made.

In short, from 1914 to 1918, Germany had to fight against fifty powers on five fronts: Russian, French, Italian, Greek, Yugoslavian.

In the summer of 1940, Hitler will be able to fight the great armies of France and the absurdly small British army on one front two thousand kilometers long—from Belgium to the French colonies in North Africa, with the acquiescence of Stalin and Mussolini—and perhaps the help of the latter! Worst of all, it will be a long time before we have achieved air parity (in March 1941, according to an article I read in an informed American magazine).

So, compared to the obvious weakness of Wilhelm's position in 1914, Hitler will have these advantages before he starts:

1. All the mineral production of Scandinavia at his disposal
2. Norwegian submarine and air bases on the Atlantic facing England
3. The ability to close off the Baltic
4. Control of Polish ore and coal
5. No enemies in the east or south, but, on the contrary, suppliers of wheat and oil, and possibly allies
6. Fifty-five percent of Romanian oil exports, without bothering to occupy the country
7. The forces of Italy, to whom he can always offer the inducement of Yugoslavia—or if that fails, the stationing of several German divisions on the Brenner—a pretty powerful "inducement"

And militarily, we have no plan of attack, because since the war began, we have entrenched ourselves comfortably and complacently behind our Maginot Line and our small inadequate defenses to the north.

The announcer said this morning on the radio: "The Allies are ready to face all eventualities." Here is our own extraordinary admission that in tactical matters, we are not willing at any point to take the military initiative (shades of Frederick, Napoleon, and Joffre!).

Further, by being diplomatically all over the place, giving a little aid to Spain, Poland, Finland, and Norway, we have played into the hands of our adversary, who attacks with considerable force in one point at a time (Austria, Czechoslovakia, Poland, Denmark, and tomorrow in the Balkans?). In his effort to forestall German aggression, your father[2] was right when he tried in 1935 to attack diplomatically at one point—Rome—and that with every means. It was not his fault if he failed.

Before I left the front the other day, two German officers were captured by chance. For two weeks, they had been spying behind our lines, trying to steal the plans of major defense works which we might have finished since September. None, alas, have ever been completed!—because our High Command doesn't know here, as they do in Germany, how to create the "mystique of work" and above all to make plans for such "eventualities." . . . Those fellows were volunteer spies. I, for one, see in the fact

---

[2]Pierre Laval.

that the Germans seek volunteers to carry out this sort of mission a sure indication of an attack this summer. There are many other indications (for instance, the growing espionage in Belgium and Holland).

I am one of the few who remained for eight months in one sector of the front. Since the beginning, we have always captured from German patrols Austrian and Czech equipment. This proves (to me, anyway) that the German High Command is holding back elsewhere, for the real attack, its formidable reserves of German equipment. Further, the German tactics at all points of the front since the beginning of the war have had but one aim—to take prisoners. Now, at the end of seven months, they know, thanks to our relief-corps system, the whole strength of our army divisions.

Again, judging by the prisoners we have taken, the spirit of the German army is magnificent. It possesses above all things Faith. The corps commander told me of the incredible boldness of the German bombers who in wave after wave dive-bombed the ships in Norway.

Now the führer of these fanatical people will be able, one year to the day after the last meeting of the Reichstag (September 1, 1939) to announce, if it has not begun by that time, the final offensive. And he can boast of a string of uninterrupted victories, above all, those since the beginning of the war—Poland, Denmark, Sweden, Norway (and the Balkans??). The position of Germany, he will say, has nothing in common with what it was in 1914. Now we have come (he can add) to the last phase of the struggle—avenge for all time the shame of 1918 and wipe out once and for all the imperial capitalism of the plutocratic democracies. And to do that, Hitler will dispose of 170 divisions, a vastly superior air force to which the Polish and Norwegian campaigns will have given confidence, and of a mass of useful technical information. Hitler will even be able to afford the luxury of sending 20 divisions to the Polish front, to keep Stalin quiet, in case all this should annoy the Soviet dictator—and still have 50 divisions more than we with which to fight against us! Moreover he will be able in the north, east, and south to strike blows where he chooses, along a line going from the North Sea to Tunisia—while trying to break through at some soft point with a massive attack on open ground, with aircraft and motorized divisions.

This can be dramatic for France!

Clare Boothe told me the other day that the only chance of drawing America into the war was to paint a very sombre picture.

Is this one sombre enough? I wrote it for her, but above all for you and your father. And I add that it isn't Paul Reynaud with his thirty-five ministers who can prepare our country in time for tomorrow's titanic struggle. . . . I love you with all my heart.

(There are two original copies of this letter. One is naturally for Clare. She or her husband can show it to Roosevelt, whom they both know well. The other is for you.)

The two signed copies of this letter were brought to Josée in Paris by a soldier who was going there on leave. I had asked her to get one of them off as quickly as possible to Carmel Offie, the secretary and factotum of Ambassador Bullitt.[3]

On May 3d, my corps commander called me to the phone and addressed me as "captain." He informed me that the French liaison officers' group had decided, on the basis of a glowing report by the British general attached to French headquarters, to recommend that I be promoted. This step up meant, unfortunately, that I would cease to serve in Lorraine. I was to report to Arras two days later.

After a sad and emotional evening in the depths of the Rotherberg, I parted from my three comrades who were to suffer the sad fate of all the defenders of the Maginot Line—encirclement and captivity.

I left this land of Lorraine with a heavy heart, little knowing that long after the disaster that befell France, because of the links I would establish with the Baccarat Crystal firm, I would come to love it as much as the Auvergne of Josée.

---

[3]U.S. ambassador in Paris.

CHAPTER 7

May 10, 1940:
The real war begins

LORD GORT'S HEADQUARTERS HAD JUST BEEN TRANSFERRED TO THE VILLAGE of Habarcq, near Arras, and there I met Colonel de Cardes, a young and brilliant cavalry officer, who was chief of staff of the French Liaison Officers' Group. He was the only man I met during the war who predicted exactly when and where the German "blitzkrieg" would strike.

"You see," he told me on the very day I arrived at Arras, "public opinion has been completely misled by official French and British communiqués. It has not been told about the intensive preparations for a spring offensive now under way in Germany. The real truth of what happened in Norway, at Narvick, has been concealed. Paul Reynaud, the French prime minister, told the Senate that 'the road to Norwegian and Swedish iron ore is barred to the Germans forever.' This is simply not true. Germany has achieved complete air superiority in Norway. She cannot afford to wait until next year for the British and French to produce a large number of tanks, planes, and antitank guns. One must therefore expect her to strike very soon, and this attack will not be directed against the Maginot Line. It will be launched in the next few weeks, when there is a full moon."

He told me that I had been appointed, for a few days only, to the 151st Infantry Brigade, until the arrival at the front of the Eleventh Division of the BEF. As things turned out, from then on I was never to see this new unit just being formed in Normandy.

On May 6th, I went to the headquarters of the 151st Infantry Brigade, located in the village of Don, south of Lille. The redbrick houses were new and spruce. Everything had been rebuilt after 1918. As far as the eye could see, the landscape was as flat as a pancake, with mine shafts, heaps of coal, and fields of sugar beet. Rows of willows marked the presence of a canal. The locks were guarded by troops who were bored to tears because they had been on duty in the same spot for months.

The headquarters of the 151st Brigade was located in a chateau, on the Canal de la Bassée, near Lille. Shortly after my arrival, I called on the mayor, an old Socialist party worker, who exuded good humor. All the mayors in this industrial area were either Socialists or Communists. He sat at his desk, and behind him, on the wall, were two photographs, one of Jean Jaurès, the great Socialist leader who was murdered in 1914, and the other of Roger Salengro, the minister of the interior in the Popular Front government who committed suicide in Lille in November 1936 after being accused by right-wing extremists of having deserted from the army in 1918.

The mayor led me to a pretty little house in the center of the village that was to be my billet. My hosts made salted butter, which they sold in the neighboring villages. They had several children, and all the family gathered around the radio in the dining room to listen to music and to the news. It was here that I heard the first reports of the offensive of May 10th.

I was suddenly awakened before daybreak by a steady barrage of antiaircraft fire. One of the batteries was only a couple of hundred yards from my window, which rattled each time a shot was fired. I naturally had no idea at the time that I was witnessing part of the biggest air attack ever launched in the history of warfare. Lille and its industrial suburbs were protected by a number of antiaircraft batteries, but in the area where the ten British divisions were stationed, there was a density of guns that the French army corps could not remotely match.

Shortly after the antiaircraft barrage got under way, I heard the sinister drone of the heavy bombers and the bombs exploding on their targets. I jumped into my clothes and leaned out of the window. Dawn was just breaking, and I could see groups of Heinkels flying in all directions. Shortly after, a few British fighters took to the air, and I distinctly heard the rattle of their machine guns.

The unit to which I was attached was in reserve and waiting for orders. We had nothing to do other than listen to the radio. *"Der Tag hat begonnen,"* said the guttural voice of the speaker from Stuttgart around 6 o'clock. He shouted into the mike that Germany had decided, against her will, to protect Holland, Belgium, and Luxembourg against an Allied threat!

Shortly after nine, I heard the voice of Paul-Henri Spaak, the spirited Belgian minister of foreign affairs, who was deeply upset. He related the dramatic conversation he had just had with the German ambassador, who called on him to transmit the monstrous memorandum from the Reich. Spaak said he had interrupted the envoy with the words, "No, Mr. Ambassador, today it is my turn to speak first." The minister's voice was drowned by a deafening explosion that shook the whole village and shattered all the windows in my house.

I dashed into the street. In a nearby field, a column of smoke rose from a mass of wreckage. I grabbed my revolver and ran toward it. A Heinkel was burning, and three men were slowly floating down by parachute. With a few British soldiers, I rushed up to the parachutist who hit the ground first. He was blond and lean and wore a smart gray uniform and fur-lined, zipped-up boots. As he limped a great deal, I put his arm around my shoulders, and we moved slowly back to brigade headquarters, watched by a few civilians who were observing the scene from the threshold of their homes. The pilot spoke a few words of French and as I had learned some German at school, we were able to understand one another. He told me that there were three other crew members beside himself, but that one of them had been unable to jump in time. The other survivors were the radio operator and the gunner. Once at brigade headquarters, I called for an interpreter and gave the prisoner some brandy, not from a desire to be kind but because I thought the pilot needed a pick-me-up if he were to be of any use to us. He accepted the English cigarettes we offered him and smoked while the doctor bound up his injured knee.

I then began to interrogate him. He told me he was twenty-three, had a wife and two children. His squadron of nine bombers was stationed at an airfield south of Berlin, of which he gave me the identification number. There were two other squadrons based on the same airfield. The previous night, at eleven, the squadron leader had got orders to fly his aircraft to another field on the left bank of the Rhine, near the Belgian frontier. He was given his flight plan half an hour before takeoff. At three in the morning, after refueling, thirty-six small bombs were attached to the undercarriage of each bomber. It was only then that they got the order to bomb the town of La Bassée, an important railway junction, between six and eight in the morning. They took off at four A.M.

"Were you informed that Holland, Belgium, and Luxembourg were going to be invaded by the German army?" I asked. He expressed great astonishment and said he had not the faintest idea this would be the case. "Were you told, or did you know, that other raids were to be carried out over Holland, Belgium, and France?" "No," he replied. "When we received our orders, we merely thought our two squadrons had been given the task of carrying out a major raid, which, if successful, would be mentioned in dispatches. That was why we felt we had to get to La Bassée at all costs, however strong the antiaircraft fire."

I questioned the prisoner at great length about the location of the other German airfields, and we talked about the German air force generally. I was surprised to discover that, despite his willingness to talk, he did not know anything that did not directly concern his own squadron or his personal role in it. Later, I interrogated or was present at the interrogation of many German pilots who had been shot down in the different sectors of the BEF, which I visited as liaison officer. Some refused to talk. Others were ready to tell what they knew, which was next to nothing.

After getting out of the pilot all the information I could gather, I got him on the subject of the war in general. He told me that Germany had no particular grievance against France but that she should not enjoy the same rights as the Germans, as her population was only half as large. He added that the real enemy of Germany was Britain and that she had to be destroyed. The Germans, he stressed, were a superior and privileged race, and only under German overlordship could world peace be established.

The two other prisoners, NCOs, had, in the meantime, been taken to headquarters; one of them, the gunner, was a sergeant who had won the Iron Cross in Poland. He was a man of the same stamp as his lieutenant and, like him, absolutely convinced of the philosophy of *Deutschland über Alles*. On the contrary, the wireless operator, also a sergeant, was uneducated and had no ideas at all about the war or its causes. He did what he was told, and that was that.

I quickly got to know that more than four thousand German bombers had taken off that morning. The High Command did not agree with me, but I was convinced it was highly improbable such a gigantic operation could be restaged in the near future. That day, the losses of the Luftwaffe in Holland, Belgium, and France exceeded three hundred aircraft. Afterward, hundreds more were shot down by RAF fighters and especially by the antiaircraft guns of the ten British divisions. Germany was perhaps in a position to replace these aircraft as rapidly as they were destroyed, but the training of air crews was another matter.

The brigadier whose office was on the first floor of the house that served as headquarters, and who was at work there while the prisoners were being interrogated, summoned me shortly after and told me his unit had to move the following day in the direction of Brussels. I was to go ahead of it and arrange for the necessary quarters with the local Belgian authorities. He gave me some printed forms that had to be signed by the mayors and a small booklet of instructions on billeting procedures in France and Belgium. The authors of this booklet had not taken into account what might happen in a country swept by panic. The officer in charge of transport gave me the keys of the only staff car, which I was able to bring back to base after the Flanders campaign, and I left shortly before midday for the north.

A few miles farther, my car was stopped by a long column of tanks, armored cars, automobiles, and motorcycles. The men in them wore helmets camouflaged with leaves and stood head and shoulder out of the turrets of the tanks, ready to open fire with their machine guns on enemy aircraft. All this armor, which had obviously been produced after the outbreak of war, was impressive. It belonged to one of the units of the corps of motorized cavalry commanded by General Prioux.

Military historians who wrote about the terrible Allied rout in the north have not laid sufficient emphasis on the extraordinary bravery displayed by General Prioux's corps. For twenty-five days and nights, without a moment's letup, these men fought German units, which were constantly relieved and always enjoyed superiority in numbers and armaments. They covered the retreat of the French, Belgian, and British troops in Belgium. Then, when the Allied defenses at Sedan were breached by German motorized divisions, what was left of this band of heroes was dispatched to the southern flank of the Northern Army Group. Their stubborn resistance made the evacuation of 335,000 British troops through Dunkerque possible, after the Belgian capitulation. But even then, the exploits of General Prioux's men were not over. Adopting a formation akin to the ancient Greek phalanx, they broke through enemy lines and reached the coast, where they covered the embarkation itself.

I overtook the leading tanks of the cavalry corps in my small car and arrived in the zone close to the Belgian frontier where, during the seven months of "phony war," we had built blockhouses and dugouts linked by thick barbed-wire entanglements—a sort of little Maginot Line.

CHAPTER 8

The Belgian trap

How can I describe the fourteen moves of Division HQ that took place from then on in the short space of two weeks?

The easternmost location was reached the second night. It was two miles away from the grim site of Waterloo, where the Prussians fought alongside the British against the French.

It would require the talent of a Victor Hugo, the precision of a Thiers [statesman of the time], and several Michelin guides to give an accurate and striking description of these moves, under attack by dive bombers and amid the endless flood of refugees.

In order not to break the thread of this story, which will take the reader by rapid stages to Washington, President Roosevelt, and the White House, I will merely relate a few striking memories. At the time and shortly after the events, I made notes and quoted from them in the course of the long speaking tour that Roosevelt and Harry Hopkins asked me to make through the Midwest in July 1940.

The first of these recollections is of dive bombing. While my car was stuck in the middle of an uninterrupted flood of refugees, I heard a peculiar screeching sound above my head and a high-pitched whine at high altitude. It was my first encounter with three Stukas. The burst of the bombs deafened me momentarily. Not far from me, another car with a small family on board was annihilated. Death was instantaneous. I felt horrified, revolted. But what could I do?

During one of my interminable stops on the road to Brussels, I got out of my car and was assailed by fantastic rumors: Italy had declared war, revolution had broken out in Paris, Louvain was on fire. When I called on the gendarmerie at Brake to try to make a phone call, I found the Belgian police interrogating persons accused of a new crime—spreading false news.

Farther on, a car was hooting desperately to try to force its way through the crowded thoroughfare. A man perched on the running board was shouting to all and sundry, "Run! German tanks are entering Brussels. Hurry!" I stopped my car in front of theirs and ran after the man as he tried to escape across a field. I drew my revolver and shot him in the legs. With the help of two or three Belgian soldiers, I was able to catch him and to hand him over to the police at the next village. My one and only prisoner in this war talked readily. He said he was a "Rexist," a Belgian Fascist, who lived in a suburb of Brussels and had been given orders by his chief, whose name he told me, to spread false news.

My second recollection is of my arrival at Alost to establish the first headquarters of our division. Night fell, and the road was so completely congested that, a few miles from the town, I grabbed an abandoned bicycle and told the driver of the car to join me later as best he could. I made straight for the railway station, but there was no station left. What was to have been the rear supply base of our division was only a mass of wreckage, of dead and wounded. Two military police from the division had got ahead of me to the hotel earmarked as an officers' assembly point. I admired their composure in the midst of all this desolation. They did not bat an eyelid and looked like dummies on a stage.

My third recollection was of my meeting with the commander of one of the forts of the Belgian Maginot Line along the German frontier, at Braine l'Alleux, south of Brussels. While divisional headquarters was still at Braine, I was awakened one night by a heavy raid on a neighboring suburb. As I listened to the drone of aircraft engines, the unceasing explosions, and the rattle of antiaircraft fire, I came to the conclusion that this raid was intended to swell the flood of refugees by throwing onto the roads all those who had remained in their homes. The Germans were obviously trying to block all movement of the Allied forces. The cost in terms of bombers shot down was high, but it paid off.

At Braine, the following morning, I looked out of the window and saw on the sidewalk a captain who wore the flash of the Belgian Maginot Line. He was with a group of soldiers who had just got off an army truck and were all unarmed. I knew that they came from a line of forts that we believed was still strongly defended at the time, and I came down to see what they were doing there.

The Belgian captain saw my own Maginot Line flash, and a couple of minutes later, he began pouring his heart out to me. He was so agitated that he could talk of nothing but what had happened to him and his men the previous night:

> I am a regular, and I was in command of one of the forts in our line of defense forts reputed to be impregnable. We had orders to stick it out if we were encircled. We could shut ourselves in, had enough food to last a month, and 800,000 rounds of ammunition. Since last September, we were given the occasional order to perform this or that maneuver just to keep in trim.

On May 10th, our commander was told to abandon the fort without firing a shot and to regroup north of Brussels. Dumbfounded, he checked to see if the order was genuine by calling up GHQ, as it seemed to him unbelievable. He told me afterward what had happened. When the German offensive began, two of the bridges on the southern part of the Albert Canal failed to be blown up, and the German armor poured over them and took the Belgian defenses from the rear. "It's incredible, it's incredible!," he repeated over and over again, mopping his brow with his handkerchief and waving his arms. "This line of defenses cost us billions to build. It could have saved Belgium from invasion. I wanted to die in my fort with my men," he added. "And now, what can we do here without even a gun?"

My fourth recollection is of a meeting with the major of a regiment of Belgian light infantry who told me about the breakthrough of Hitler's tanks in the Ardennes. It was a few hours before our retreat to the coast. He came up to me and asked me where he could find the headquarters of General Billotte, because he had been instructed by his battalion commander to get in touch with General Blanchard, the head of the French First Army. Before I gave him the information, I demanded to see his identity card, for I had become suspicious after my repeated interrogation of suspects. His papers were in order. It was from him that I learned of the disaster at Sedan.

"It is also our fault," he said. "This is what happened. Have you ever been in the Belgian Ardennes?" he asked, as he lit a cigarette. "No," I replied. "It is one of the thickest forests in Europe," he went on. "In order to prevent the German armor from driving through it, we were to sow mines and fell trees as antitank obstacles. Incredible as it may seem, the mines had been left in unguarded depots. So they all went up in smoke on the night of May 9th. Then the German armored divisions found all the petrol they needed in one or two dumps, which had been carefully camouflaged. Obviously, we should have foreseen all this but we did not dream it could happen. Now, it's too late. I can tell you that a huge number of tanks and armored cars are pouring through the front of your Ninth Army. With the roads in their present state, you will never be able to get your troops up to counterattack."

I accompanied the major back to his car and stood for a while on the side of the road, watching the sad procession of refugees. A man whose face was familiar walked past me. He had a blanket rolled over his shoulders and a small child in one arm; he carried a suitcase with his free hand. I recognized him as a lawyer from Louvain who had come to consult me in Paris a few months before the war:

"I left Louvain yesterday," he said, "when street fighting broke out. My car ran out of petrol a few miles away, and I have decided to walk as far as France and try to save my wife and child."

In exchange for a few Belgian cigarettes, I gave him all the francs I had in my pocket, as well as some bacon and beer from my British rations. As the army post office had ceased to function, I scribbled a few lines to Josée and entrusted them to him in the hope that he would reach Paris in a few days.

The sight of the Belgian highways thronged with refugees made my heart ache, and a strong feeling of despondency came over me. The British officers, on the other hand, did not seem greatly affected by these tragic scenes. Perhaps because they themselves, their fathers, and grandfathers had been accustomed to fighting wars on foreign soil, and the tragedy they witnessed was not that of their own people.

After the sixth day of the German offensive, we moved south of Waterloo, and our sinister retreat, punctuated by insignificant, delaying counterattacks, led in the end to our final encirclement.

CHAPTER 9
Encirclement—Dunkerque:
A toss-up between
life and death

On May 26th, the sixteenth day of the German offensive, practically the whole of the French Northern Army, including the British Expeditionary Forces, was encircled by the Germans. The Wehrmacht had reached the channel at Abbeville, and communications were cut off between the North and the South. It had become difficult to know the exact whereabouts of the enemy. His tanks and armored cars penetrated deeply and in large numbers through the gap at Sedan and had then begun to fan out toward the North. We ran the risk day and night of coming up against them where they were least expected.

On that afternoon, I was able to reach the headquarters of the Liaison Officers' Group at Hazebrouck and reported to Colonel de Cardes, whose self-control was remarkable. This, textually, on the basis of the notes I took practically day by day, is what he told me:

> It has happened. I told you so. It is all very painful to me, but one must try to get a grip on oneself, to hope, to believe in a miracle, or rather in two miracles: the first, that a bridgehead will be held in Dunkerque, thanks to our navy and to the British air force, which has come to our rescue. The second miracle is that the Germans will be stopped on the line of the Somme.
>
> On this hypothesis, I have drawn up a plan for the reorganization of the Liaison Group with the arrival of British reinforcements for a reorganized expeditionary corps. I want you to leave immediately for Dunkerque, London, and Vincennes. The French air attaché in London, for whom I will give you a letter, will certainly find room for you on a plane for Paris so that you can hand over this envelope with documents for General Weygand, the commander in chief, to Gasser, his ADC [aide-de-camp].

I gathered my belongings and arrived at the headquarters of General Blanchard, set up in a small chateau beside a wood in which staff cars, concealed under camouflage nets, were parked among the trees. I asked a group of drivers if one of them would volunteer to take me to the coast. They all wanted to. I chose the youngest, an unmarried man, and got into the small Renault. I then studied the map to select the least hazardous route.

I had learned the proper technique for taking cover from the Stukas' machine-gun fire: as soon as I heard the whine of their engines, or saw one of them draw close, I would stop the car and jump into the ditch on one side of the road, while the driver did the same on the other. We had to do this several times on the way to Dunkerque.

It was getting dark, and we were crawling along a secondary road crowded with refugees. Suddenly, a few hundred yards to our left, German tanks, which had come to a halt, began strafing the refugees with machine-gun fire, causing a panic among them and scattering them in all directions. My own reaction was to get the driver to reverse a few hundred yards, and I told him to return to Hazebrouck as quickly as possible, if he could. As for myself, I made for a small wood to the north and worked out my position on my map. I reckoned that, by discarding some of my gear, I could get to Dunkerque, which was only fifteen miles away, by daybreak on foot if I kept on right through the night. I got going and took brief two-hour breaks at regular intervals. About halfway to Dunkerque, I reached a canal guarded by a British patrol. I was exhausted and had to have some rest before going any farther. I asked the sergeant to wake me up an hour later, which he did very precisely, and I resumed my march with much dragging of feet. As day broke, the port was under bombardment by an increasing number of Heinkels. Finally, very footsore, I stopped about one hundred yards from the heavy steel doors of the dockyards.

On either side of the doors, there was a sentry box in front of which stood an officer, a petty officer, and a marine. The sight of those smartly dressed sailors with their blue caps, red pompoms, and white gaiters each holding a musket with a short bayonet that flashed in the sunshine made me realize that I looked like a tramp in my dusty, stained uniform. I tried to spruce myself up as best I could and moved forward. The officer drew close to me to check my identity and led me to the chief of staff of Admiral Abrial.

While I waited outside his office, I gazed out of a window at the vast dockyard and discovered a new world very different from the one I had known after sixteen days and nights of retreat and rout, of sadness and suffering. The sight was indeed comforting: officers, petty officers, and ratings were walking or rushing about all over the place with a purposeful air. I felt that a major operation was under way. For the past few days,

Admiral Abrial and his staff had been working around the clock in one of the bastions on the major plan for the evacuation of 335,000 men. It began that night and saved the troops of the BEF five long years of captivity.

It was a strange fate for this old citadel of Dunkerque, built a few centuries before to protect France against the British threat from the sea, to be now converted by the admiral and the French navy into a fortress to cover the retreat and embarkation of British troops, who had become our allies.

I was ushered into the office of the chief of staff. Our conversation was short because I realized he was snowed under with work. He told me that "unfortunately, I do not have time to accompany you, but one of my deputies will do so. Two launches are leaving for Dover quite soon, and he will take you to the embarkation point in his car. You will be taking a small risk," he added, "if you really want to leave this morning because the cruisers and destroyers lying offshore to provide protection will only take up their stations this evening. This afternoon, we will only send one or two thousand men. The real job will be done at night."

The officer led me to a small car. The driver made for the other side of the town, zigzagging hell for leather between the shell holes as if the devil were on his tail. Along the wharfs, large blocks of stone loosened by the bombing fell into the murky waters of the harbor; houses that had withstood the shelling of the First World War were badly hit. All their windows were smashed, and their roofs had caved in.

At the embarkation point, there was a long trench where about twenty British officers were waiting for the launches. The officer in charge of the evacuation explained that we had to split into two groups and, when he blew his whistle, make a run for one or the other of the boats. The first would stop in front of the trench; the second, about twenty yards away.

As a child, I was brought up in the United States by my American mother who had taught me the equivalent of the French: *Am, stram, gram,* or eenie, meenie, minie, moe. Why not try it this time to decide which launch to choose? I did and got into the second one. The first sank somewhere between Dunkerque and Dover.

As the officer blew his whistle, we ran to the launches and jumped in with our kit. We could see the German bombers out at sea, flying in wide circles over the Pas de Calais. "What are they doing?" I asked the skipper, as our launch drew away. "They are laying mines. They began a few days ago," was his reply. As we left the French coast, three squadrons of Heinkels, twenty-seven in all, converged from three directions. As if by some prearranged signal, six British fighters, flying at very high altitude, appeared in the sky and at the precise moment when the Germans jettisoned their mines, they dived onto them. They fought under our eyes the finest air battle I have ever seen. In a few minutes, almost all the Heinkels had been hit and fell in the sea, leaving behind them long trails of smoke. Only when I reached Dover did I learn the news: the first "Bolton Defiants," with their revolving turrets, had been sent that very morning over the channel by the RAF.

This extraordinary sight, which has come to my mind very often since, convinced me, with absolute certainty, that any German attempt at a landing on British soil would be doomed to fail.

Were it not for the presence of a few warships in the harbor, Dover had a prewar aspect. Not a single bomb had fallen on that side of the channel during the raids, which had gone on day and night over the French coast. Whereas the station of Alost had been smashed to smithereens in a few minutes, the one at Dover was intact. I was familiar with the rail journey to London in the small, clattering, swaying carriages. Britain seemed still at peace. The playing fields were full of schoolboys enjoying games of football, rugby, or cricket, and the tennis courts were all in use.

But Victoria Station, at the end of this beautiful day in May, was beginning to look like the Gare de l'Est in Paris, where Josée had come to bid me good-bye nine months before. Newsboys were shouting the banner headline, printed in huge letters, all over the front page of the *Evening Standard: Calais Falls*. Thus it was that this French port, which England had held for two centuries and whose name was said to be engraved on the heart of Mary Tudor (who lost it), fell to Hitler's war machine in sixteen days, the first serious blow struck at the might of the British empire.

I jumped into a taxi and made for the Savoy Hotel. After plunging into a huge bath of hot water, I fell into bed and was soon sound asleep, without even taking time for a meal, as Britain began her first night of real war.

CHAPTER 10

From London to Paris
in a "grasshopper" plane

THE FOLLOWING MORNING, I CALLED ON THE FRENCH AIR ATTACHÉ AT THE embassy with the envelope of urgent documents for General Weygand. He told me he could arrange for me to leave London that same night in an RAF bomber or, better still, as I was in a great hurry, in a light aircraft reserved for special missions. I asked what these special missions were exactly. He explained that, before the war, a young reserve air force lieutenant he knew had been in the habit of piloting a private aircraft. He had volunteered to carry out delicate missions such as flying officers to places not accessible to standard military aircraft. If Robaud—that was the lieutenant's name—was able to return safe and sound from Dunkerque, to which he had just flown a senior officer, the air attaché would inform me immediately.

An hour later, I got a phone call informing me that Robaud had returned and was already on his way to my hotel to pick me up. A few minutes later, he was there, and I quickly realized that he was the kind of man France produces in times of crisis. Danger was his business, and this he had in common with many French air force pilots I had known. He dreamed of heroic exploits.

When I asked him on which airfield he had landed, he replied that he had left his aircraft in a small field, beyond a London suburb, and would easily find it again on his map. We got into a taxi and drove through the East End, at which point Robaud began, with the help of the map, to give the driver the necessary directions. I felt a little worried when I saw what he called his "machine." It looked like a large grasshopper crouching in a meadow. I wondered how on earth we could reach Paris without coming under antiaircraft attack from the moment we crossed the French coast. Robaud told me that the real advantage of this plane, which he had designed himself, was precisely its small size, which made it look inoffensive. It was also, according to him, the best camouflaged machine in France. He had himself painted the wings green and sky blue.

As we drew close to it, he explained that by hedgehopping too low to cast a shadow on the ground, which could be spotted at high altitude, it was difficult for enemy aircraft to detect. He asked if my eyesight was good. I told him, that, unfortunately, I was a little shortsighted and had lost my glasses in Belgium. "It doesn't matter," he said. "The only thing I will ask you to do is to keep an eye on what is going on behind us. If you spot an enemy plane swooping down on us, give me a warning shout, and I will try to land somewhere immediately. When I do, don't lose a second, jump out of the plane and dive into the first ditch or hole close at hand. It is the best way of avoiding machine-gun fire, and I have used it successfully on a few occasions." He added that our flight would probably seem to me a little long, as our cruising speed would not exceed 120 miles an hour!

I did not feel very reassured, and when I got into the machine I felt as though I were sitting in a bathtub that had suddenly sprouted a pair of wings. We took off and flew just over the treetops. I watched the sky carefully and spotted a few British reconnaissance planes. I was beginning to realize that I was probably in the hands of a very remarkable pilot.

After an hour, we reached the sea, and he landed on a beach. I saw him jump out of the cockpit, and break off a small stick from a tree in a nearby field. As he came back, he plucked all the leaves from the stick. I wondered what on earth he was doing when he removed the cap on his reservoir and measured the quantity of fuel that remained. After examining his stick, he announced calmly that he did not have quite enough to fly by way of Le Havre and that he would take a chance and cross the channel by the shortest route, hitting the coast just south of Abbeville. That was just about the line reached by the German offensive.

We took off again and skimmed just above the crest of the waves, until the French coast came into view. As we crossed it, I saw an antiaircraft gun firing at us. He had seen it too and went into a sharp climb. Having got up to about four thousand feet, he concluded that the gun was a French one. He then rocked the plane from side to side in order, he told me, to give the people on the ground a good view of the French tricolor markings on the wings. The firing ceased, and we headed for Paris.

At that moment, we noticed two squadrons of Heinkel bombers flying overhead in the direction of Le Havre. Perhaps they did not see us. But I am inclined to think they took us for a couple of people on an excursion in a light aircraft who did not deserve bursts of machine-gun fire. Shortly after, my pilot spotted three German fighter planes, very high and very far away, which seemed to be making directly for us. Fortunately, we were above level ground and landed immediately in a field. I jumped out of the machine and fell flat on my face behind a tree. Two Messerschmitts dived toward us at high speed but went into a climb immediately without firing a round. An hour later, we reached Paris.

I expressed my gratitude to the pilot and told him that he deserved to be given a fighter aircraft. "You see," he said, "the trouble is we were complacent for many years, and today, while in Germany they have too many aircraft for the pilots available, we, in France, have the pilots but not the aircraft."

I jumped into a taxi and told the driver to take me as quickly as possible to Vincennes. Once I got to the fortress, which was General Weygand's headquarters, I handed over the documents to an officer on the general's staff and dashed back to my home on the Place du Palais-Bourbon. Josée was at home. She had got none of the letters I had given to Belgian refugees fleeing to France. My wholly unexpected appearance was one of the happiest moments in our lives.

CHAPTER 11

Ambassador Bullitt, General Weygand, Marshal Pétain, and a "forgotten Frenchman"

Barely a quarter of an hour after I had got home, the telephone rang. Carmel Offie, the personal assistant to William Bullitt, the American ambassador, was on the line, wanting to speak to my wife. She told him that I had just turned up, and Offie suggested that I come to the embassy straight away.

William Bullitt

The American embassy is very near our home, on the other side of the Seine. I crossed the bridge and the Place de la Concorde and was greeted by the familiar smile of the black porter who stands at the entrance, under the star-spangled banner.

I had got to know William Bullitt during my years in the United States, in the early thirties. He was very fond of France and spoke French fluently. He always preferred to speak it with me, and very quickly, we switched to the familiar *tu*. The list of towns of which he had been given the freedom would be difficult to draw up, such was the sympathy he enjoyed in all parts of the country.

After we had embraced effusively, we settled down in deep leather armchairs in his huge ambassadorial office. Our conversation, which was long and intimate, has remained graven in my mind. Bullitt had a telephone within arm's reach on a small table by his side, and every time it rang, and I would take a few steps toward the secretaries' room next door, he signaled to me to stay.

He spoke first, after a pause, "René, do you think *we* are done for?" That "we" on his lips gave me a measure of his love of France. To this, I replied, "It's going to be terrible for France. But England cannot be invaded. The fighters of the RAF are more than a match for German bombers, and she has the Home Fleet as well." I went on to tell him about the enormous losses of the Heinkel squadrons in the air space over the British divisions in northern France, the interrogation of pilots that I had attended, and that incredible air battle over the channel in which I had seen five or six Bolton Defiants shoot down three squadrons of Heinkels.

"But," he objected, "they are very pessimistic in Washington—Roosevelt, Cordell Hull, with whom you heard me speak on the phone a moment ago, and others. Would you be ready to go to Washington at very short notice? It would be important." To which I replied that I could only go there on orders of my military superiors. "I have an appointment tomorrow with Paul Reynaud [the prime minister], and I shall ask him that you be sent," he said (see exhibit 1).

General Weygand

The ambassador did not lose any time because, the following day around noon, I received a call from General Weygand's chief of staff, asking me to come round that same evening at seven. He hinted that I would be asked to take the Clipper leaving Lisbon for the United States at short notice.

As I made my way through eastern Paris toward General Weygand's headquarters, the sun was setting behind the trees of the Bois de Vincennes. Here and there, I overtook groups of workers cycling peacefully home after their day's work or children returning for supper after play. Around the old Vincennes fortress, there was an unbelievable atmosphere of calm and peace. It was only broken by the occasional roar of a dispatch rider's motorcycle setting off with orders for some unknown destination.

A guard led me through the long bare corridors to the ADC's office. Captain Gasser told me that General Weygand had spent the better part of the preceding night visiting the headquarters of the different armies in the field and had attended a cabinet meeting in the morning.

In the general's waiting room, I could see, through the tall windows, the dungeon of Vincennes and the moat where, at a tragic period in French history, the Duc d'Enghien, the last of the Condés, had been shot in 1804. An NCO led me into the general's office, a vast room whose walls were covered with large maps. With the briskness of a young battalion commander, the general, who had been ADC to Marshal Foch in the First World War and was now over seventy, came over to greet me, shook my hand, and said, "I saw Mr. Bullitt this morning in Mr. Paul Reynaud's office, and he asked that you be sent immediately to the United States. I have decided to appoint you assistant military attaché at our embassy in Washington, and I want you to get onto the first Clipper leaving Portugal.

PARIS SENDS US ENVOY
FROM FLANDERS 'HELL'

Count Rene de Chambrun to Tell
Roosevelt of Operations

PARIS, June 2 (UP)—A survivor of the "Flanders Hell" is en route to Washington to inform President Roosevelt regarding Allied war operations, it was revealed tonight.

Capt. Count Rene de Chambrun, evacuated by sea from the Flanders pocket of encirclement, is en route by clipper to the United States as new assisant military attaché to the French Embassy in Washington.

An honorary American citizen because of his direct descent from Lafayette and a son of the late Clara Longworth of Cincinnati, Count de Chambrun is charged with the special mission of acquainting President Roosevelt and other American officials with anything they desire to know about the military operations.

The count left Paris last night for Lisbon to board the American Clipper for New York.

His special mission, it was revealed, was entrusted to him by Premier Paul Reynaud and General Maxime Weygand.

Count de Chambrun was liaison officer between the British Expeditionary Force and the French First Army trapped in the Flanders pocket but was evacuated by sea to England, whence he returned to France.

His father retired recently as a general of the French Army after a long colonial career.

Exhibit 1. A United Press cable was sent to U.S. newspapers announcing René de Chambrun's departure to "inform" President Roosevelt regarding war operations.

Before you depart, at the latest tomorrow evening, you must see Mr. Dautry (the minister for armaments) in the morning, to speed up as much as possible the processing of our arms procurement orders, and also Marshal Pétain and the president of the republic. The appointments will be made for you."

He got up suddenly and led me over to the largest of the maps on the wall, which was crisscrossed with red and blue pencil marks. I also noticed little flags bearing the swastika pinned deep into French territory, showing the extreme limit of the German advance. He showed me the front, which he intended to hold with what troops he had left.

"We shall soon be attacked again, and it will be the decisive battle, into which I will have to throw all my reserves. Between Sedan and the sea, Gamelin had a front of two hundred kilometers along which, either in the line or in reserve, were deployed three of the finest French armies—the First, the Seventh, and the Ninth—the twenty-five Belgian divisions, and the ten divisions of the British Expeditionary Forces. Today, I have a front longer by a third, which extends from Montmedy to the English Channel, near Abbeville.

"We are going to run short of men, equipment, and especially of arms. Explain to the Americans how great are the odds against us. Make sure especially to ask Roosevelt to bring pressure to bear on Churchill to send over to France the whole of his fighter force. We have the airfields to accommodate them. The British must realize at last that their destiny too is at stake here. The overall picture is not cheerful," he concluded. "But a miracle can always happen, and I have not lost hope." He stopped for a second and added, "In any case, a commander must never lose hope."

Before saying good-bye, the general asked me to write for him, that same evening, a report on my impressions of the military situation I had briefly summed up in the course of our conversation. Back home, and after a light supper, I got to work on it and have kept a copy. Here it is:

In the field, June 2, 1940

Captain R. de Chambrun to General Weygand,
    commander in chief of the army

My dear general:

Following your request, I have the honor to sum up my impressions of the events I have witnessed between May 10 and 30, during my service as liaison officer between the First Army headquarters and the divisions of the British Expeditionary Forces.

I noticed from the very first days of the German attack, and after driving along the highways of Belgium, that the flight of refugees had been systematically organized. I had two agents arrested in the commune of Ogy and the city of Niuvic whose role was to cause panic around them by spreading false rumors about the approach of the Germans and their methods of warfare. The procedure used by these men was always the same: to make the Belgians believe that the arrival of motorized German units was imminent. Thanks to this method, the Germans in Belgium found the roads deserted, while millions of refugees, most of whom fled in heavy horse-drawn vehicles, were obstructing the means of communication used by the British. During the retreat to the Scarpe, I happened to try, under air bombardment, to clear a road on which British columns of troops had been held up for more than eight hours.

I noticed that this exodus had a depressing effect on our troops and sometimes even on our officers. It had no effect on the British, perhaps because they are less emotional than we and accustomed to fighting on foreign battlefields.

South of the British sector lay the Belgian Ardennes, opposite the Sedan gap. Had this forest area been prepared for defense by felling trees and laying mines, it would have been extremely difficult for German armored divisions to penetrate it. Because of the utter negligence of the Ardennes Chasseurs responsible for this task, the German units got through this dense forest in less than forty-eight hours. I learned from a certain Belgian source that they were even able to obtain petrol thanks to hidden depots set up in advance.

I found that behind the lines in France and in certain large cities such as Arras, Lens, Valenciennes, Douai, Seclin, Roubaix, and Tourcoing, a large number of civilian officials had hardly shown courage and a sense of duty. The mayors of almost all the townships in the North had fled. This contributed greatly to the increase in the general panic.

Isolated groups of civilians, antiaircraft and army service corps units, and officials retreated without orders. Thus in the North, it was impossible for two British divisions, who were to hold the fixed defenses on the Franco-Belgian frontier after they had withdrawn that far, to find in Lille the documents pertaining to that sector since those who had been in charge of them had gone. It would seem desirable, in towns situated immediately behind the line in the Somme and the Aisne and even farther, to entrust the command, not to officers with a bureaucratic conception of their duties but to men determined to fight and to eliminate all cowardice. It would also seem advisable to give precise instructions to all local officials on how to deal with tanks, motorcyclists, parachutists, and other new methods of warfare. The conduct of certain reserve units that fled from the fighting zone left much to be desired. Their appearance and behavior were deplorable, their morale bad. The propaganda of the Popular Front reproduced by German pamphlets made an impact. I heard several soldiers making such remarks as this: "I am sick and tired of risking my life for the two hundred Families (the Left's expression for the financial 'rulers' of France)."

I had many occasions to be with British units, and their behavior was good. I noted particularly the calm resolve of General Gort as well as the decisiveness shown by his divisional commanders such as Martell and Curtis. During this extremely difficult period, the chief of staff of the French Liaison Mission, Lieutenant Colonel de Cardes, worked prodigiously and succeeded in maintaining contact between the two armies. His task, as well as that of the First Army staff, was made very delicate by the daily moves of headquarters. The headquarters of the First Army were constantly bombed (Lens, Estaires, Attiches), which proved the effectiveness of the enemy's intelligence, while we never knew where the German headquarters were. Despite the painful impression caused by these continual raids, the officers' morale remained excellent. The motorized cavalry corps of General Prioux, constantly in the breach, never failed to distinguish itself.

I mention also the urgent necessity of securing from Britain several squadrons of fighter planes, which would operate in the Dunkerque region. These squadrons are stationed on bases at home where they are doing nothing since no British towns are being bombed at this time. If they were in action in France, they would bring down many German bombers, which will one day raid England. During my brief trip to London, I brought this fact to the attention of an influential member of the Privy Council, who asked me to go with him the next day to see Mr. Churchill. As I had to leave the next morning by plane, he took it upon himself to transmit my suggestion and to recommend it.

Tomorrow morning, I shall see M. Dautry, Marshal Pétain, and the president of the republic. I will leave the day after tomorrow for Lisbon, after receiving your final instructions. Your ADC can always reach me at Inv.29.97.

René de Chambrun.

Raoul Dautry

Late that evening, while I was working on my report, a secretary to the minister for armaments told me that he would see me the following morning at seven. I asked her to repeat the time of the appointment, for never in my life had I been given such an early one. I arrived a few minutes before at the Hotel Majestic, near the Arc de Triomphe, which had been converted into a ministry at the outbreak of war.

Two armed guards in sentry boxes on either side of the entrance were surrounded by police inspectors in plain clothes. I told one of them that I had an appointment with the minister. He led me into the main hall, which was deserted. A secretary came down the stairs and took me to what must have been one of the luxury suites on the first floor, now turned into an office for the minister.

Dautry opened the door into the antechamber, where I was waiting. Short, stocky, energetic, and strong-willed, he greeted me and bade me take a seat. We knew each other well, for he was one of the nine board members of the French Information Office in the United States, whose president was Marshal Pétain and of which I was the founder. Our conversation fell into two parts: First, he got me to relate my impressions of my twenty days at the front after the outbreak of the German offensive. Then he asked me to call on the French Purchasing Commission in New York on my way to Washington, and talk to the director, Bloch-Lainé, and his assistants. "We must do everything to make them feel that our orders for arms and materials should be shipped immediately," and he went on to deplore the administrative delays on the American side.

As I left him, I came across the men and women of the ministry who were arriving for work with an unhurried air. The peaceful atmosphere of the place seemed to me quite out of tune with the tragedy that was unfolding in northern France.

Marshal Pétain

Marshal Pétain, whom I saw at the end of the morning at the Hôtel des Invalides, where he had an office, was an acquaintance of several years' standing. I had met him the first time in 1917, when I was ten years of age. He was then commander in chief of the French forces. My father, a colonel at the time, acted as liaison officer between him and General Pershing, the commander in chief of the American Expeditionary Corps.

Pershing, a widower, had an only son, Warren, of exactly my same age, and it was agreed by our parents that I would keep young Warren company and be his playmate. For this reason, I spent the last year of the First World War with him, in the retinue of Generals Pershing and Pétain, at their respective headquarters. My most vivid memory of that war was the triumphal entry of the two generals into Metz, which had just been liberated by Franco-American troops. We went to the arsenal where General Pétain, grabbing two German spiked helmets that were lying around, rammed them on our heads, right up to our ears, and exclaimed, "It's all over! We got the Boches!"

At the time of the dramatic events of the Rif war, in Morocco in 1925, when Abd-el-Krim led a revolt against the French protectorate authorities, my father commanded the shock troops ordered to stop the rebel forces at all costs at the gates of Fez. This is not the place for me to relate the circumstances in which Pétain, who had by then become a marshal of France, conducted the operations that led to the capture of Abd-el-Krim. He stayed at my father's residence, and my relations with him became even closer.

In 1931, accompanied by my father, he went to the United States to represent France at the 150th anniversary of the Battle of Yorktown. I drafted his speech and acted as his interpreter. When he returned to France, he sent me a photograph with the following dedication: "To the little Bunny [the nickname I was given by my family], in memory of the visit to the United States in 1931, when he was so thoughtful and affectionate for his old friend. Ph. Pétain."

A few years later, after my four years in a New York law office, I went back to France, alarmed at the damage done by Nazi propaganda in the United States and anxious to set up the French Information Office to counter it. On the advice of all the personalities I met in this connection, such as the American ambassador, Jesse Isidor Straus, the rector of the University of Paris, Raoul Dautry, and Governor General Olivier, a leading colonial administrator, I called on Marshal Pétain to ask him if he would agree to become president of this new institution. As I was the moving spirit behind it, I saw the marshal two or three times a week very regularly at that time, until war broke out and I was called up on active service.

When, that morning, I walked into the office where we had met so many times, I was struck by his calm and serenity. He gave me the impression that I had left a world in turmoil to enter a haven of peace and tranquillity. He questioned me at length and asked me to call as soon as possible after my arrival in Washington on his great friend, General Pershing. This I naturally promised to do. We did not discuss the military situation, for he knew I had done so with General Weygand, but we exchanged reminiscences until I took my leave. When I got home for lunch, a message was waiting for me saying that I should be at the Elysée Palace in the late afternoon.

President Albert Lebrun

My most urgent problem was to go to a shop in the area of the Ecole Militaire and buy myself a ready-made uniform with the three bars of a captain. Later, a taxi dropped me off in the courtyard of the Elysée Palace, wearing my brand-new uniform, and I had the impression that the guard and the ushers viewed me with a faint trace of condescension. Not many captains, I imagine, arrived in a taxi to call on the president of the republic!

The usher who showed me into his study carried a list of the president's appointments that afternoon. Casting a sidelong glance at it, I discovered that the head of state had seen the Romanian ambassador at three and Mr. Paul Reynaud at three-thirty. Mine was the last of the day's meetings.

Along the corridor that led to the study, the Aubusson carpets stood rolled up in corners. Everything in the palace seemed ready for a hasty retreat. Some furniture had even been removed from the grand drawing room, and I noticed that only the president's study seemed to be still wholly furnished.

Albert Lebrun welcomed me warmly and offered me a seat on the left of his big desk. After asking me to hand over a personal message to President Roosevelt, he began to talk about the military campaign, which he seemed to know inside out. He was familiar with the names of all the generals, be they army, corps, or divisional commanders. I asked him if he knew of the whereabouts of his son Jean (Jean Lebrun was a personal friend, a signals officer in one of the divisions on the Lorraine front during the winter of 1940). "I have had no news of him since the outbreak of the German offensive," he replied, with sadness in his look.

In the course of our conversation, I would occasionally glance at the big Louis XVI clock on the mantlepiece. After thirty minutes, I said, "Mr. President, I am taking too much of your time in these tragic hours for our country." "No, no," he replied, drawing his armchair a little closer to me. "You see, this evening, I am not disturbed either by the telephone or by visitors, and I have no more appointments after yours." He paused and added, "It is the first time in some weeks, for generally, my meetings and audiences hardly ever end before seven or eight o'clock."

He began to talk about the attitude of the king of the Belgians, which had shocked him deeply. Then he got onto Edouard Daladier and his successor, Paul Reynaud. "Their task is difficult because of the slowness with which democratic principles evolve in this country. Your father-in-law knows something about it. I wish he would come and see me," he said.

Then, sadly and with a touch of philosophy, he added,

It is strange. I am sure our forefathers who set up the republic as a transitional regime after the defeat of 1870, in order to reconstruct France, would not recognize their offspring if they saw it today. In 1871, thirty-six million French peasants, workers, and bourgeois, who came to the conclusion that, individually, they were not competent to manage the affairs of the state and that they could not all govern together, decided to entrust to my predecessors the choice of the prime minister, whose task was to pilot the ship in all weathers. The prime minister was just like the head of an industrial company, to be retained or dismissed at intervals by the people's elected representatives. If the people were satisfied, the prime minister could continue in office; otherwise, he was compelled to resign. That was true democracy.

Alas, the Chamber of Deputies and the Senate, yielding gradually to popular pressure, have, a little more each day, curtailed the authority of the executive arm of the state. Committees and commissions have been set up, the unions have grown steadily in strength and in power. Public opinion, which is not necessarily the opinion of the majority, has, through the impact of the press, the cinema, and the radio, grown so much in influence that it now completely dominates the prime minister. But if the duty of a prime minister is to conform to the will of the people, it is also to provide leadership and guidance!

Do you know that President Paul Reynaud, who only obtained a majority of one in the last vote in the Chamber, is the forty-fourth president of the Council of Ministers since the Third Republic was proclaimed in 1871 and that it has seen more than one thousand ministers come and go?

He then went on to question me about the advantages of the American Constitution and, in the field of justice, of the Supreme Court with its irremovable justices.

I noticed that since the start of our conversation, the minute hand of the clock had moved full circle almost twice. Nothing had broken the silence apart from the sound of our voices. The president saw me out to his antechamber. I expressed the hope that he would soon have news of his son. I declined, with thanks, the offer of a car and driver to take me home. As was the case that morning in the huge empty Hotel Majestic, my reception at the Elysée Palace had a gloomy and surrealist character. I thought to myself, as I left, that everything would have been much the same if, instead, I had been received by the chief curator of the museums of France at the Louvre, after closing time. And I wondered, while I crossed the Place de la Concorde to go back to the Place du Palais-Bourbon, whether I had not shaken the hand of the last president of the Third Republic.

CHAPTER 12
Paris—Lisbon—Washington

THERE COULD BE NO QUESTION OF MY STAYING A DAY LONGER IN PARIS. I just had to catch the big Pan Am Clipper that left Lisbon on June 9th. I therefore decided to take the overnight train to Bordeaux, the Spanish frontier, and Lisbon the following morning.

For the first time since the two gendarmes had rung at my door nine months before with my call-up papers, our two families, mine and Josée's, on the eve of my departure, got together for dinner at the Place du Palais-Bourbon under *The Circus,* the ceiling painted by my friend José María Sert. To celebrate the occasion, Josée had brought up from the cellar a magnum of Cheval Blanc '29.

I wanted Josée to come with me to the United States and tried to persuade her. But she had studied law, and I had lost the art of pleading. Her parents, however, who were good negotiators, suggested that she come with me as far as the Spanish frontier. At the time of general mobilization, in August 1939, she had got a diploma in first aid and, in May 1940, had obtained at the Gare d'Austerlitz, from which I was due to leave, premises that, with the help of a few friends, she turned into a dormitory where refugees could rest after being given some food. In a neighboring room, nurses were tending walking wounded. She insisted that I visit her place of work before we boarded the train.

Our fellow passengers gave no sign of the panic that would reign a few days later on that same Paris–Bordeaux line. Frenchmen were still confident that the army would win the battle of the Somme. And beyond that there was the Marne, where the tide had miraculously turned, almost at the gates of Paris, in September 1914. The weather was gorgeous, and the Loire as peaceful and languid as ever. I have always liked Bordeaux. It was the neutral ground on which my Paris team, the Stade Français, which was captained by the celebrated Adolphe Jaureguy and was packed with southerners, would play the quarter and semifinals of rugby tournaments.

The train stopped at the frontier. But Josée came on with me as far as Irun, which was still nursing its wounds from the Spanish Civil War. It was there that Spaniards told us the Battle of France had begun. Slowly, the train drew out of the dark, ill-lit station. Through my carriage window,

I could just make out the spare and energetic silhouette of Josée returning to the war while I pursued my journey to a world at peace.

I have always slept well in trains, even Spanish ones. The following morning, when I drew the curtains of my sleeping-car window, the train was steaming at a brisk pace along the picturesque valley of the Tagus, between Salamanca and Lisbon. The Aviz, once the residence of a rich Portuguese, had been turned into a hotel for millionaires and was packed. In the lobby I caught sight of wealthy Paris friends who had put their names down on the waiting list for the Pan Am plane to New York. There were only four a week. When I arrived, I learned that the departure of my flight had been delayed twenty-four hours because of a problem that occurred frequently—waves in the Tagus estuary whipped up by the wind.

The prestige attached to a French uniform enabled me to get a servant's room for the night. The news from the front got worse by the hour, while Portuguese newspapers, sympathetic to the Allied cause, indulged in wishful thinking and wrote about hypothetical counteroffensives and the destruction of hundreds of German tanks. My uniform also made an impression on the hotel porter. He had fought in the 1914–1918 war with the Portuguese division, incorporated in a French army corps. Every time I went past him, he would tell me, "We will get them all the same, mon capitaine!"

The following day, I had a serious setback but also a small consolation: the Clipper was delayed another twenty-four hours, and I was able to discover the beauty of the bay of the Tagus. On returning from my walk, I called on the American minister, Herbert Pell, a personal friend of President Roosevelt's. There I met Admiral Charles Courteney, the commander of the American squadron in European waters. He was waiting to leave by the same flying boat as I. Pell gave me the latest copy of the *New York Times* he had received, containing a cable from the United Press, with the curious title that read: "Paris sends to the United States an envoy straight from the hell of Flanders"; and the subtitle: "Count René de Chambrun will give Roosevelt details of the military operations" (see exhibit 1).

Pell, Courteney, and I could only talk about the lightning advance of the German army into France, and the two men were very pessimistic about Britain's capacity to repel an invasion. So I rehearsed the same arguments I had put forward in my talk with Bullitt and got the impression I carried a little more conviction with the soldier than with the diplomat.

On June 10th, in the morning, on the long landing stage, the names of the happy few allowed to board the Clipper were called. After the flight from Paris to London in my extra-light aircraft, I had the impression, as I stepped aboard, of getting into the bowels of a Leviathan.

Josée usually chided me for talking rashly. She had not failed to warn me once again on our journey from Paris to Irun to keep silent, and I had decided to abide scrupulously by her advice during the long flight, which, with two stopovers in the Azores and Bermuda, was to last thirty-six hours. I read a lot during the trip, put my notes in order, prepared the statement I would make to American civilians and military, and pondered at length over my past meetings with Roosevelt, whom I was to see again in profoundly dramatic circumstances for France.

As a preamble to the conversations I was to have with the American president on his yacht or in his White House office, in June, July, and August 1940, I feel it necessary to give the reader some details about our past relations.

My American mother had an elder brother, Nicholas Longworth, who was to achieve celebrity on two counts: he would become the only speaker of the House of Representatives who was allowed to have a Baldwin piano in his office on Capitol Hill, the better to charm the members of the opposition whom he received! and he married the only daughter of Theodore Roosevelt, my aunt, whose name was Alice. She was to become an outstanding personality. Her honeymoon was spent on a world tour, which, at the time, turned into a triumphal progress, with calls on King Edward VII, President Loubet of France, the kaiser, Tsar Nicholas II, the emperors of China and Japan, and others. The blue of her eyes was legendary and became known as "Alice blue."

For Franklin Roosevelt, the nephew of Theodore, I was to be "my cousin" once removed. When I arrived in New York in 1930 to spend my first four years with a law firm, Franklin Roosevelt was the state governor. I saw him for the first time on the occasion of the grand banquet that took place once a year on Lafayette-Kościuszko-Marne Day, the date of birth of the two heroes of the War of Independence and of the Battle of the Marne in 1914. The governor, who was a real political animal, never missed this banquet, for New York was the largest Polish city in the world after Warsaw. He would seat the Polish consul general on his right and "my cousin" on his left.

Then, in 1934, when he had been elected president of the United States, a great ceremony took place on May 20th, the first centenary of Lafayette's death. The United States and Roosevelt decided that it would be the same as that which had marked his death in 1834, when the news got to Washington with several weeks' delay. At the solemn session of Congress, in the presence of the state governors, the Diplomatic Corps, the Supreme Court, as I was on the spot, I was called upon to represent Lafayette's descendants.

After the ceremony, I was invited to the "family" lunch, which followed at the White House, at which Mrs. Eleanor Roosevelt and Aunt Alice were present. Those two strong characters, the one, Eleanor, a left-wing Democrat (more so than her husband), and Aunt Alice, as far right as her father,[1] were on their best behavior out of respect for Lafayette's memory!

Such, rapidly sketched, is the background of my relations with the statesman I was to get to know intimately in the course of many conversations during that summer, especially on the morning and evening of August 1, which offered me one of the greatest joys of my life.

In the following chapters, and especially in the conclusion to this book, much will be said about Roosevelt's "number two" at the White House, Harry Hopkins. We had become friends during the depression years— 1930–1932—which followed the stock market crash on "black Friday," October 29th.

Harry had begun life the hard way. His father was a saddler in a small town in Iowa. As a social worker, gifted, intelligent, totally devoted to the relief to the unemployed and the poor, he rapidly became one of Franklin and Eleanor Roosevelt's protégés and was appointed president of TERA (Temporary Emergency Relief Administration), which distributed millions of dollars in relief. After Roosevelt's first election as president, Hopkins became head of the WPA (Works Progress Administration), which proved the most useful and effective of Roosevelt's New Deal projects. After my years of law practice in France—from 1935 to 1939—we were to meet again on June 14, 1940, at the White House, where Hopkins had become secretary of commerce and Roosevelt's intimate friend and adviser. He could not be closer to his "chief." I found him living in the famous Lincoln Room at the White House.

On June 12th, at noon, the Yankee Clipper landed softly on the waters of the Bay of Long Island. A Pan Am official handed me a message to call Miss LeHand, Roosevelt's private secretary at the White House, as soon as I got to my hotel.

Friends who had come to meet me helped to waylay the reporters, and one of them drove me to the old Ritz, where I had stayed so often and had in my early days danced through the night with the debutantes in the Crystal Room—and even, why not admit it, indulged in some flirtation in the Japanese Garden. This hotel had become for me a kind of historic monument. A few years later, it was to fall victim to the destructive frenzy of developers.

---

[1] He died in 1919.

CHAPTER 13.

My Cruise on the Potomac with Franklin Roosevelt: I return with his handwritten list of twenty-three persons I must meet and convince within the next thirty-six hours

I SETTLED DOWN IN A COMFORTABLE ROOM AND CALLED MISS LeHAND. I remembered her and particularly her pleasant and welcoming voice, for we had spoken to one another several times before the ceremonies to mark the first centenary of the death of Lafayette, on May 20, 1934. She warned me that my talk on the radio, sandwiched between that of the president and of the governor of New York, was to have lasted six minutes, then a week later, five minutes, and finally four. Straight away, she told me that "the president wants to see you as soon and as long as possible." And she added, "We felt the best thing would be for you to come round tomorrow morning. He is having a couple of friends in for lunch, and the ideal solution would be for you to spend the weekend on the *Potomac* with him, the Averell Harrimans, who, I believe, are also friends of yours, and Harry Hopkins, whom you know well. We could leave around four, return on Sunday about noon, and have lunch after at the White House." I replied, "Nothing would give me greater pleasure."

"In this way," I added, "I shall have time, by taking the midnight train, to call on the military attaché, who is my chief since I have become his deputy, and Ambassador de Saint Quentin, and I shall be at the White House at noon."

The dramatic surge of German armor and the scale of the disaster naturally made me think with no little sadness of the mission of "encouragement" that Dautry had entrusted to me. But I had no right to skip a visit downtown, to 15 Broad Street and the French Purchasing Commission, where I found Bloch-Lainé, and his assistants, whom I knew—Bizot, Quellennec and d'Ornano—completely demoralized. What was I to do?

I returned by way of the French Information Center, which I had founded, where meetings of the Action Committee, led by André Vulliet and Le Blanchu, took place. There, everyone was putting on a brave face in the light of events, and that was comforting to me.

I dined with Clarence Dillon, the leading banker, and Frank Polk, who had been detailed to represent the United States on the board of directors of the French Information Center, whom France had made commanders of the Legion of Honor. Both gave me tips about the people I would meet in Washington, and I left them in time to get onto the midnight train.

The next day, a few minutes before twelve, I entered the White House, carrying my suitcase, which I entrusted to Miss LeHand, who was expecting me. I was to find it again on board the *Potomac,* and this saved me the trouble of going back to the hotel to fetch it after my appointments. She took me into the office of Harry Hopkins, whom I had not set eyes on since my departure from New York in 1934. He in turn took me into the president's oval office. The door between them was open. I sensed the complete intimacy between the two men, which was to last until their deaths, less than a year apart.[1]

The president was sitting behind his desk, in his wheelchair. The "my cousin" of earlier days was forgotten, and he called me René. The broad communicative smile he usually wore had also vanished. I noticed that he spoke his first few words slowly, "It is good to have you here with us. During these last months, I have often thought of the general and of Clara.[2]

"We are going to spend a family weekend with the Harrimans and Harry, and you will tell me everything you told Bill Bullitt. But now, talk to me about your war, and how you came to work with the British?"

I summed up the first nine months of the war, my pessimism after Narvick, my letter to Clare Luce, which I thought Henry Luce might have passed on to him, my conviction that the Luftwaffe, whose bombers had suffered far greater losses than was generally believed, could do nothing against the RAF, 85 percent of which had remained in Britain, where the best fighters in the world were coming off the assembly lines.

Harry Hopkins had returned to his own office after the start of our

---

[1]Roosevelt died on April 12, 1945; Harry Hopkins, on January 29, 1946.

[2]My father and mother, General de Chambrun and Clara Longworth.

conversation, and the two of us were alone when Roosevelt replied in essence as follows: "Harry and Averell must hear what you have to say. It's very important. As you probably noticed already in New York, yesterday, and here today, a wave of pessimism and isolationism has been sweeping over the country in the past few days, even among cabinet members; and we decided the day before yesterday that the antiaircraft guns, the aircraft, and small arms, of which the greater part had already been ordered by France and was already awaiting shipment in Norfolk, Baltimore, and New York, should be withheld for our country's own defense."

In the meantime, Miss LeHand had come in to whisper in his ear that his luncheon guests had arrived. She saw me out and had me taken by her personal driver to the French embassy, where I had lunch with Saint Quentin, Truelle, the minister, and my "chief," Colonel Lombard. The morale of the two diplomats could not have been lower. That of my chief was a little higher.

I left immediately after coffee and stopped off in the hall of the Mayflower Hotel to go over my notes on the military operations in Belgium and on the statements of captured German airmen. I also reread my report to General Weygand and arrived at the White House a little before four.

The black usher led me into the reception room looking out onto the garden and beckoned me to a chair under the portrait of Lafayette. This was obviously the gathering place for the "family" cruise. Harry Hopkins turned up first, then Averell Harriman and his wife, Mary, and, a few moments later, the president, again escorted by Miss LeHand. We left in two large Cadillacs for the Navy Yard, where the yacht was waiting for us.

As soon as we got on board, tea was served on the rear deck. The heat was terrible. When the radio operator brought a telegram for Roosevelt, he read it and handed it to me: "The Germans have crossed the Seine near Paris and are marching towards the Loire." He seemed a little more depressed than a few hours earlier and remarked, as he dropped his arms on either side of the wheelchair, "René, the show is over," then he added, with a sigh, "I really think Britain will be unable to hold out." I replied that he was unfortunately right as far as France was concerned, but, as I had told him a few hours earlier, he was completely mistaken in the case of Britain.

Bullitt had said the same thing to Cordell Hull and me on more than one occasion. "So tell us how you really feel," Roosevelt went on. I then launched, before this small court of five judges, three men and two women, into a plea that lasted more than an hour. It had been mulled over and worked out with a clear mind in midheaven over the Atlantic while the Yankee Clipper was taking me farther and farther away from the turmoil of war. A few days earlier, in Ambassador Bullitt's office in Paris, I had expressed a conviction. On the *Potomac,* that conviction had turned into cast-iron certainty. I explained the incredible "kills" carried out before my very eyes among three squadrons of Heinkels by those new Bolton Defiants with revolving turrets, scattering death and destruction around them:

> The air attaché in London told me the factories in Coventry are turning out between seven and eight of them each day.
>
> Britain had not taken the war seriously so far. She has only mobilized completely since the fall of Calais. The one success we scored in the military collapse of France was that of our navy, which was complete: it carried out the reembarkation of the entire British Expeditionary Forces.
>
> British morale is unimpaired. Throughout the "phony war," the British made the serious psychological error of seeing matters through rose-tinted spectacles; and now, Ambassador de Saint Quentin, with whom I have just had lunch, tells me that Lord Lothian and his staff are describing it to you as almost desperate, in the hope of obtaining from you some emergency aid.
>
> I maintain that Britain, entrenched in her island, is invincible, thanks to her fleet, her fighter force, which is becoming the best in the world, a good antiaircraft defense, which must be reinforced immediately, and ground forces, which have been miraculously rescued. These, thanks to air superiority, can be switched within twenty-four hours to any spot where a landing—which has become more and more improbable—is attempted.
>
> Do not forget that the Reich overwhelmed Poland in a few days and then, alas, France, in a few weeks, thanks to the massive exodus and helplessness of the Belgian population, and its own air supremacy.
>
> I also maintain that, from today, no German bombers can carry out daylight raids over Britain, and this is a key point. They can only fly at night, and as you have in store more than two thousand quick-firing antiaircraft guns ordered by France, it is madness to keep them here.

The deeper I go into my demonstration—it is a professional failing to which most lawyers are prone—the more I feel convinced of the case I am defending.

At that moment, for the second time, I saw the president hit the arm of his wheelchair and grab it. He then told me point-blank, "René, you have convinced me." Then, after a moment's thought, he looked at Hopkins and Harriman and said, in a paternal tone of voice, "And how about you, boys?" Harriman, turning to his friend and calling Roosevelt by the nickname of "chief," replied, "I think we feel as you do."

After a brief pause for thought, and looking me straight in the eye, Roosevelt went on, "René, I am going to ask you to do a job." I was, of course, curious to know which "job." In his stride, speaking a little more slowly and stressing the last word, he added, "And that job is to convince this country." I could only reply with a wry smile, "That is much more difficult, Mr. President. There are in this country more than 130 million Americans, and the vast majority seem to believe in a German victory." Smiling in turn, and turning to Hopkins, as if seeking his approval, he remarked, "The task is perhaps less difficult than the one you have just accomplished."

As he undoubtedly wished to consult Harry and Averell on a "possible strategy" out of my presence, he suggested that Miss LeHand ("Missy," for him) and Mary Harriman show me over the *Potomac*. It was a former destroyer, refitted with taste and efficiency from the standpoint of communications with the shore. Every cabin had a telephone and a bathroom. Harry Hopkins's also had an office, which communicated on one side with the president's and on the other with my cabin.

We returned to the rear deck, after casting a glance at the fast-receding banks of the river, for we had almost reached its mouth.

It was at this point that the President declared,

> Averell, Harry, and I have taken a decision, but naturally, it all depends on whether you agree, as Missy had invited you for a weekend cruise. We propose to cut it short, and to return tomorrow, Saturday, around four. Missy and Harry will make appointments for you. Tomorrow night, you dine with William Knutsen, who has been put in charge of all armaments. It is essential that before Tuesday, you have talked to every member of the cabinet, which I will call together in the morning, and that you are heard at length by the Foreign Relations Committee of the Senate. You will see President Barkley tomorrow in late afternoon, and I think he will be able to organize a lunch meeting Monday at the Senate, which is in session morning and afternoon.

Roosevelt then took a *Potomac* radiogram form and, while consulting Hopkins and Missy, drew up the list of people I should see as soon as possible. It contained twenty-two names, to which were added the initials of a twenty-third. It is reproduced in exhibit 2.

Before writing down the initials of Mrs. FDR, Mary Harriman had remarked, "What are you doing about the most important women?" In reply, Roosevelt added his wife's initials and remarked jokingly, "She rep-

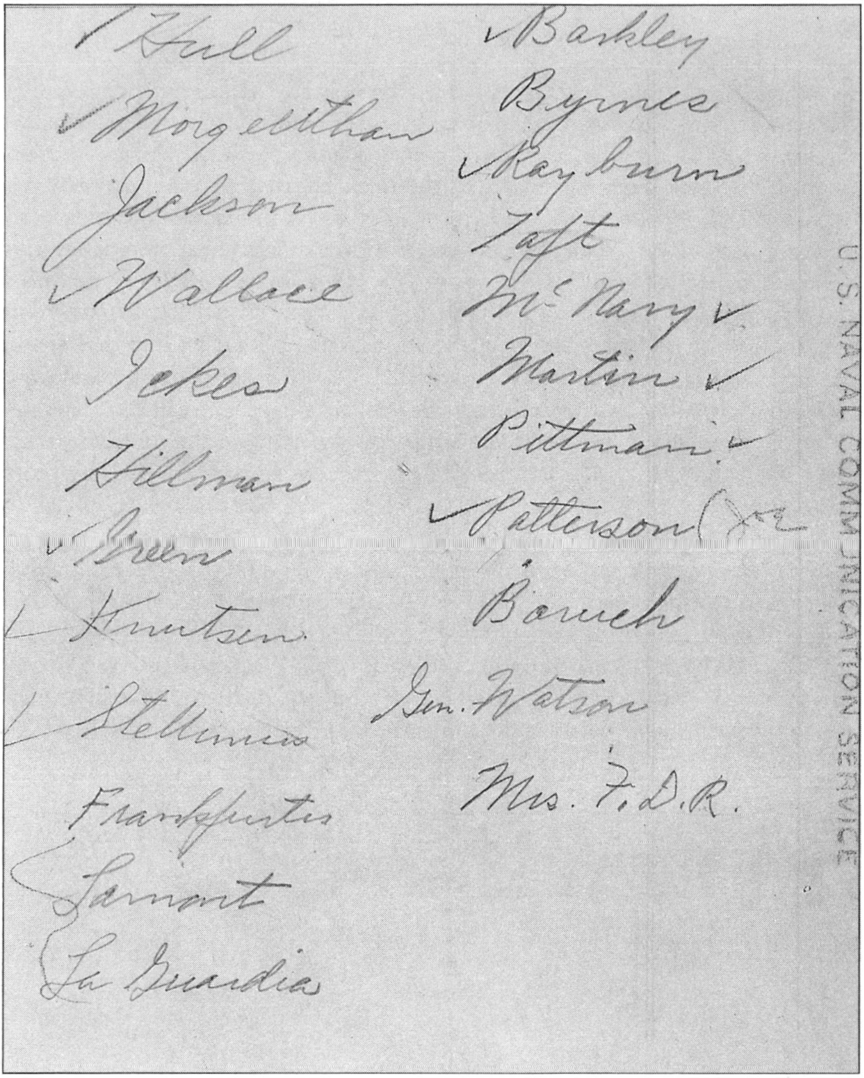

Exhibit 2. Franklin Roosevelt's handwritten list of important people that I was to persuade to the cause of Britain. The list, written on a radiogram form from FDR's yacht, is as follows: Hull, Morgenthau, Jackson, Wallace, Ickes, Hillman, Green, Knutsen, Stettinius, Frankfurter, Lamont, La Guardia, Barkley, Byrnes, Rayburn, Taft, McNary, Martin, Pittman, Patterson (Joe), Baruch, Gen. Watson, Mrs. FDR.

resents all the 'right-thinking' ladies in the country who read her column, 'My Day.'" I was to see her in person the following day.[3]

Roosevelt had included in his list two leading personalities of the opposition, Senator Taft, the leader of the Republicans in Congress, and Baruch. Referring to them, Roosevelt said to me, "Your Aunt Alice could fix these meetings." My reply went without saying, "Why not? She is an intimate friend of Taft's, and malicious gossip claims (wrongly) that she has a weakness for Baruch."

Because of the heat, and of the magnificent sunset, we had dinner out on deck. When I returned after having changed, Roosevelt sadly, and with a look of sympathy and understanding—he had deep down in his character a touch of sincerity in such circumstances—handed me a radiogram announcing the Germans had entered the northern suburbs of Paris without firing a shot.

I thought back sadly of Aubervilliers, Pierre Laval's constituency north of Paris, which he loved as much as his own village of Châteldon. During dinner, the conversation was rambling. Roosevelt, who had always had left-wing sympathies, which became more marked under the influence of Harry and Eleanor (both of whom had contacts until their death with Earl Browder, the head of the American Communist party), said to my stupefaction as we indulged in philosophical recollections of the years immediately preceding the present catastrophe, "René, I believe that if the French Senate had not overthrown Léon Blum, France would not have been defeated like that." As I did not wish to contradict him head on, I simply replied, "I believe the outcome would have been just the same."

The following morning, after breakfast in bed served by a U.S. Navy rating, Harry Hopkins knocked on my door to pay me a visit. He had already phoned Barkley, the chairman of the Foreign Affairs Committee of the Senate, and the lunch was fixed there for Monday at one.

Everyone on board was taking it easy. Dressed in the ship's bathrobes bearing in blue letters the name SS *Potomac,* Harry Hopkins and I went to see the president in his huge cabin. He received us in bed.

I recall that it was there I told him that the tragic events that had taken

---

[3]There was, at this time, only one cabinet member, a woman, Frances Perkins, who did not appear on Roosevelt's list, although she held the important post of secretary for Labor. Harry Hopkins thought it important for me to see her. And he called her on the telephone from the White House on that Saturday to introduce her to me "telephonically." She came the following morning, Sunday, to have breakfast with me at the Mayflower. It was the prelude to many meetings, including a fascinating dinner she organized on Wednesday, June 26, with the representatives of the most important unions, whom she got to come to Washington.

place in France made him the only man "who could stop Hitler." I felt what I said touched a soft spot and had really pleased him.

Miss LeHand, who was already dressed, joined us. She had been in touch with the Mayflower Hotel to ask that my things be moved to a large suite where I could receive friends and members of the opposition. Our arrival was due at four o'clock, and before sitting down to a quick lunch, Harry Hopkins and I worked on the text of a cable that I would send to Paul Reynaud, in French naturally, through the embassy.

Here is the text:

> I have just spent two days with the president and his closest adviser, Harry Hopkins. STOP. He is convinced that his country, the British empire, and what is left tomorrow of the French fleet and colonies constitute the only rampart against German domination of the world. STOP. As champion of a cause, he has an almost mystical confidence that events make him the only man who can stop Hitler. STOP. He will do everything to carry public opinion. STOP. It will follow him, even into war, on two conditions: one, that Britain, instead of demoralizing the Americans by defeatist propaganda, which plays into the hands of Germany, declares that she will win through, in spite of setbacks; and two, that France holds on to her fleet and her colonial empire.

To make certain that the cable went off immediately after we landed, I sent a telegram to Truelle, asking him to meet me at the White House a little after four on our return. He was waiting in the small lobby next to the entrance and sent the telegram as soon as he got back to the embassy.

Harry Hopkins suggested that I try to get Paul Reynaud on the telephone, to confirm the telegram, but communications with France had become increasingly difficult. The operator of the White House said they might improve later. I therefore left the number of the restaurant where Harriman took me to dine with William Knutsen. Miss LeHand rang me there to say that a call to Bordeaux would almost certainly come through between 10 and 11 P.M. She suggested I return to the White House as soon as possible.

Roosevelt was still in his study with Harry Hopkins when I arrived. While waiting for the call, we drew up a program for the next couple of days. Roosevelt left us to go and get some sleep, and shortly after eleven, I heard, on and off, very clearly, the voice of Paul Reynaud, in spite of breaks in the connection and sound distortions. Here is exactly what was said:

R.C. Monsieur le président?

P.R. I can hear you. Where are you?

R.C. I am calling you from the White House where I have just spent the day with the president, and we are fully agreed.

P.R. But do you know that I have handed in my resignation?

R.C. We did not know.

P.R. Yes, I have resigned, and Marshal Pétain is forming the new government.

At this point, fearing that it might be impossible to renew the call, I wished to make the following point:

R.C. But, Monsieur le président, I am afraid we may not be able to get in touch with the marshal. Can we ask you to pass a message on to him?

P.R. Yes, of course.

R.C. The president is convinced there is no solution other than an armistice, which brings the war to an honorable end on French soil, but on the sole condition that the fleet is not handed over.

P.R. It is six in the morning here, and I will report what you have told me as soon as the marshal is awake and I can see him.

R.C. Thank you.

The final words of this conversation, which was my last between the two continents, were the following:

R.C. Where is Roger?[4]

P.R. He has been taken prisoner.

I returned to the Mayflower around midnight. A fairy godmother had turned my bachelor bedroom into a luxurious suite, put my few possessions on the table of the drawing room, and propped up a cable against the telephone, on the bedside table! It was from Josée—the first from Irun. She must have felt that I was very very far away. My spirits revived. I fell asleep with her presence at my side.

---

[4]Roger Dernis was Paul Reynaud's son-in-law. I had known him intimately, first at St. Cyr and when we had both begun our legal careers as assistants of his own father, Louis Dernis, a Paris attorney.

Epilogue concerning
Franklin Roosevelt's List

Under Truman's presidency, eight years later, the list of twenty-three names surfaced again.

When, after the war, I resumed the rhythm of my twice yearly visits to New York, in the spring and the autumn, President Harry Truman had succeeded President Roosevelt, who died on April 12, 1945. Truman had been triumphantly reelected after completing his predecessor's unfinished term of office.

This Week magazine had become the publication with the largest circulation in the world, as it was subscribed to by some thirty of the most important newspapers from the East to the West Coast. Each of them reproduced it under its own title and printed the contents in its Sunday edition.

In the spring of 1948, William Nichols, the editor in chief of the magazine—who remembered the details of my mission to the United States and my cruise on the *Potomac* and had discovered that President Truman, "Roosevelt's future vice-president," had not been regarded as one of the twenty-three leading personalities of the time I must see—asked me for permission to publish the list as an exclusive, along with a brief summary of my mission. This was announced on the front page, followed by a two-page spread of photographs of the twenty-three persons, in reverse order, with Mrs. Roosevelt in the lead. A subtitle on the third page stated that the name of the incumbent president, Harry Truman, did not appear on the list. (See in appendix A the text of the article that appeared in the *Los Angeles Times*.)

For sentimental reasons, it was decided that this reminder of those dramatic days would be published on June 20, 1948, eight years after my arrival in Washington and the signature of that fateful armistice.

CHAPTER 14

My own 18th of June 1940

SUNDAY, JUNE 16, FOLLOWING THE ABRIDGED CRUISE ON THE *Potomac*, WAS going to be no holiday for me. As soon as I was awake, and before giving Harry Hopkins the call he was expecting, I rang Aunt Alice and two or three friends in New York. I had breakfast with Frances Perkins[1] and arrived at the White House where Harry Hopkins received me in the same garb as on the ship, save that his bathrobe was not the same color. Together we planned the meetings for the following day.

I lunched with Aunt Alice at her picturesque house on Massachusetts Avenue. It was a fond reunion, for she has always been, and would remain until her death on February 20, 1980, my favorite aunt on both sides of the Atlantic. She had a strong and dominating personality. The whole United States laughed at her comment on the second attempt of Thomas Dewey to beat the unbeatable Roosevelt, whom Aunt Alice did not like. To reporters who came to ask her what she thought of this, she replied, "All French chefs know that you cannot make the same souffle rise twice." This catty remark, which was published in the whole press, did some damage to the candidate.

After the heartrending part of our conversation concerning Josée, my parents, and the collapse of France, about which she wanted to know everything, we went on to talk about my budding relationship with Franklin and Eleanor Roosevelt, whom she could mimic to perfection. She agreed, without excessive enthusiasm, to help in my campaign on behalf of Britain and promised that she would organize a small dinner party for me with the Tafts and Joe Patterson.[2]

I then spent the greater part of that Sunday afternoon with one of the secretaries on duty at the White House drawing up the memorandum for the president and the cabinet. When the first draft was completed and cor-

---

[1]Harry Hopkins had phoned her and suggested the breakfast with me at the Mayflower.
[2]The Republican journalist tycoon.

rected the title became "Duplicate of Report for President Roosevelt."[3]

On the following day, Monday, June 17, Miss LeHand had two original copies made because she wanted me to have one as a souvenir. Roosevelt marked in pencil in the margin those paragraphs he advised me to stress when speaking to the senators. The only word he altered was in the last line before one. I had written "the forces that today, as they did in 1918, struggle consciously or unconsciously to prevent Germany from dominating the world." On the two original copies, Roosevelt crossed out the word *Germany* and substituted *the Nazis*.

Miss LeHand made me sign both copies and gave me one. The pages were tied together with a little red ribbon, which I have kept.

The president's last words, when he dropped in to see me hard at work, were "good luck" in my Senate hearing with this historic reminder, in his frequently picturesque language, "Don't forget that it was the Senate that threw the Versailles Treaty into the wastepaper basket, and here we are today holding the bag for the mistakes of others."

The Day of Monday, June 17

I rang up Frank Polk in New York, who, with John Davis, was the head of the law firm where I had worked for four years. He had been under secretary of state in President Wilson's day, and I sought his advice as to how I should handle the Senate.

I then met Lord Lothian at the British embassy. He had invited the Australian ambassador, Casey, to come in on our conversation. Both were to become firm friends. Purvis, the head of the British Purchasing Board, was also there.

I thought that we could easily discuss things on the telephone and meet over breakfast—an American habit, which has today spread to France. We agreed to see each other again the following day, before the meeting of the cabinet.

Lunch at the Senate was a particularly moving occasion. The vice president of the United States is de facto president of the Senate, and Key Pittman, the chairman of the Foreign Relations Committee, had asked me to take the chair, with John Garner, the vice president, on my right and Senator Barkley on my left. Pittman sat opposite me.

All the members of the Foreign Relations Committee and the heads of the other committees were present at the lunch. When we sat down,

---

[3]See appendix B.

Senator Barkley made a little speech of presentation, in which he said simply that the Senate was very happy to receive an officer of the French army who happened to be a descendant of Lafayette, also an officer of the French army when he came to America. He recalled that I was "Nick" Longworth's nephew. Most of the senators had known him, for he had been Speaker of the House of Representatives for two terms. Everything went very well, and Key Pittman accompanied me back through the Capitol to Harry Hopkins's car. After dropping in at the Mayflower, I returned to the White House, where I arrived around four in the office of Harry Hopkins to talk about the press conference due to take place later at the Mayflower.

The president asked us to come in and see him, and, raising his right arm in the Fascist—or perhaps I should say Roman—manner, he told me that Pittman had just rung him up to tell him that "the French captain hit a home run," an expression taken from baseball that corresponds to a converted touchdown in rugby football. He advised me to give a slightly intimate character to the press conference by receiving the reporters in my own suite. He suggested that I introduce myself as an officer who had been in the battle of Dunkerque, and who was sent by the French government to inform the French ambassador about the situation, simply adding that President Roosevelt, who knew me and my parents, had invited me to spend the weekend on the *Potomac.*

Harry and the president advised me to stress the naked German aggression, without an ultimatum, against Belgium, the onslaught of tanks, the dive-bombers, the panic of the Belgian population partly instigated by the fifth column, the machine-gunning of men, women, and children on the roads. Mobilization of the Belgian army proved impossible. "Naturally, you must emphasize that you have come via Britain and have noted that the spirit of the RAF is undaunted; that the success of the reembarkation of the Expeditionary Corps was complete, thanks to the combined efforts of both the French and British fleets and of the RAF; that the RAF is about to achieve mastery of the air over its own territory, and that Britain and the British empire are going to hold out."

Back at the Mayflower, a few minutes before six, the reporters started to come, but they were so numerous that I could not follow the president's suggestion of receiving them in my suite. So the press conference, in fact, took place in a large hall downstairs. There must have been over fifty, and because of all the questions I had to answer, it lasted until seven thirty when I offered drinks to those who seemed not to want to go home.

With my breakfast the next morning, I received the *Washington Post* and the *New York Times,* and I was told that all the leading papers of the country had given excellent reports of the press conference (see exhibit 3).

CHAMBRUN DEPICTS BELGIAN DEBACLE

Frenchman Says Allies Were Hamstrung by 5th Column Operations in Rear

Special to THE NEW YORK TIMES.

WASHINGTON, June 17—A remarkable story of the fiendish perfection of the fifth column methods with which Germany hamstrung the Allied armies in Flanders was related to newspaper men today by Count René de Chambrun, descendant of Lafayette and French liaison officer with the British armies in Belgium.

The French Army, he said, was knocked out by an opponent who used brass knuckles. But it had exhausted the German forces to an extent unrealized on this side of the Atlantic, said the slim young soldier, and he expressed perfect confidence that Great Britain, with what assistance America could give her, could still hold out.

Count de Chambrun, who, under an old Maryland statute passed two years before the Constitution, can call himself, as a descendant of Lafayette, an American citizen, is a member of the New York Bar. When war broke out he was called up as a lieutenant of infantry, served in the Maginot Line and was then made captain and liaison officer with the British forces.

He was in Flanders from the time the Allied forces arrived until he crossed the Channel in a speedboat from Dunkerque to England, never for twenty-eight days having been able to take off his clothes.

Found Foes in Rear

He came to Washington to report to the French Ambassador and incidentally, in a talk with President Roosevelt, acquainted the Chief Executive with Germany's new methods of waging war.

"When Belgium was invaded without an ultimatum," said Count de Chambrun, "we of the Allied armies thought we were going to fight on the battle front. Very soon we found that the greater part of the battle was to take place behind us. In every town and village in Belgium fifth columnists spread rumors to induce the people to flee. As a result, our divisions found every road and field blocked by refugees, rendering movement almost impossible.

"A day after the invasion we discovered that behind every billboard advertising certain products was a map of Belgium in full detail, posted there the night before. Among the wagons of the refugees were carts in which German soldiers, sometimes in civilian clothes, lay concealed. They carried light machine-guns with which to attack us from behind. Telephone wires were cut, almost as fast as we laid them, by spies hidden among the refugees. The German armored divisions in the Ardennes were supplied with fuel from secret stores which had been accumulated in advance by fifth columnists."

Parachutists Kill 3 Generals

Three generals, said the Count, were killed by parachutists or fifth columnists at their own headquarters.

"During the whole campaign," he said, "I felt that the enemy was behind me. We were totally unprepared for that. For instance, when I left the front line to bring dispatches to Cassel, a distance of 100 kilometers, the first thing I saw there was a detachment of German tanks firing on civilians. When I arrived in a peaceful village near the coast itself the first thing I heard was the scream of the sirens of the dive-bombing Stukas.

"This whole system of tactics had been prepared for months by Col. Gen. Wilhelm Keitel while Chancellor Adolf Hitler and Foreign Minister Joachim von Ribbentrop were assuring and reassuring the Netherlands and Belgium that they would not be attacked.

"Speaking as a liaison officer who saw the British Expeditionary Force fighting, let me say I have complete faith in the British Empire. I think it is farther from being beaten by Hitler, who dominates half of Europe, than it was by Napoleon when he dominated all Europe. I do not believe the German and Italian fleets combined are any match for the British fleet.

Says Nazis Are Weakened

The thousands of French soldiers, sailors, pilots and civilians who gave their lives did not die in vain, for France's resistance has exhausted the German Army to a greater degree than is realized here.

"In the beginning we underestimated the German Army; now you are overestimating them. While France was defending her soil she was wearing down Germany. Britain, while supporting France was preparing. She is now producing the best planes in the war. The last sight I saw when I left Dunkerque was six Boulton Paul Defiants bringing down twenty Hienkels without loss. I am sure that Britain is prepared for the battle that faces her and with what assistance the United States can give she can save herself."

Exhibit 3. Two-column article that appeared in the *New York Times* Tuesday, June 18, 1940.

The Days of June 18 and 19

It is, of course, known today that the "official" call of General De Gaulle on the BBC (British Broadcasting Corporation) from London on June 18, 1940, commonly called "l'Appel du 18 Juin," was heard by very few Frenchmen at the time, whereas all France listened to the solemn and pathetic address of Marshal Pétain on the previous day, June 17th. I have always been very pleased that my press conference and my memorandum to the cabinet and to the Senate Foreign Affairs Committee antedated by twelve hours the "Appel du 18 Juin." But my greatest satisfaction during those sad days was to come, when Franklin Roosevelt told me that the cabinet had decided the day before that the embargo to dispatch the tanks, antiaircraft guns, and machine guns, which had been ordered and manufactured for France, had been lifted and that these would be shipped very rapidly to England.

I had my second breakfast with Lord Lothian at the Mayflower. He told me that "my country will never forget." To this I replied, "But this decision would certainly have been taken a few weeks or a couple of months later." He added that I would have to continue the good work, especially in the Midwest, where people were very isolationist. I told him I was about to do so and that I was dining that very evening with a hard core of isolationists.

Indeed, I dined that evening with Alice Roosevelt Longworth, herself very much an isolationist. She agreed to invite Robert Taft, the leader of the Republican opposition, and his wife, Martha. Taft was senator for Ohio, born in Cincinnati, and an intimate friend of my mother's. Roosevelt, whom I informed about the dinner, alluding to my aunt, his cousin, and Taft, said with a laugh, "Those two will be hard nuts for you to crack!"

I seized the opportunity of this friendly and relaxed talk with Lothian to reveal my secret to him, "Since I arrived and am battling to turn the tide of defeatism, I have been increasingly obsessed by a thought that has spurred me to action: southern France, where there are millions of refugees, is going to suffer from famine, along with our millions of prisoners of war. They must be sent supplies by cargo from America to Marseilles. Britain's gesture, in authorizing navicerts[4] for the passage through the Straits of

---

[4]Navigation certificates issued by British officials that exempted noncontraband consignments from seizure or search by British blockade patrols.

Gibraltar, could only make her more popular in the United States." I was very pleased to note that he raised no objection to the idea.

During this second talk with Lothian, I had the feeling that we were on the same wavelength. He was many years my senior and acted as secretary to Lloyd George during the Versailles peace talks, after the First World War. He had become a firm friend of the United States and visited practically every state, giving interviews, lecturing, and writing books. I was deeply shocked when I learned of his sudden death in December, five months later. He suffered from acute uremic poisoning, and his life would have been saved had he not refused treatment because of his strong Christian Science convictions.

After our long breakfast talk, Henry Morgenthau, the secretary to the treasury, had set up a meeting in the imposing Treasury Building with Henry Stimson, the secretary for war. (There was not yet a minister for defense, but two secretaries: one for war and one for the navy. Stimson was to become secretary for defense, and William Knutsen was to be the arms program director, without the title of secretary of state.)

Morgenthau asked me to try my hand at a second report, elaborating on what I had already written about Britain's fighter force. I got the work done with the help of the British air attaché, whom Lothian had put in touch with me.

In spite of my deep affection for my favorite aunt, Alice Roosevelt Longworth, who was very fond of Josée and myself and had crossed the Atlantic to attend our wedding, I was a little apprehensive about the dinner. Neither Taft nor Alice had any liking for Britain, and I was going to plead her cause, as a kind of spokesman for Franklin Roosevelt for whom neither had particularly fond feelings!

Alice had lost her husband, Nick Longworth, my mother's brother. She had borne him a little girl, a charming latecomer, my cousin Paulina. At the time, she was fifteen and lived with her. The hors d'oeuvre of the meal was a stunt that I remember to this day. As soon as all five of us were gathered together, the anti-Roosevelt tease began: Paulina was training a very young fox terrier and had taught it to do its business on a newspaper. Any number of newspapers and magazines carried photographs of the president, and, as a curtain raiser to the evening, young Paulina put down in the middle of the drawing room floor a magazine with the picture on the front page of the president of the United States, all smiles and slightly prominent teeth. The little dog immediately performed as expected and disappeared into the kitchen.

In spite of this, I came away with a pleasant recollection of the evening, which ended after midnight. Without agreeing to "unconditional aid" for Britain, my three dinner companions, who were fundamentally isolationist, admitted, as was to be the case with Lindbergh himself, that the United States should significantly step up its defense expenditure, in addition to what was spent on the navy, which in the past had always been substantial. It was a decision which would also lead to an increase in aid to Britain and the Soviet Union.

CHAPTER 15

Generals John Pershing
and George Marshall

THE FOLLOWING DAYS—JUNE 20, 21, AND 22—WERE CERTAINLY THE MOST
painful and tense in my whole life. They culminated, on the 22d, with the
conclusion of the Armistice. Roosevelt was satisfied because the French fleet
had been saved, and France still had a government, an administration, and
a so-called southern free zone, but my heart was bleeding.

A Private Lunch with
General Pershing

At the end of the last morning in May, I was at the Invalides, in the office
of Marshal Pétain. He had given me this last and most pressing recommendation: not to fail to call on his great wartime friend, General Pershing.

I phoned the general immediately after the trying days of June 17 and
18, and he invited me to lunch with him alone, at the Army and Navy
Club, on Friday, June 21. I gathered from his tone of voice that he was
deeply moved to hear that his old friend the marshal had accepted the
daunting task of coming for a second time to the assistance of his country.
I went to this luncheon with feelings of great emotion as General Pershing
had crossed the Atlantic to act as best man at our wedding in Paris at Sainte-
Clotilde.

Very few French people, I think, know about the tragedy that befell
Pershing while he commanded a battalion of an army of which he would
one day become supreme commander. One night, when out on maneuvers,
his wooden frame house near San Francisco caught fire. His wife carried
their one-year-old son, Warren, out of the blaze and put him down on the
lawn. She then went back into the house to fetch her three daughters. All
four were burned alive. When Pershing landed at Dunkerque, in April
1917, he brought his son, then aged eight, along with him. I was a few
months older, and my father took me out of the College Stanislas, in Paris,
to become the playmate of the young Pershing.

I remained in touch with Warren in New York. He was, alas, to pass away before his father. The long and moving talk I had with Pershing at the Army and Navy Club, a few hours before the armistice was signed in the forest of Rethondes near Compiègne, has remained graven in my memory.

A few months ago, when I had begun to write these memoirs, I was sorting out my father's papers. He had been in attendance on the marshal in 1931, at the festivities to mark the 150th anniversary of Yorktown. I came upon a letter that I had never seen before (see exhibit 4). I have been too closely associated with all these events to comment on the surprising hypothesis raised at the close of the general's letter, save to write this startling conclusion: I was to dine the following day in Washington with the man who, fifteen years later, liberated Marshal Pétain, then a prisoner of the Germans, and whom France, "allied" to the United States under the leadership of General de Gaulle, was to sentence to life imprisonment.

On Saturday, June 22, I attended Colonel Lombard's reception. He had brought together some leading Americans to try to explain to them what was happening in France. I learned that among the two and a half million prisoners of war—reduced to two million at the end of the summer because of the harvest—was almost the whole of the Third Army responsible for the Maginot Line, and I kept thinking, day after day, about my three comrades, Bentz, Billet, and Saint-Guily, until my return to France in 1941.

I left Colonel Lombard to go and dine with General George Marshall, who had invited me that evening to his country house in Virginia, on the other side of the Potomac. He had known my father well at the end of the 1914–1918 war, when he was on the staff of General Pershing. My father, who had fought as a colonel at Verdun, on the Somme, and at the Chemin des Dames, had been appointed in May 1917 liaison officer between Generals Pershing and Pétain (see cartoon on p. 86).

Mrs. Marshall had come to represent her husband at the small private gathering at the French military attaché's. We left together, as I was dining at her home. "Send your chauffeur away," she told me. "I will take you back to the Mayflower." The wife of the army chief of staff in 1942, Eisenhower's superior, was simplicity personified. She drove me to her house in Virginia, where her husband and their children gave me a warm welcome.

I saw him for the last time in England on the night of December 15, 1947. I had come to London by plane that morning, knowing that he was there to attend an important conference with Molotov, Bevin, and Bidault.

I called Ambassador Lou Douglas's secretary to advise her that I had come on purpose to see General Marshall. She asked me to wait at Brown's Hotel for her to call back. Much to my surprise, she soon was on the phone again to advise me of the sudden breakup of the conference. General

November 16, 1931.

General Adelbert de Chambrun,

Paris, France.

My dear de Chambrun:

I hear nothing but the highest praise of the
Marshal. He left a fine impression everywhere by his simple
dignity and friendly attitude. His speeches, without exception, were well done and quite to the point. Each one
seemed exactly to fit the occasion for which prepared. He
was especially felicitous at my luncheon at the Army and Navy
Club, and also at the dinner given by the Institut Francais
de Washington.

For me the visit was the climax of our association
together beginning, as it did, in 1917. You know the story.
Whenever I needed real support in my discussions or disagree-
ments with the Allied High Command, I always knew that Petain
would give it because he has a logical mind and a personality
free from prejudice. One could always count on him to be on
the right side of every question.

It was indeed a pleasure to have the opportunity
to revive the friendship of war days with you and the Marshal.
I enjoyed every minute we were together, and was especially
pleased to have you so intimately one of the trio - or
triumvirate. What good fortune it would be, if ever our two
countries should again be fighting side by side, to have two
commanders-in-chief with the perfect confidence and friendship
that exist between Petain and myself.

I was more than delighted to have you come over,
particularly as his counsellor, as your presence added a
charm to the whole thing that would have been missing without
you.

Please extend to Madame de Chambrun and accept for
yourself my warmest regards.

Affectionately yours,

John J. Pershing

Exhibit 4. Letter from John J. Pershing to General Aldebert de Chambrun.

COL.
QUEKEMEYER   COL. DE
CHAMBRUN   COL.
MARSHALL   GEN.
PERSHING.

Marshall and Ambassador Lou Douglas would, she said, be back from Downing Street for an early dinner before leaving to get on President Truman's plane, the *Sacred Cow,* which was to fly them back to Washington. His chief of staff, Colonel Hummerline, called me a little later to invite me to dinner with the ambassador and the general. It was then that I explained the reason for my impromptu visit to London to see him. The reason was this: I wished to obtain his permission that top-secret documents, in the possession of Robert Jackson, the American chief prosecutor at the Nuremberg War Crimes Trials, should be communicated to me. Those documents dealing with the German aircraft industry during the war, and seized from the archives of the Luftwaffe, provided irrefutable evidence of the patriotism of Pierre Laval. They showed how he had played a game of hide-and-seek with the Germans—preventing them from seizing all the shares of France's nationalized aircraft industry and obstructing German attempts to have workers or machinery transferred to Germany.

"Your request places me in a difficult position with respect to our British Allies and especially with the Soviets. In principle," Marshall said, "I should refuse. But I don't think I can say no to Josée Laval." A few weeks later, a Captain Ullman, head of the information division of the American War Crimes team, brought a first batch of documents to my office, and he made thirteen trips in the following year, each time with a new batch—several thousand pages altogether.

CHAPTER 16

Harry Hopkins gives me a secret mission to boost Roosevelt's morale with the cooperation of the representatives of the British empire. An encouraging evening with Frances Perkins and the unions

On the following day, Sunday, June 23, I decided to go and spend two days in New York. A great friend of mine, Thayer Hobson, who ran a publishing firm, had phoned me in Washington as soon as he had read about my statement to the press of June 17. He begged me to write an account of my own personal experiences of the war as quickly as possible in order to beat the competition. He added that he would put a secretary permanently at my disposal, so that I could dictate to her a text that would appear simultaneously in book form and condensed in two installments of the *Ladies' Home Journal,* a magazine owned by a friend, which, in those days, had the largest circulation in the United States, bigger than *Life* and *Look.*

On the train to New York, I began to think that this might, through the substantial royalties I would receive and hand over entirely to the Red Cross, be a way for me to get a large number of parcels sent to French prisoners of war through Gibraltar and Marseilles, as we had just heard that part of France had remained unoccupied.

With each day that went by, this question of the prisoners assumed increasing importance in my mind. I was obsessed by the thought that all those I had known in the 162d Fortress Infantry Regiment might be lingering in prisoner-of-war camps while I was living in luxury in a country and among people who had everything they could wish for.

That was the trend of my thoughts when I had my first talk, soon after my return to the old Ritz in New York, with Thayer Hobson. He was eager to go and had no trouble in convincing me. He had even thought of the title of the book himself: *I Saw France Fall*, with the subtitle *She Will Rise Again*.

He introduced to me a secretary with glasses and freckles who would raise no eyebrows during the tough journey into the most isolationist areas of the United States, which Harry Hopkins and Henry Wallace were fixing up for me, starting with Chicago on July 1, the first stop on a ten- to twelve-day campaign.

I devoted my two days in New York to my lawyer friends and to the two directors of the French Information Center, which pursued its useful work since news from France was very scanty.

On Wednesday, June 26, I left for Washington on the morning train in order to have time to think things over and to lunch quietly alone. When I arrived at the Mayflower, I found a message for me on the notice board that said, "Urgent—On arrival, call Mr. Harry Hopkins at the White House."

He asked me if I could come over straightaway. I did and he greeted me with the words, "The chief's morale is falling again." It was all the fault of the British: Lothian and the ambassadors of Canada and Australia came to see him, one after the other, and paid the same calls on Cordell Hull. The president and the head of the State Department got the impression that they were unduly pessimistic.

"You should go and talk to Casey,[1] who is the most intelligent of the three, and see what he thinks of my idea. I feel, on second thoughts, that it had better come from you rather than me. You ask him for an appointment. You will simply allude to the fact that I told you the 'chief' felt the British were very pessimistic, and as you know his character and reactions well, you could make the following suggestion: The representatives of the British empire should request a joint meeting with the president, not for the purpose of discussing supplies but simply to review the situation in general and to express complete solidarity with Britain, bearing out your conviction that the British empire will fight to a man until final victory."[2]

Hopkins added that it would be useful for the visit to coincide with a rousing appeal by Churchill and the prime minister of Canada, Mackenzie King.

---

[1]Casey was the Australian ambassador.

[2]The plan unfolded as arranged, thanks to Casey.

I called Casey from Harry Hopkins's office, and while he listened in on our conversation, I arranged for a breakfast meeting the following day. As I rang off, he looked at me with a satisfied smile and said, "Good work, doctor!" I came to the conclusion that, in his eyes, I had become a doctor in international psychology!

I returned to the Mayflower on foot, thinking, as I went along, about the evening to come with Frances Perkins and the union leaders but even more perhaps about my talks with Harry Hopkins, this American Machiavelli.

As I have already said, I had known him during the four years I spent in New York between 1930 and 1934. He was exactly fifteen years older than I. We were both born in the last week of August in two different centuries, and I still recall one of our joint birthday dinners in a small restaurant of the Village. In his friendly company, I always had the impression that we were the same age.

Much later, when Roosevelt was serving his third term, I believe he played with the idea that Hopkins might become his successor and his political executor. But Harry's health was too poor. He died a few months after his leader in the winter of 1946.

The Dinner with the Union Leaders

But let us now come to the encouraging evening I spent with Frances Perkins and the union leaders a few hours later at the Mayflower. She had sent me the list of the eight or nine persons concerned with details of their positions; some had come specially to Washington for the occasion. Here it is:

—Harvey W. Brown, president, International Association of Machinists
—Boris Shishkin, economist, American Federation of Labor
—Edward Keating, editor of *Labor*
—W. D. Johnson, national legislative representative, Railway Drivers
—Sidney Hillman, general president, Amalgamated Clothing Workers of America
—Ralph Hetzel, Jr., director of employment, Congress of Industrial Organizations
—D. W. Tracy, president, International Brotherhood of Electrical Workers of America
—Francis P. Fenton, national director of organization, American Federation of Labor.

To this list should be added two of Frances Perkins's assistants and especially one of her friends, Mrs. Ruth Shipley, the head of the Service of Admissions and Visas in the State Department. Close and confident relations were to grow between her, Miss Perkins, and myself in the months to follow over the assistance to be given to French Jewish refugees in France and even to famous German writers who had fled to France, like Thomas, Heinrich and Golo Mann, and Franz Werfel, for whom Josée made arrangements in Vichy to leave unoccupied France and get to Canada or Portugal, pending their permanent entry into the United States.

All the requests I forwarded to Frances Perkins and Mrs. Shipley were granted (see, by way of example, exhibit 5 concerning the visa given to René Mayer, who was to hold important cabinet posts in the government after the liberation of France).

Frances Perkins had booked a private dining room at the Mayflower. She kindly informed me, in advance of the scenario she planned for the meeting, I would be seated at her side. Opposite would be Edward Keating, the boss of the powerful newspaper *Labor*. By the time coffee was served, she would suggest that he put a question to me about the fall of France, which had caused deep shock throughout the United States. As I anticipated I would have to speak at length and reply to lots of questions, I ordered, around six, that wonderful triple mixture, "half milk, half cream, and Graham crackers," so that I should not need to eat much during the meal.

The Mayflower had put in the center of the table some flowers surrounded by little French and American flags. Edward Keating, in a very courteous tone of voice, asked me, as arranged, the first question: "Count de Chambrun, could you tell us why France lost the war?"

I replied,

> I will try to answer this sweeping question. It is not an easy one. First of all, you must remember that the First World War claimed more than one and a half million dead and more than a million wounded in France alone. She had become, in the years that followed the armistice, the most pacifist country in the world (along, perhaps, with her Swiss neighbor). The most striking proof of her pacifism was her decision not to raise or maintain an offensive military force. Do you know that the building of the Maginot Line, which was purely defensive, cost France more than the building of their fleets by the United States and Britain combined?
>
> Out of the last ten years, from 1930 on, I spent almost the whole of four years here, in my second mother country. I returned to France during the winter of 1934–1935. I now call upon you to think for a moment about the situation in France, during that winter, when I left America, and what it was four years later on September 3, 1939, when she declared war on Hitler.
>
> On December 31, 1935, France had a center-right government. Her budget and that of her colonial empire were in surplus. She had the second largest gold reserves in the world, after those of Fort Knox. The 3 percent

DEPARTMENT OF STATE

WASHINGTON

September 14, 1940.

My dear Mr. de Chambrun:

I have just been told by the Visa Division that a report has been received from the American Consul at Montreal stating that a transit visa was issued on September 11 to René Mayer.

Sincerely yours,

Ruth Shipley

Chief, Passport Division

Mr. René de Chambrun,

C/o Ritz-Carlton Hotel,

Madison Avenue and Forty-Sixth Street,

New York, New York.

Exhibit 5. Letter from Mrs. Shipley, head of the Passport Division at the Immigration Department.

treasury bonds (*emprunt perpétuel*) had risen to par. Her air force was the strongest in the world.

A few months before I left, I remember saying goodbye to Codos and Rossi, who were taking off from Roosevelt Field in Long Island, in an attempt to beat Alcock and Brown's long-distance flying record of 9,500 kilometers. They landed at Aleppo, in Syria, which, at that time, was a French protectorate, along with Lebanon. They had covered 10,400 kilometers nonstop in a plane with a French Hispano engine and a French Bréguet fuselage.

The German army, 100,000 strong, was banned from the left bank of the Rhine. Hitler had just had Dollfuss, the Austrian chancellor, assassinated, as a prelude to his first attempt at annexation, and had suffered a major setback because Mussolini sent two divisions to the Brenner Pass, mobilized a first contingent of reservists, and welcomed the widow of Dollfuss in Rimini. In the wake of those events, Pierre Laval was to negotiate and sign an offensive and defensive alliance with Mussolini to guarantee the independence of Austria.

France, at that time, still had treaty arrangements with the Little Entente (defensive alliance of France, Czechoslovakia, Yugoslavia, and Romania) and Poland. Hitler's Germany was completely encircled.

From the time of the fatal elections of May 1936, which produced in the Chamber of Deputies a Radical-Socialist-Communist majority (the Popular Front), the decline was sharp. Mass strike action and a reduction in working hours increasingly curtailed the output of arms factories and arsenals, while working hours in strike-free Germany steadily increased. France declared war with, as her only ally, Britain, which was not ready to wage it—the total strength of her army on September 3, 1939, did not exceed the equivalent of two divisions. We had 60, underequipped, pitted against 170 highly armed German divisions, one tank to every three German ones, and practically no bomber aircraft.

To give you food for thought, I will tell you of two events that I witnessed personally.

The first occurred in 1937, two years before the outbreak of war. From the time of my return to France from the United States and my marriage, my wife and I lived in what is still our present home on the Place du Palais-Bourbon, a hundred meters away from the Chamber of Deputies. Sometimes, in the evening, on my return from work, and before going home to dinner, I would go to the public gallery of the chamber, for which I had a permanent pass, and listen in on the debates for a short while. At that time, Léon Blum was prime minister. On the extreme left sat 73 Communist deputies, next to them 155 Socialists, and, nearer the center, 100 Radicals. The Socialists and Communists, with a few left-wing Radicals, made up the government majority.

On that day, the government had tabled a motion of confidence, and I saw Maurice Thorez, the leader of the Communist party, rise to his feet to ask for a half-hour's adjournment. The government needed the seventy-three communist votes to carry the day and agreed. The former miner from Lens then left his seat, slowly descended the steps of the aisle, and went to a telephone outside the chamber. A few minutes later, he returned with the all clear from Moscow to support the government of France.

I recollected this two years later, on September 26, 1939, when a ministerial circular addressed to the officers of the Third Army and signed by Edouard Daladier, prime minister and minister of war, ordered the arrest of Maurice Thorez, the former secretary general of the Communist party, charged with desertion. The order was to be passed down to noncommissioned officers and privates. We did not know at the time that the government had arrested a few Communists but that the three leaders of the party, Thorez, Duclos, and Ramette, had fled the country. The first was already in Moscow. Stalin had just signed his nonaggression pact with Hitler. The other event took place in September 1939, a week after France had gone to war.

I then explained to my audience the claustrophobia that I experienced underground, in one of the forts of the Maginot Line. I told them that there were still a few unfinished pillboxes, in front of the big fortifications, which were to be manned by volunteer machine gunners. Two "African Battalions," made up of common-law criminals—they were French because Algeria was under French rule—had just arrived to finish the work on one of them under the supervision of officers. Some from my regiment were asked to volunteer for this task.

I had given my name because of the chance it gave me to breathe fresh air. It was stipulated that the hours of work had to be those laid down by the law of 1936, that is to say, a maximum of forty hours a week, and night work was forbidden. To our great surprise, we received an order from the War Ministry to the effect that overtime could be called for at weekends only with a special authorization, issued by the staff of the general commanding the Third Army. And here I added for the benefit of my union leaders: "During all that time, a few kilometers away, on the hills of the Warndt, all round the clock and at night under arc lamps, the Germans poured concrete to build the fortifications of what was to be called the Siegfried Line, which later made it possible for them, without any risk of counterattack, to launch their blitzkrieg through Belgium at the time of their choosing."

Without wishing to criticize the president of the United States in any way, I pointed out that I had been taken aback when he told me, over dinner on the *Potomac,* ten days or so earlier, "René, I believe that if the French Senate had not overthrown the Blum government, France would not have been defeated like that." As we say in France, *je me suis mis un boeuf sur la langue,* I held my tongue and simply replied, "I believe, Mr. President, that the result would have just been the same."

And I added,

> This evening, in the presence of all of you, the representatives of the workers of this country, which I love almost as dearly as I do my own and want to see becoming ever stronger in this dangerous world we live in, I owe you the whole truth. When faced with events of the kind I have related, which came after so many others, the officers from Lorraine, who belonged to one of the crack regiments in France, all asked themselves the same question: "How can we fail to lose this war?"

After making this reply to Edward Keating, in which I tried to explain the real reasons for our defeat, I spent nearly two hours speaking of the future, of my conviction that Britain could not be invaded because of the air superiority she was about to acquire thanks to her fighter force, of the strength of the Home Fleet, and of my certainty that she would win the war if she got the full support of the United States. I read extracts from the report that I had prepared for President Roosevelt and members of the government and ended by saying that, once peace had returned, France would surprise the United States, which today was far too incredulous and skeptical about her future.

The more the evening wore on, the more I felt a growing bond of understanding between those men and women and myself. It was almost one in the morning when we parted.

I had been impressed by the lunch meeting with the Foreign Relations Committee of the Senate. But the warmth of the evening with the union leaders made a lasting impression on me and was a precious encouragement as I left, full of confidence, three days later for the huge agricultural states of America, which I did not know well.

My Last Two Days in Washington and New York before Departing for the Prairies

The following day, Thursday, I had a long meeting with Henry Wallace, the secretary for agriculture, in the presence of a captain of the U.S. Air Force to whom General Marshall had given the task of arranging for the loan of a plane to fly me to those cities on my itinerary with bad rail connections.

I noted that everything had been planned in great detail by the secretary of state's private office—the meetings with state governors, with journalists, with farm unions. I was to leave New York for Chicago by the New York Central on Sunday night and take in Saint Paul, Minneapolis, Des Moines, Kansas City, Denver, Topeka, Saint Louis, Cincinnati, and Columbus.

Harry Hopkins, Henry Wallace, and, for that matter, myself had come to the conclusion that it was preferable for me, since Ambassador Saint Quentin and Colonel Lombard entirely agreed, to resign from my post of assistant military attaché. The war was over. I was a reserve officer, and to carry out my mission effectively, it was better to introduce myself as a Frenchman, a descendant of Lafayette, since the Americans were so keen on this, and as a "citizen" of Maryland.

To celebrate my "demobilization," I invited to my last dinner in Washington my chief, Colonel Lombard, who had become a good friend. It amused us both to think that my father had been one of his predecessors as military attaché in Washington with the same rank as myself! My godfather was none other than William Taft, who was to succeed Theodore Roosevelt, the father of my Aunt Alice, as president. It so happened that Taft was, like my own mother, a native of Cincinnati and her intimate friend. Thus, for my parents, the White House became a kind of second home.

Taft was a huge man, at least one or two inches taller than General de Gaulle. He was very straightforward, full of humor, and a great tease. He often took it out on my father. Never would he fail to invite him to inaugurations of statues of Lafayette, of which forty-four towns already bore the name. One day, he told him point-blank, "Aldebert, I will see whether you are a good sport. If you are, you will come tomorrow to attend the inauguration of the statue of a German, General Steuben, at the corner of Lafayette Square." He then, for a good twenty minutes, launched into a panegyric of Steuben that eclipsed Lafayette. My father, who had a sense of fair play, was present at the inauguration, and Taft, who was having dinner that evening at our home, immediately turned on him:

"I was rather good, wasn't I?"

"I don't agree, Mr. President. You were unfair, and I protest in the name of Lafayette's descendants."

"I regret to tell you, Aldebert, that, for a native of Washington,[3] you don't understand a thing about inauguration speeches. They adhere to a

---

[3]My father was born in Washington where my grandfather was legal adviser to the French embassy.

very strict pattern: to praise someone to whom a statue has been dedicated is necessarily to diminish the merits of another. So if you care to consider that I inaugurate a statue of Steuben every two years, and one of Lafayette every two months, you will agree that you can't talk of unfairness, since I have spoken twelve times more in praise of Lafayette than I have of Steuben. In any case, I am inaugurating a statue of Lafayette in Charleston in two weeks' time, and I invite Clara and yourself to travel there in my special train. You will then learn what I really think of this ham-fisted Steuben— a brutal Prussian officer, that's all!"

When Taft entertained my parents privately, Suzy, my sister, who was five years older than I, was allowed to be present at dinner. I only made a brief appearance, and after the president had waved benignly to his "little French godson," my governess, Katy Hearts, took me off to the huge kitchens, where the staff was exclusively black and where I had a wonderful feast before being put to bed. From that time on, I have liked black people. My first meetings with them were through the years of my youth and in the Pullman sleeping cars and dining cars of the trains on which I traveled.

When my father was promoted to the rank of major and posted back to France to the Fortieth Artillery Regiment of the Iron Division in Lorraine at the end of 1913,[4] Taft gave a dinner to celebrate his fourth bar. He had invited the ambassador and all his staff and two days later, on the eve of our departure, gave another intimate dinner, attended by my grandmother, who had come over from Cincinnati, and my sister Suzy, then twelve and considered worthy of being present with the grown-ups. On that occasion, Taft staged a different scenario as far as I was concerned. He took out of his pocket a dollar bill and some small change and asked me to give him an exact reckoning of the lot. I ran off to the kitchens where Katy, of course, counted it all up for me. I came back and informed the president proudly, "You have two dollars and eighty-seven cents." "All right, keep them," he replied. That is how I got to know the kitchens of the White House, before I was a guest on the presidential yacht thirty-six years later.

My parents bought me a piggy bank, which, eight months later, at Saint-Mihiel, fell into the hands of the Germans. How could I possibly have imagined that so many years later, I was going to lose to another generation of German invaders, in the dead of night, in May 1940, my second uniform and my other possessions, too bulky to be carried on foot on the road from Cassel to Dunkerque?

---

[4] This regiment of covering troops was stationed at Saint-Mihiel, between Toul and Verdun.

CHAPTER 17

I become a traveling salesman for the commodity "Britain" in the deep and isolationist heart of America— First lap: New York–Chicago. The end of a boyhood Dream. My penultimate journey by Pullman

I ARRIVED AROUND NOON IN NEW YORK. AT THE OLD RITZ, I FELT A LITTLE closer to France than in Washington. I had set up a meeting with my friends from the French Information Center and its two directors, along with the two American members of the French board and those of its Action Committee whom I wished to see. We gathered on the premises of the Maison Française in Rockefeller Center.

It was a great satisfaction for me to discover that the institution had become so useful. We agreed it would open half an hour earlier and close an hour later. The documentation in its possession on France was enormous. The staff maps of North Africa in its files were donated to the U.S. command after the United States entered the war. The funds available in Paris were used to finance the American Library of the Rue de Téhéran, which my mother ran during the whole of the German occupation, and over 100,000 American books were saved.

I devoted my dinner and evening to Thayer Hobson, the publisher. We signed a contract, and I promised him a completed manuscript before the end of August. He had already spoken to the editors of the *Ladies Home Journal* and was certain that they would use an abridged version, which could appear in two installments immediately after the book's publication.

I had decided to devote all the royalties to the dispatch of parcels to French prisoners of war and to dedicate the book to Bentz, Saint-Guily, and Billet, the three lieutenants who, together with myself, belonged to B Company of the First Battalion of the 162d Regiment of Fortress Infantry. I had, alas, received confirmation that all three were prisoners of war in the same camp.

The following day, I had lunch with Averell Harriman. President Roosevelt was then at his home in Hyde Park, and at the end of the meal, he decided to call him. I had already appreciated, during the weekend on the *Potomac,* how intimate their relations were. He was later to be chosen by Roosevelt and Harry Hopkins for the post of ambassador to Moscow and to take part in the Casablanca, Tehran, and Yalta conferences. He discussed my trip with the president and handed over the phone to me. Roosevelt's advice was summed up in four words and so was his parting wish for my success, "Be your own self," he said. "God bless you, René." He always seemed to have a gift for the attractive catch phrase.

On Saturday, I lunched with Josée's and my oldest friend, Roy Howard. As a boy, he sold newspapers in Cincinnati, my mother's birthplace, and she was one of his clients. In 1940, he was fifty and had become the Jean Prouvost (owner of *Paris Soir, Match,* and many out-of-town newspapers) of American journalism. His chain of newspapers included, in New York, the *World Telegram* and about twenty local papers, radio stations, and the Scripps Howard Press, which controlled the United Press. He was, in 1959, to become the first American member of our Josée and René de Chambrun Foundation. His advice to me about my book was short and to the point, "Tell what you saw, and no propaganda."

Roy Howard was a conservative Republican through and through. He barely forgave me for consorting with Roosevelt but decided all the same to help me to the full in the battle for Britain, in spite of his somewhat isolationist prejudices. He phoned the governor of Minnesota, Harold Stassen, one of the leading lights of the Republican party, who agreed to give a big dinner for me with the representatives of the farmers' unions in the area.

In the afternoon, I went shopping alone on Fifth Avenue. It was to be my own personal contribution to the campaign for Britain in the heartlands of isolationism. I needed a light bag for my rail journeys and my short hops by air, by car, and on foot. I also needed a handsome briefcase. As I am used to wearing a clean shirt every day, and there would be no laundry facilities, I had to buy a number of shirts, shorts, and socks to be sent by express mail to different places along my route.

The contribution of Uncle Sam to the campaign was a U.S. Army Air Force plane with pilot and radio operator, and the publisher's was the train fare for the author and secretary. The author took care of the hotel bills.

I spent the night on Long Island at the home of Mona Williams. Her house in New York was to be my refuge when I tiptoed back to the United States, so to speak, six years later, after being charged with intelligence with a foreign power and of plotting against the security of my country (see the epilogue of this book).

While the millionaires of Long Island were having a long lie-in next morning, I began to write up my notes for *I Saw France Fall: She Will Rise Again,* which I would dictate from Chicago onward. For lunch at the wonderful Piping Rock Club, Mona Williams had invited my former boss, John Davis, and a few other friends. The club's self-service buffet is certainly the best in the world. Two French chefs would point to the baby Long Island scallops, the small Maine lobsters, and the chocolate mousse "with whipped cream"!

I got back to the Ritz to continue to sort out my notes taken day after day, with which I would dictate my book, and I felt that, in spite of the advice of cautious friends to the contrary, it would be necessary to inject into it a little propaganda all the same in order to defend the honor of France, in spite of her defeat.

Grand Central Station was a few blocks away from the hotel. One crossed Madison Avenue and came upon the great marble monster astride Park Avenue. I got there early, with my kit, feeling like a fiancé setting out for his wedding. In the days of my boyhood, I loved American night trains: the Cincinnati Limited of the Pennsylvania Railroad and the Twentieth Century of the New York Central.

The competition was such between the New York Central of the Vanderbilts and the Pennsylvania Railroad of the Fricks that the Cincinnati Limited left at 5 P.M. and arrived at Cincinnati at nine sharp the following morning. The company offered refunds of 10 to 30 percent of the fare for delays of ten to thirty minutes. Most of the passengers, including my parents, naturally looked forward to delays to obtain a refund, but, as a child, I sympathized with the drivers in their cloth caps and goggles, out in the open on the platform of their big locomotives. Because of my battle for Britain, I was to make my last two trips on those wonderful trains, the first on the Twentieth Century to Chicago, and the second on the return journey, from Cincinnati to New York.

I had always been impressed by the long row of Pullman cars, with their splendid black attendants in black trousers and white coats standing at attention at the doors. They would help the passengers to set foot on small stools at the bottom of the steps. I liked to hear their repeated calls of "All aboard!" Each gave the impression of being the echo of his neighbor, all the way down the line. And when a couple lingered before parting at the last moment, the black attendant, in a protective tone of voice, would say, "Lady, please kiss the gentleman good-bye. We are off. All aboard!"

I was about to make the last of these dreamlike trips because war and the development of air travel throughout the world were to sound the death knell of the Twentieth Century and the Cincinnati Limited. The only reminders of those two empires today are Vanderbilt Avenue and the Frick Collection in New York. I still have a vivid memory of those two nights because my publisher had been particularly generous in reserving for me the upper and lower bunks so that my cubicle had double the breathing space. The green curtains that hung from the ceiling of the Pullman car gave me the impression of being a Hindu potentate in his palanquin or, even further back in time, Cardinal de Richelieu traveling in his litter.

The following morning, I met Mary Mayer, the secretary, in the dining car for an American breakfast and explained that before arriving at Chicago Central Station, we would go through a town in the eastern suburbs called La Grange.

La Grange was the name of the château where Lafayette had retired after his five years of imprisonment in Prussia and Austria. In the course of his triumphal visit to the United States in 1824–1825 no fewer than six towns were given the name of the estate where he was to spend the last thirty-four years of his life. It became our property in 1935.

I do not remember whether, on that morning of July, 1940, steaming through that particular La Grange, the thought crossed my mind, which recurred on two or three occasions during that campaign for Britain: In 1777, a lieutenant of dragoons in the regiment of Noailles, Lafayette, arrived on American soil as a volunteer in the war against England. One hundred and sixty-three years later, one of his descendants, a captain in the stricken French army, had just been entrusted by the thirty-second president of the United States with the task of traveling around the country to muster support for that same England. The first president, George Washington, with Lafayette at his side, had received the surrender of Cornwallis at Yorktown!

At the end of the morning, I settled down at the Drake Hotel in Chicago, where Frances Perkins had reserved a bedroom and small adjoining sitting room where the secretary came to work with me for the rest of the day, as the meetings set up for me in Washington by Averell Harriman, Henry Wallace, and herself only started the following morning.

CHAPTER 18

The prairie agrees to provide a modest support to Britain but refuses to take part in the war

Chicago, Illinois

This was my first trip to Chicago. The weather was sunny and very warm. I suggested to Mary Mayer that I dictate the first chapters of the book on the banks of Lake Michigan. For the newcomer, it is a huge inland sea. Facing one another, on a bench, my secretary and I gave official birth to the book dedicated to my "pals" of the Maginot Line, which would appear in print less than three months later.

After lunch at the Drake Hotel, she spent the afternoon transcribing the morning's dictation while I sneaked off for an outing in a sightseeing boat on which tea and drinks were served. It was an afternoon of relaxation, solitary and restful, before broaching the meetings of the following days in the defense of Britain's cause, before audiences that I thought would become more and more indifferent the farther I moved away from the East Coast.

The following day, I had three important engagements. The morning was set aside for the one organized from Washington by Frances Perkins with the AAA, the Automobile, Aerospace, and Agricultural Implement Workers Union, with headquarters in Detroit. Fifteen or so of its representatives were arriving on the early morning train, and my talk was due to take place in one of the private dining rooms of the Drake. I got there early after having breakfast.

When the group arrived about nine, a snack was served. The meeting lasted until noon. As far as I was concerned, it was as warm and friendly as the dinner with union leaders at the Mayflower in New York, which Frances Perkins had set up. Most of the delegates who came to Chicago were employed in the three great rival automobile firms: General Motors, Ford, Chrysler.

My problem was to break the ice and thaw the atmosphere. I decided to start off with an anecdote that might amuse them, coming as it did from a French captain straight out of the "blitz." I began therefore by stating that I knew the city of Detroit very well for having spent three fascinating days there and penetrating some of the secrets of its industry. That was back in 1933, during the third year of my apprenticeship with the great New York law firm headed by John W. Davis.

I had a visit from the youngest of the four brothers of the Dubonnet empire, André, who was a do-it-yourself and automobile enthusiast. Thanks to his great flair for business, he had bought from an Italian inventor the world patents of a significant technical breakthrough that was to be very lucrative for one of the big Detroit automobile manufacturers. It consisted of an independent wheel suspension. The patent had been taken out in Germany, the United States, France, Switzerland, etc., and John Davis had fixed up a meeting with General Motors for me and Dubonnet who, by reason of our long-standing friendship, preferred that I should assist him rather than one of the seasoned lawyers of the firm. Alfred Sloan, the president, received us in his stately office along with William Spencer, a patent lawyer who knew about the invention, and one or two other people whose names I did not record.

Without beating about the bush, and in a very friendly manner, Sloan said to us, "Gentlemen, we are very interested in your invention. We want to have it. I suggest you make us an offer." We withdrew for consultation, agreeably surprised. André Dubonnet, in France, had known a Mr. Repusseau, the inventor of shock absorbers of the same name, who, a good many years back, had obtained from General Motors for his invention a cash payment as an advance on royalties. He whispered into my ear, "Of course, you will tell Sloan that I speak no English" (he understood it very well). And off we go with a request for a cash payment of $100,000—they were good sound dollars at the time—and royalties ranging from fifty cents on the cheaper model to two dollars for Cadillacs.

I quietly announced our figures, but Sloan retorted, "Our company has never made any cash payments." Dubonnet gave me a broad wink when Sloan put forward the additional argument, "We always practice the system of royalties per car." And he repeated, "Cash payments, never!" His offer was twenty cents for the cheapest model and one dollar for Cadillacs.

After taking note of the pious deceit—I say *pious* because it was in the interests of the shareholders of General Motors—André Dubonnet shrewdly got me to reply that the offer was inadequate and that he could well afford to wait. I translated and added that, in any case, he was spending two days in Detroit, where he was due to visit a factory, and would think the matter over. We withdrew.

Back at the hotel, I was a little surprised to find a message to call Edsel

Ford, the big competitor of General Motors. But I was even more astonished, an hour later, to receive a call from Sloan himself suggesting a second meeting. Dubonnet and I began to think that walls had ears in Detroit!

At this point, I asked my audience, "How many of you here are from General Motors?" Three hands went up. "And from Ford?" Two hands rose. And, to a burst of laughter all round, I pointed out that, in 1933, General Motors had lied by telling me no inventor had ever received a cash payment and that Ford had at least one spy at General Motors because the secret negotiations with them had lasted only one hour.

Then, in a relaxed atmosphere, I finished my story: The contract with General Motors, for a duration of seventeen years, which was as long as the life of the patent, provided for fifty thousand dollars in cash and royalties ranging from thirty cents to one dollar. We proposed a rebate of 5 percent on those figures on condition that the new system would be advertised as the Dubonnet System. But this was contrary to General Motors's policy, and the Dubonnet System was for a good many years to be known the world over as the "knee action" invented by General Motors.

Faced with a distinctly more receptive audience, I was able to embark on the subject of my crusade, calling for questions as I went along. Those men were intelligent and appealed to me. I took my remarks a stage further than in Washington, although Miss LeHand and Harry Hopkins had urged me to exercise a degree of caution.

Every day that passed without any sign of a German invasion of Britain, while the rate of production of Bolton Defiants rose steadily, led me to say—and I would repeat it from time to time during my journey through the prairies—"Britain is now invincible, provided she gets unlimited aid from the United States (she already enjoys that of the Dominions). Full American support will prove decisive in this war, as it did when you gave it to France and her allies in 1917."

I detected signs of complete agreement in the little group of listeners and felt much more at ease than face to face with the Foreign Relations Committee of the Senate. From the way they grasped my hand when we parted and asked me to return to Detroit, I felt myself becoming an American once again, as I had done during my four years in New York when I was practicing law and watching baseball games on Sundays.

Delayed by the prolonged leave-taking, I hurried a few blocks from the hotel to the club where Averell Harriman's associates had invited about one hundred people: businessmen, company presidents, bankers, journalists. There, my statement was brief and to the point. There were few questions, as everyone was in a hurry to get back to work. But the atmosphere was good and less isolationist than I had feared.

That afternoon, around four, Henry Wallace had collected a group of farm operators in a big air-conditioned warehouse, located in a southern suburb. To them, Britain seemed as remote as Siberia! In this job of traveling salesman, if one misses a trick—and on this occasion I felt it was the case—one must not lose confidence.

Saint Paul, Minnesota

On my way to the station, I picked up Mary Mayer at the hotel, and we settled down in the dining car to resume dictation of the book. The following morning, we were at Saint Paul, the capital of the farm state of Minnesota, located on the banks of the Mississippi. The twin city of Minneapolis, on the other side of the river, is linked to it by a splendid suspension bridge.

As I came out of the station, I was a little taken aback to be met by a superb Lincoln and a chauffeur who explained that he worked for Mr. John Cowles, the owner of the *Minneapolis Star,* the *Herald,* and the *Journal.* I knew he had got a call from his friend, colleague, and competitor Roy Howard in New York and had promised to organize my visit to the Twin Cities. The chauffeur informed me that Cowles had also reserved for the duration of my stay a suite at the hotel with the pretty French name of Nicollet and a room for the secretary.

The chauffeur also knew that I was dining that evening with the state governor, Harold Stassen. He therefore suggested taking the secretary right away to the hotel, on the other side of the Mississippi, and coming to collect me around eleven, after dinner at the governor's mansion, to drive me back to it.

In the meantime, he dropped me off at the best hotel in town, where Henry Wallace's staff had arranged for me to have a room where I could rest before, between, and after the two meetings with the farmers. One took place in the morning and the other in the afternoon. I was, of course, shown the names of all those present. Practically all were of Scandinavian or German descent.

Mr. Wiggin, whose first name I do not recollect, was the owner of the *Pioneer Press,* the great Saint Paul newspaper. He had organized at his club a lunch party of about thirty journalists, politicians, and businessmen. At dinner, Governor Stassen had invited one of the state senators and two Republican congressmen who had been unable to make the lunch to meet me. Stassen had lost the nomination at the Republican party convention, which had taken place the month before in Philadelphia during my stay in Washington. The majority of the delegates preferred Wendell Wilkie, a more liberal Republican, who was to bite the dust in the presidential contest the following November, when Roosevelt was reelected for a third term in violation of a historic precedent set by Washington.

Encouraged by the welcome I had received the day before from the union representatives in Detroit, I went so far as to say to this small group of isolationists, when coffee and cigars were produced, that if the United States did not back Britain up to the hilt and if, by some remote chance, she lost the war, the Americans would lose their economic and commercial standing in the world, and there would be no one left to buy their farm surpluses other than the poorer countries and the bad debtors of Latin America.

I took leave of the governor around eleven. It was very hot; the sky was studded with stars; the moon was shining. Although the springs of the Mississippi are in one of the lakes near the Canadian border, not far away, it is already broad and fast-flowing at Saint Paul. I asked the driver to slow down so that I could take in the scene. On the way to Denver, in the Rockies, I flew over the river, and walked along the quayside at Saint Louis. I recollected, during that trip, that much further down the river, during his triumphal tour, Lafayette was sailing upstream in a packed steamer when it sank. Several people drowned, and the "guest of the nation" had a narrow escape from death.

On a Saturday, some months ago, while writing this book, I was browsing through the thousands of documents in the archives of La Grange and discovered the dictionary of Indian words Lafayette used to communicate with the Indian servant he had brought back to France. In it, I came upon the word *Meshacebe,* which in the Indian language means "Father of Rivers" and in English has become "Mississippi."[1]

Minneapolis, Minnesota

It was midnight when the driver dropped me off at the Nicollet, where the hotel manager had waited up for me. A maid led me to a small suite, and on the table, I found a tricolor bouquet, surrounded by all the publications of the Cowles Group.

Calling at the hotel early that morning were the pilot and radio oper-

---

[1] Few Americans appreciate that the Mississippi is only the second largest river in the United States. The Missouri, which has its springs in the Rockies at an altitude of 1,500 meters, flows north toward the Canadian frontier before turning west and coming down in a succession of wide curves to join the Mississippi. Just north of Saint Louis, where the two flow together, the Missouri is more than two miles wide, to the Mississippi's one.

ator of the U.S. Army Air Force aircraft assigned to me. It had a cabin with room for six and a writing table and was waiting at a military airfield a few miles from the western airport of Minneapolis. The following day, it would fly me to Des Moines, the capital of Iowa, then to Kansas City, Denver, Colorado, and back to Saint Louis, in Missouri.

At the morning meeting set up by John Cowles, I noted, as I had done on the other side of the Mississippi, that all the names of those taking part were of Scandinavian or German origin. The John Cowles Building, where the two big morning newspapers, the *Star* and the *Herald,* and the evening *Journal* were produced, looked like a large factory. But it had a big auditorium where all those members of the staff were gathered who could take time off to come and listen to my talk without disrupting production. I made it short, as Cowles and I, with a few local personalities, were to lunch together at his club.

In the afternoon, there was a gathering of farmers and unionists organized by Henry Wallace, and the following morning, we left by plane, the secretary and I, for Des Moines.

Des Moines, Iowa

I had already met John Cowles's brother, Gardner Cowles, during my years of law practice in New York. It did not take me long in Des Moines to realize that Gardner ("Mike") was the giant of the two. He entertained me with his wife in his splendid home, which resembled a private house of the "belle epoque" in Paris. The couple ran a lavish establishment with an army of servants.

Mike's wife, Fleur, had a hobby—painting and drawing. Her paintings on china were well known. Mike was the owner of the famous *Des Moines Register* and headed *Look* magazine, which, from the Atlantic to the Pacific coasts, had an even larger circulation than Henry Luce's *Life.*

Shortly after my arrival, I got a phone call from Harry Hopkins. Miss LeHand was at his side, and I was happy to hear that the first convoy of more than two thousand antiaircraft guns, four dozen fighter planes, and a large number of machine guns was on its way to England. He added, "René, it's your doing. Keep on." Miss LeHand at that point gave me the message that the president had asked Bill Bullitt to come and spend a few days with him around the 15th of July. This was good news as I was certain that his pro-French sentiments would prompt him to back the sending of food to the unoccupied zone of France.

Mike Cowles had organized a meeting at the club of which he was president and a dinner with the leading personalities of the city and the state. The following day, as he drove with me to the airport, he spoke these few simple moving words, "You convinced us. *Look* will defend England." Since then, we met on each one of his trips to Paris, and he was one of the first visitors "admitted" by Josée at La Grange. She showed him all she had done in the first year, the bedrooms of Lafayette and Adrienne and the library that she had restored in every detail with reverence and devotion. She only drew the line at one thing, as in the case of our friend Henry Luce, the owner of *Life:* the taking of pictures in return for a big donation to our foundation. Mike Cowles wanted to be the first to do so. "Never," she said. "The soul of this house must remain unsullied. It has been preserved since the death of René's uncle, Louis de Lasteyrie, thirty-five years ago."

Kansas City, Missouri

I was welcomed at the airport by Mr. Haskell, the owner of the *Kansas City Star.* He took me to the Muelebach Hotel and explained the lunch he had organized around the governor, Lloyd Stard, who was coming from Jefferson, the state capital. He had made his reputation as the scourge of the Democratic machine, known by the name of its boss, Joe Prendergast, whom Stard had sent to jail.

Among the guests at the lunch were the executives of New York Life, the big insurance company, which had its head office in Kansas City. The dinner was given by the celebrated William Allen White, owner of the *Emporia Gazette,* who had just agreed to establish a committee "to defend the United States by aiding the Allies." He explained that I was traveling all over the United States as the "salesman" of his committee. On that occasion, I met Alfred Landon, the former governor of Kansas and unlucky contender for the presidency when Roosevelt was reelected in 1936. He was won over to the policy of aid to Britain.

Denver, Colorado

I had promised to attend at Denver, Colorado, a meeting of the United Mineworkers of America, organized by Frances Perkins the day after my stopover in Kansas City, and I was due in Saint Louis forty-eight hours later. The pilot said it could be done, on condition we started very early in the morning and left Denver at five in order to get to Saint Louis by nightfall. I owed to this tight schedule the privilege of seeing one of the finest sights of my whole journey: the approach to the Rockies, at the end of the prairies just after sunrise and the return just before dusk over the spot where the Missouri and the Mississippi flow together.

The mineworkers' union is one of the oldest in the United States. In 1940, it was celebrating its fiftieth anniversary, and today, it is a century old. Those miners gathered at their union headquarters, and the time I spent with them, before the governor's lunch, was as fascinating as my meeting with the automobile workers and with the union leaders at the Mayflower. The questions I was asked were all to the point. My audience admitted the need to help Britain when I pointed out that if the German Reich won the war, America would lose most of its markets in the world and the output of all her mines would fall dramatically.

Ralph Carr, the governor, a powerful figure in the Republican party, had got together a few local personalities and the owner of the *Denver Post,* along with some of his staff. Toward the end of the meal, when the time came for questions, the editor in chief of the newspaper asked in a slightly irritating tone of voice, "If I get it right, you Frenchmen are quitters!" To which I replied, "On September 3d, 1939, we declared war to defend democracy, and *you* were acting the quitters then. We were defeated, after calling upon you in vain. You remained quitters. And you are still quitters today where Britain is concerned. I suggest, under those circumstances, that we refrain from calling one another quitters."

Upon which, he then asked me nicely, "Could you appear on our radio program tonight and say what you have just said?" I replied, "If you come to the airport with a tape recorder and interview me, we can set up the program together. But I must get to Saint Louis before the night." Everyone burst out laughing, and the "entente cordiale" between "quitters" of both nations was signed and sealed then and there.

I have always been struck by the fact that it is much easier, when one can field the right arguments, to convince an Anglo-Saxon audience than a Latin one.

Saint Louis, Missouri

The sun had not yet set when the plane drew close to Saint Louis and the pilot made a detour of a few extra miles to the north in order to fly over the spot where the two giant rivers flow together. It is located only a few miles from the city. In the reign of Louis XV, Saint Louis was a township of about a thousand Frenchmen, the size of Châteldon. Much later, tens of thousands of German immigrants moved in to swell the population.

The day's program included a meeting with the Brotherhood of Electrical Workers, one of the more left-wing unions. Almost all those present came from Emerson Electric, which had its head office and main plant in Saint Louis. Everything went off smoothly.

Pulitzer, the founder of the famous prize that bears his name and owner of the *Saint Louis Post Dispatch,* had organized a lunch with representatives of the leading banks and industries of the city. At the end of the day, forsaking the plane, I took the train to Cincinnati. It too was named the *Spirit of Saint Louis,* after the aircraft in which Lindbergh, who was a native of the city, flew successfully across the Atlantic for the first time. One could not but spare a passing thought for him during the journey.

Here is another: I had just completed my six months' course as a reserve officer cadet at Saint Cyr and was in the huge crowd that waited in the night at Le Bourget for him to arrive. When the little plane touched down, there was a mad rush. I still had my French junior rugby team scrum-half legs and, in the crush, found myself close enough to see this young Icarus, turned into a hero without knowing it, climb out of the cockpit and say simply, "I am Charles Lindbergh!"

Cincinnati and Columbus, Ohio

At last, I reached Cincinnati, my mother's native city. I was to spend three days there resting, the first letup I had had since the Maginot Line. As a child of three, four, and five, I spent the summer vacation with my grandmother. My father was a captain at the time and French military attaché in Washington. It was at my grandmother's picturesque home, where in 1940 my aunt, Alice Roosevelt Longworth, was living, that I was to spend those three days of "rest and recreation." She was my mother's sister-in-law. My cousins, her nephews, lived on the estate. After the Rockies, the vast prairies, the Mississippi, I suddenly had the feeling that I had got back a little closer to Josée and to France.

Mary Mayer had returned to New York with about two-thirds of the book. I would now be able to do at last what I would not have dared during my mission and watch a night game of baseball, my favorite American sport. I did, however, something for Britain also on the occasion of a ceremony when the mayor of Cincinnati made me a citizen of the city and presented me with a golden key, "to enter it at night." Aid to Britain through sending fighters and antiaircraft guns was the gist of my speech.

The next day, before getting onto my last Pullman of the Cincinnati Limited, on the way back to New York, I spent some time in Columbus, the capital of the state of Ohio. My Aunt Alice had lent me for the day her luxurious limousine and her genial black chauffeur, Mike Tompson, who was all smiles and wore a fine gray uniform. The prospect of the trip delighted me. Preston Wolf, the boss of the *Columbus Dispatch* and of the local radio station, was the political backer of my uncle, Nick Longworth, in the state of Ohio. He gave a lunch at the country club, presided over by the governor. The invitations read as follows: "To meet Count de Chambrun, a soldier of France, descendant of Lafayette, who will speak in defense of England."

The task described on the invitation was easy, and I thanked Heaven for this last day of my "holiday." I would be alone with my thoughts and rest during the long drive in both directions on a fine three-lane highway.

CHAPTER 19

New York: My July 14th.
Bullitt's return: Vers l'espoir

SUNDAY, JULY 14TH, "BASTILLE DAY": THE CINCINNATI LIMITED GLIDED slowly through the deep tunnel under the Hudson and into Pennsylvania Station, more than an hour late. The dusty, ill-lit dome struck me as gloomy. The marble frame of the booking offices was yellowed. The black porters with their red caps were nowhere to be seen. I had the impression that the great battle of the famous private railroad companies against faster air travel through this huge country was already a lost one.

At the Ritz, where I resumed residence, I got a call from Miss LeHand toward the end of the afternoon, telling me the president wished to speak to me, and she transferred the call immediately. Through Henry Wallace and Frances Perkins, he had, he said, very favorable reports of my journey. He thanked me for undertaking it and added that he had just heard on the radio a "very dignified" speech by Churchill on the subject of France. He also informed me of his latest telephone conversations with Bill Bullitt and confirmed that the ambassador was returning to Washington by Clipper at the end of the week.

As the conversation went on and as he seemed relaxed on this late afternoon, I spoke for the first time with him of a possible dispatch of food supplies to the unoccupied zone of France, which was still submerged with refugees from all over the country and even from Holland and Belgium. He suggested I take this up with Bullitt as soon as he was back, adding the promising phrase, "I will agree with your suggestion if Bullitt agrees." To which I replied, "I shall naturally go and meet him at the airport." I felt greatly heartened.

I spent most of that week in New York getting on with my book and busy with the French Information Office. On Saturday, July 20, I drove to La Guardia to meet the Clipper on which William Bullitt had traveled back from France via Lisbon, accompanied by his faithful assistant, Carmel Offie. As soon as I caught sight of a large group of reporters who were certainly expecting the ambassador to make a statement on arrival, I felt I must say a few words to him privately before he met the press about the ridiculous rumors current in the United States concerning Marshal Pétain and Pierre Laval.

I managed to make my way to the foot of the gangway and, with a warm embrace to Offie and his boss, whispered in his ear, "There are many reporters around." He remarked, "I don't intend to say anything." But I immediately retorted, "You must certainly say something because of the stupid rumors about Pétain, a Fascist working for Hitler, etc." He replied, "All right, I will speak."

Very calmly, he made a statement that was just what was needed and proved all the more important because the *New York Times* and the *Herald* published it word for word. While he was chatting to Sumner Wells, the assistant secretary of state who had come over from Washington, Offie handed me some mail, including a precious letter from Josée, and suggested meeting for a quiet talk. I told him I would be staying put at the Ritz, where I intended to work all the rest of the afternoon and evening. "We will probably come by around seven, on our way to dinner next door," he said.

They both turned up, and we talked for nearly an hour. After describing the atmosphere in New York, I suggested supplies be shipped by the United States to unoccupied France. Bullitt agreed wholeheartedly. "It is a must," he added. Roosevelt had invited him to spend two or three days at his Hyde Park home, and he would raise the subject with him there.

Two days later, I returned to Washington, where I had a lunch appointment with Lord Lothian and with Casey, the Australian ambassador. The atmosphere was set fair. Lothian expressed his gratitude for my journey to the West of which he had already had a report from the British consul general in Chicago. He confirmed the figure of antiaircraft guns, fighter planes, and light machine guns shipped or about to be shipped before the end of the month and the increase in the number of planes coming off the Coventry assembly lines. When he repeated to me what he had said the day after the American Cabinet had lifted the embargo on these shipments, "All this is your work," I simply replied, "No, I merely acted as an accelerator."

We spoke freely to one another, and I told him about my two conversations—the one on the phone with Roosevelt when I got back to New York a week before and especially the one with Bullitt on his return from France. I added that the ambassador would certainly see him after his stay at Hyde Park. I sensed that Casey shared Bullitt's conviction that a majority of American public opinion would regard the granting by Britain of the necessary navicerts for the shipment of food supplies to France as a handsome gesture.

That evening, I dined with General George Marshall and his wife at their pretty little frame house in Virginia, on the banks of the Potomac, not far from Mount Vernon. He suggested that I should make a tour of all the regional commands to tell their commanders and their staff officers about the German infantry's new methods of warfare.

I begged for a little time to finish off my book, of which the proceeds were earmarked for parcels to prisoners of war, because I felt under a moral obligation. We worked out a compromise solution. I would call on General Caffrey a few days later at the Pentagon, and he would summon the regional commanders for a meeting with me at a date to be set later.

In the meantime, on the following morning, Harry Hopkins had asked Frances Perkins, Henry Wallace, and me to drop in at the White House for a four-cornered talk. He received us in his office in shirtsleeves and slippers, and I got the impression that when the president was absent, he really ran the place. He began by saying that Bullitt had convinced "the chief" that Pétain was "the right man" and that the new French ambassador, Henry-Haye, a senator and mayor of Versailles, very friendly toward the United States, who was due to take up his new post in Washington in a few weeks' time, would, in Bullitt's words, also be "a good man."

He asked me to have another talk with Morgenthau, the secretary to the treasury, who, according to him, was the only member of the Cabinet who seemed ill-disposed toward Marshal Pétain. Then and there, he fixed a meeting for the following morning and also suggested I see Cordell Hull. With the latter, I had no problem. Everything was plain sailing. I had already met him twice before my trip to the prairies. He was a calm, intelligent, and moderate Southerner. He had understood the need for the armistice with Germany, for a government which would save the French colonies and the fleet from falling into the hands of the Germans, and he did not regard Marshal Pétain as a "Fascist."

I saw Morgenthau along with his assistant, Harry Dexter White. This other Harry was then his leading adviser on relations with foreign countries. Some years later, in September 1944, he produced the vast plan for the "pastoralization" and partition of Germany. The United States discovered with amazement, after Roosevelt's death, that he was one of the Soviet spies firmly entrenched in the seat of power, the other one being Alger Hiss. Harry Dexter White was the favorite of the KGB.

I recall that he remained silent and looked interested as I tried to reply to Henry Morgenthau's questions and to explain all about the armistice, Marshal Pétain, the fleet, the salvaging of our colonial empire, our two million prisoners of war, and much else.

I returned to New York on the last weekend of July to spend the remaining days at the splendid home of the Harrison Williamses on Long Island, getting on with my book.

CHAPTER 20

Washington, August 1st:
Morning: My longest talk with Roosevelt—he says yes.
Afternoon: Churchill says yes— Roosevelt confirms the deal— one of the great moments of my life.

Upon returning to the Ritz, where I had invited Simone and André Maurois for dinner, I found an urgent message to call Harry Hopkins at the White House. He asked if I could arrange to take the midnight train to Washington and be there at ten-thirty next morning for a meeting that President Roosevelt regarded as important.

I naturally agreed. Hopkins took the opportunity to say that he had had a private talk with Lothian the day before. The latter had referred to what he called "René de Chambrun's crusade for Britain," adding that he thought Winston Churchill would agree if Roosevelt asked him to authorize the issue of navicerts for successive shipments of food to Marseilles, on condition that the tonnage involved was limited. Here, I thought to myself, was an opening at last.

He hinted that Roosevelt wished to discuss the situation in France after the tragedy of Mers-el-Kebir, the man whom he described as "the Pétain of today," the men "in charge" of North Africa, and what I thought of de Gaulle, about whom people were beginning to talk. It was a crowded agenda. He suggested I drop into his office a few minutes before seeing the president.

Roosevelt greeted me warmly and spoke of the good reports he had had of my tour of the prairies. "Now tell me what you think is going to happen in France. Pétain worries me," he said. I reassured him and tried to make him understand the immense drama France had been through, the scale of which was not appreciated here: an army of six million men in total rout, the massive exodus of millions of Belgians and Frenchmen. "It was not only Pétain who called for an armistice; it was the whole of France!" I demonstrated to him that the fact of having saved from complete German occupation the whole of the southern part of the country, its access to the Mediterranean, its colonial empire, and the fleet was an enormous advantage over a wholesale capitulation that would have meant immediate occupation by the Germans of North Africa as well.

I made him appreciate the usefulness of having a government on the spot and especially of a prefectoral and municipal administration that had already secured the mass return to their homes of hundreds of thousands who could not have found enough to eat in the unoccupied zone. The government had already obtained that 400,000 agricultural workers should not be sent to prisoner-of-war camps in Germany but stay in France to bring in the harvest.

I maintained that the sinking of the French fleet by the British at Mers-el-Kebir, near Oran, in July 1940, had been a serious blunder, if not worse, as neither Pétain nor Darlan would ever have surrendered it to the Germans. Churchill had reluctantly decided on the operation for fear the fleet would be seized by them, in contravention of the terms of the armistice, at a time when Britain was fighting for survival. Units of the British navy, under orders of Admiral Somerville, shelled the French ships, which were at their moorings and therefore incapable of retaliating. All were scuppered or rendered unusable, except the battleship *Strasbourg,* which managed to make for Toulon. Fifteen hundred French sailors lost their lives in the engagement, which had a disastrous effect on French public opinion and gave a boost to the propaganda of the advocates of collaboration with the Nazis. The president did not know that, before the signing of the armistice, as early as June 12, Admiral Darlan had ordered the battleship *Richelieu* to sail from Brest to Dakar and the *Strasbourg* from Saint-Nazaire to Casablanca. He did not know either that ships' captains had been given secret orders to scuttle if the Germans broke one of the main clauses of their own armistice and tried to lay hands on any of them.

I replied to his questions about my own journey and public sentiment, which in my opinion was evolving with each passing day in favor of stepped-up assistance to Britain. After expressing his gratitude to me for undertaking the mission, he asked me point-blank, "What do you think I can do for France?" My reply was short and immediate, "The only thing that must be done for France today is to feed the unoccupied zone." To which he replied, "I would like to do it. But if we send food there, the Nazis will grab it."

My retort was as follows, "Do you really think the Germans would dare to violate the demarcation line laid down by the armistice in order to take from the mouths of the Frenchmen in Marseilles the condensed milk that America will send them? It is true they have committed many crimes and will continue to commit more. But I am certain they will not commit that one because it would have far too many adverse repercussions for them. If they did something of the sort, the French people would not forgive them for many years. On the other hand, they would never forget that the United States had given them a helping hand in the hour of their greatest need."

I explained in detail the plan that I had worked out and that I had thought over many times, often at night before falling asleep. I had discussed it with Lothian, Casey, and Harry Hopkins. It consisted of food shipments at two-, three-, or four-week intervals, thereby limiting the risk of confiscation of one single consignment. So long as, for instance, the Germans allowed tins of condensed milk to be distributed in France, the United States would continue to reap the political and moral advantages of their generosity, which would grow steadily until a possible but highly improbable seizure by the Germans turned the whole of French public opinion against them.

At that point, Roosevelt seemed impressed by the argument and interrupted me suddenly with this remark, "Why didn't I think of it?" To which I replied that he had hundreds of problems on his mind and it was more than natural I should be the one to have had the idea since it was really the only question about which I was constantly thinking since my arrival in the United States, especially when I heard that all my comrades of the Maginot Line were prisoners of war in Germany.

He then asked me if I would be prepared to go to Vichy in order to put a proposal to Marshal Pétain. The prospect of such a journey upset all my plans, but I replied, "I could leave at short notice, if you so wished." He thought the matter over for a moment and, after reminding me of the violent attacks that Paul Baudouin, the foreign minister of the Vichy government, continued to level against Britain after the Mers-el-Kebir tragedy, he said word for word, "Here is the proposition you can transmit from me to the marshal: if he agrees to call a meeting of American reporters in Vichy and to make a statement in favor of our rearmament and our democratic ideals, if he puts an end to Baudouin's attacks against Britain, I will see to it that the free zone of France gets regular shipments of food, in particular of condensed milk, until the end of hostilities."

The proposition seemed to me so vital that I took a sheet of paper from his desk and asked him to be good enough to repeat it under dictation. I mentioned the navicerts Britain would have to issue to enable supply ships to sail through the Strait of Gibraltar should the marshal accept his conditions. He replied with a smile, "They can't refuse that to you," and I answered tit for tat, smiling in turn, "Mr. President, they will be even less able to refuse it to you." He laughed again, with his good loud laugh and said, "I see what you want: I should do the dirty work. Then tell Lothian to come and see Harry and myself this afternoon." He insisted on the secret nature of my mission to France, cautioning me not to speak about it to anyone and to have contact with no one but the marshal and "your wife, since you are going to bring her back with you."

Under his dictation, I wrote down the broad lines of the statement he wished the marshal to make on Franco-American relations, as well as the substance of the letter that the latter was to address to him, emphasizing the appalling straits in which the French people found themselves and authorizing the use of official French gold reserves to pay for the food shipments.

Speaking of the document Pétain was supposed to write, he added literally, "Bring me back a good letter from the marshal, and I will make it public at one of my press conferences with my comments."

It was exactly ten past one when I came out of the Oval Office. In the hall, I was met by reporters who were puzzled by the length of my talk with the president and the fact that one or two other appointments on his schedule had been canceled. I tried to dodge their questions and spoke in general terms of the president's queries about France. I added that the armistice had been the lesser of the evils and that I hoped for recovery after our great ordeal.

To avoid being followed by an inquisitive reporter, I did not drive away in the car lent me by Harry Hopkins but hailed a taxi to return to the Mayflower, from where I phoned Lothian, who was lunching alone and suggested I come straightaway. I was at the embassy a few minutes later. I asked the ambassador to give me his word that no one in Washington would learn what I was about to tell him. He agreed wholeheartedly. He also considered that his country's gesture in granting the required navicerts would have a very positive impact on American public opinion. He was going to call London and would go over to the White House straight after to see Harry Hopkins. We arranged to meet again at six P.M.

I went round to the French embassy and informed Saint Quentin. He promised to keep the matter secret and appeared very satisfied. I then went to see Sumner Wells and Adolphe Berle, with whom Miss LeHand had set up appointments. Punctually at six, I was again with Lothian. He had talked to Churchill, and seen Harry Hopkins and Roosevelt. He said to me, "My government agrees, on condition that the shipments involved are reasonable and that the tonnage of the ships is relatively low." When I expressed my gratitude, he added, "You deserve this."

I told him I would be leaving that very evening for New York, where I would be completing my book, before taking the Clipper to Lisbon at the beginning of the following week. He undertook to have a letter of introduction sent to the governor of Bermuda in order to inform him of my coming.

From the British embassy, I went to the White House. Hopkins took me in to see Roosevelt, who said, with a broad wink, arm upraised, "René, it's a deal." It was one of the happiest moments of my life. I went back to Hopkins's office, and we gave one another an accolade, French style, although this is not an American custom. I explained that I had promised to go to the home of Clarence Dillon late that evening, in order to devote a long weekend to my book. His estate was in New Jersey, about halfway between Washington and New York.

I rang Clarence Dillon at his office because he knew Hopkins and put the following suggestion to him: Hopkins insisted on dining with me and taking me to the station, where trains left every hour for New York. We reckoned that by catching the ten o'clock train, I would be in Trenton by half past midnight, where the Dillon limousine would pick me up. I could thus get to his Peepack home shortly after one in the morning. I naturally insisted that no one should stay up and wait for me.

Our dinner at the Mayflower took place, as far as I was concerned, in an atmosphere of complete euphoria. Hopkins insisted on ordering the most expensive bottle of claret on the list, as neither of us drank champagne. The train was nearly an hour late at Trenton. At the station exit, Clarence Dillon's Rolls was waiting for me. The butler, an old acquaintance, welcomed me to a house deep in slumber. After offering me a variety of food and drink, he led me to my bedroom.

I woke up in a happy mood at this wonderful estate located in the attractive "inland" part of the Far Hills of New Jersey. That great banker, founder of Dillon Reed, had been one of the few to forecast the stock exchange crash of 1929. He was a man of remarkable taste and style. During my four bachelor years in New York, I had made friends with his son Douglas, who later became American ambassador to France, under secretary for economic affairs, secretary of state, and finally, chairman of the board of the Metropolitan Museum.

While my father was in command of an army corps at Bordeaux before the war, he wanted to do a good turn to the owner of a famous vineyard who had been practically ruined by the crash—most of them were—and had asked him to find an American buyer for his property of Haut Brion. This was how Dillon in 1935 entered the exclusive club of owners of the great vintages for a mere pittance. At his house at Dunwalke, built exclusively of pink bricks salvaged from old southern houses, he had a special cellar built for the Haut Brion.

I let him into the secret of my conversation with Roosevelt, and he decided to celebrate the president's "yes" with a magnum of 1921 Haut

Brion. His wife and children had a good laugh when he forbade his butler to go down to the cellar, and we saw him come up the stairs, holding the bottle cradled in his arms, just like a newborn baby, and crossing the dining room with careful footsteps to avoid jolting the precious liquid, which had certainly been tossed about a good deal when crossing the Atlantic.

With the exception of Josée, I had promised Roosevelt that I would tell no living soul about the mission to Marshal Pétain with which he had entrusted me. But I want the reader to understand why I could not keep it a secret from Clarence Dillon. Since my coming to New York for my "apprenticeship," he had always been a sort of guardian angel to me. He would remain one until his dying day.

I had resolved secretly, from the time of my arrival in 1930, to prepare the New York Bar examinations without going through the necessary four years at law school. I took evening courses and was plunged in law books over the weekends. But a minor disaster occurred at the time when I put my name down for the examination, which was held twice a year.

The day after I had registered, the *New York Times* picked up the story and announced in a few lines that a descendant of Lafayette was going to sit ten days later for the bar examination. The head of my law firm, John Davis, immediately gave me a piece of salutary advice. "For the sake of your own personal reputation, and that of the firm of Davis, Polk, Wardwell, Gardiner and Reed, you cannot run the risk of failure. You must therefore report sick, take another course of evening classes, and retire for six weeks to the home of Clarence Dillon, where you will be able to concentrate on your law books. You will continue to receive your salary and will be entitled to three weeks' paid holidays a year."

I spent six weeks hard at work in this stately home of Dunwalke and passed; the honor of the descendant of Lafayette and of Davis, Polk, Wardwell, Gardiner and Reed was safe.

The second month of the "phony war" I was summoned to the headquarters of the Third Army, which covered the Maginot Line. General Condé's chief of staff handed over to me two parcels that had come by way of the American embassy and the Defense Ministry. I did not know such a circuitous route could exist. I signed the receipt, and in the car that drove me back to Rotherberg Fort, I opened the two parcels.

The smaller one came from Cartier in New York, and on it were the initials "CD" (Clarence Dillon) "to Lieutenant RC." It contained a gold watch in a waterproof case because of the damp of the Maginot Line. The other parcel, of a less anonymous character, contained a pair of braces embroidered by Mrs. Dillon, with a little accompanying note. It conjured up recollections of Broadway theaters in the Gay Nineties of my youth, when the stage Frenchman always had a beard and, when he took off his coat, wore both a belt and a pair of braces, in case the belt should let him down. Mrs. Dillon had embroidered with black silk thread on one of the white silk braces "God hates a coward," and on the other, "But he loves a prudent man." That pair of lucky and cautionary braces may have helped me to get to Dunkerque and to England without too much difficulty. For my part, I always thought Mrs. Dillon was a saint.

Be that as it may, it was during that weekend, which followed the wonderful piece of news, spent with charming friends, that I worked out my schedule for the last week before my return to Lisbon, Josée, Vichy, and Marshal Pétain.

CHAPTER 21

Eight more days to convince

Henry Luce's empire:—Time, Life, Fortune, March of Time, *the* Scripps Howard Press—*and to finish off my book*

AFTER THIS RESTFUL WEEKEND, CLARENCE DILLON DROVE ME BACK TO NEW York. We chatted about everything under the sun, and even the cavernous depths of the interminable Holland Tunnel did not interfere with our conversation.

To enable me to enjoy peace and quiet and finish off my book, Dillon suggested I spend the last four days of the week at Peepack, where I would not be bothered by phone calls. Mary Mayer, the secretary who accompanied me on my trip to the prairies, was to come at least twice to take dictation and pick up what I had time to write myself. I would thus be in a position to hand in the complete manuscript to the publisher the following Monday.

I lunched with Henry Luce, and we spoke at length about the French Information Center, which his publications used extensively. I had, of course, made strong recommendations that the institution should remain aloof from the controversies of French residents in New York, who seemed to be already dividing into two camps. The word *resistance* had not yet been invented nor that of *collaborator*. But those who took Marshal Pétain's defense and stood up for the armistice were beginning to be called "Fascists"! As time wore on, they would become "collaborators" and "pro-Nazis." And some, who had been liable for National Service on September 1939 and had chosen to remain in New York, would soon discover that they were "Fifth Avenue resistance fighters!"

After lunch, we went to the Time-Life Building where, at three o'clock, a meeting was held of the editorial staff of all the group's publications. Luce gave me the recommendation, when I said my "spiel" on Britain, to reply fully to the questions that I would certainly be asked about what was really going on in France.

My unshakable conviction about the growing superiority of the RAF fighter force, the Bolton Defiants and Spitfires, over the Messerschmidts had been boosted further still by the three successive conversations I had with Lothian, who informed me confidentially of the rate of production of these planes, which rose steadily from week to week.

Under the influence of Lord Beaverbrook, whom Churchill was well inspired to switch from journalism to war production, the progress made was astounding. It was our lamentable "phony war" period in reverse. This man of extraordinary vitality knew how to mobilize the workers of the aircraft industry in support of the nation at war. They agreed to work seven days a week, as they did thirty years later during the Falklands conflict. Beaverbrook also had a hunch that production of bombers should be reduced and everything concentrated on turning out fighters. "Where bombers are concerned," he would say, "we shall see later, when we have won the battle of Britain." The men on the job quickly came to call him "Beaver Tornado," and that "Beaver" was to become the great victor against Goering.

A strange set of circumstances led me to go to the West Indies shortly after the war for some business negotiations. Josée, who was leaving France for the first time after her great bereavement, came along with me. The client had hired a yacht in Florida. We spent two or three fascinating days on board with the "Beaver" and his French girlfriend. The happy relationship between them—she was an attractive person—had not been affected in any way by the sinking of the French fleet at Mers-el-Kebir in 1940. And he went out of his way to demonstrate his esteem for Pierre Laval by the respect he showed his daughter. I have never forgotten it.

Faced with very direct and hard-hitting reporters trained in the school of Henry Luce, I believe I did reasonably well in my replies to their questions. The session was followed by a three-cornered talk in his office with the editor in chief of *Time,* Frank Norris.

I had told Luce that I was returning to France the following week in order to bring Josée back to New York and naturally kept the real purpose of my journey a close secret. He asked me whether I would agree to "meet" Norris and the magazine's best photographer, entirely by chance, as it were in the Clipper to Lisbon. I could thus arrange their journey through Portugal and Spain, and especially into France, and help them on their way to Vichy. It would enable them to produce the first American story out of Vichy France. In agreeing to the proposal, I think I was guilty of my only white lie during the whole period covered by these recollections.

The meeting with the press the following day—a group of reporters from

Scripps Howard and the United Press—went off smoothly. The "boss," as I said, was a great friend of Josée and myself, past, present, and future, which certainly helped a great deal.

At the end of the day, Clarence Dillon came to pick me up, and we headed back to Peepack. I had signed my contract with Thayer Hobson, who told me that I would receive twenty-five thousand dollars of those days for my condensed version of the book. After paying about one-quarter in tax, the remainder would make it possible for me to arrange for ten thousand parcels worth $1.50 each to be sent to the prisoners of war, beginning as early as October.

On that Monday evening of August 6, 1940, before falling asleep in that haven of beauty and peace, I could not help remembering that it was almost a year since, on August 22, 1939, in the morning, I had left Josée to go and serve underground in the Maginot Line and that from then on, I had not had one single really free weekend. During this long one at Peepack, my time would be all my own. I would rest, reflect, dream, and hope.

When dining with Harry Hopkins at the Mayflower a few days before, I had put at about fifty-fifty the chances of Marshal Pétain agreeing to Roosevelt's proposal. But as I did not know what the atmosphere of Vichy was like, I kept fearing some last-minute hitch. Buoyed up by the atmosphere at Peepack, I raised my estimates of the chances of success with Marshal Pétain and of the number of parcels that would be sent to the prisoners. Words flowed from my pen more easily. I found the right slant to defend in this book the honor of France and of her empire.

Thanks to those four privileged days, and after lunch with the whole of the Dillon family, including the son, Douglas, and the daughter, Dorothy, I returned to New York and the Ritz, where I found a flattering letter of introduction[1] that Ambassador Lothian had written to the governor of Bermuda, whom I would meet during the only stopover of the Yankee Clipper on its transatlantic flight.

I had promised, before returning to Peepack, to spend that Sunday evening with old friends, the Jimmy van Allens, who were entertaining Charlie Chaplin. The prospect of meeting him amused me a great deal. Although I very rarely went to the movies, I had seen *The Gold Rush* over and over again. Our meeting was not a happy one, for at the very outset, he put the following question to me, "Have you seen *The Great Dictator?*" I was forced to say that I had not. This visibly upset him and had a depressing effect on the atmosphere. Many years later, I tried to repair my

---

[1]See appendix C, p.195.

faux pas by acting as counsel to his son Sydney, who had married a charming Frenchwoman.

Back at the Ritz, I corrected the last chapters of my book, while waiting for midnight to ring up Josée, who always, very punctually, awoke at six. She gave me a piece of good news: François Piétri, a friend of her father's, had been appointed ambassador to Madrid, and, as soon as I arrived there, he would have me driven to Perpignan, where another car sent by the préfecture would speed me on to Châteldon and Vichy with the *Time-Life* team.

CHAPTER 22

New York—Lisbon—Madrid—Vichy: Petain's enthusiastic yes to Roosevelt—his press conference

My last day in New York was devoted to the French Information Center and the New York Committee of the Center composed of two Americans, Clarence Dillon and Frank Polk, and the only member of the French board residing in the United States, the famous writer André Maurois.[1]

In the afternoon, I worked out details of the publication of my book with Thayer Hobson, the publisher. He got the *Ladies' Home Journal* magazine to agree to make two successive payments of royalties three weeks before the appearance of each installment. I would therefore be able to leave New York with the assurance that the dispatch of parcels could begin from the end of September and would continue until December, when the royalties from the book, dedicated to the prisoners of war, would take over.

The following morning, in the Yankee Clipper, which took off from the bay of Long Island, opposite La Guardia airport, I met, as prearranged, Frank Norris and his photographer, Ed Riley, who, with all his cameras hanging about him, looked like an advertisement for the Michelin Man.

In the morning, we reached Bermuda. As we were told there would be a five-hour delay for an engine check, I decided, after my visit to the governor, who was warned of my coming by Lothian, to hire a bicycle.[2] My

---

[1]The board of directors of the center was made up as follows: Chairman: Marshal Pétain; French members: Raoul Dautry (industrialist), Emile Moreau (governor of the Bank of France), Sébastien Charléty (rector of the University of Paris), André Maurois (French Academy), Général de Chambrun; Clarence Dillon and Frank Polk, representing the board in the United States.

[2]Cars were banned in this already ecological island.

little cycling interlude made me think of our wedding anniversary in Bermuda when Josée and I had to get on our bicycles again. In the course of our first outing, I discovered one of the traits of my wife's character, a native of Auvergne, a region renowned for its extinct volcanos and hills. The largest of the islands is made up of a series of rather steep hillocks, and I noticed that Josée pedaled up each one of them, while she dismounted to go downhill, thus combining the two essential facets of the Auvergnat character: energy and caution.

The long flight to Bermuda, with a brief stopover in the Azores, turned Norris and the photographer into firm friends. They came along with me to the French embassy in Lisbon, which was able to secure berths for us on one of the night trains. From Lisbon to Madrid, these were always packed. After giving us a light meal at the embassy, François Piétri recommended an early start, as we had to make a long detour by the east coast in order to cross the frontier directly into the unoccupied zone of France. I wanted to reach Barcelona, and especially Perpignan, before nightfall.

We found rooms for the night in Perpignan, still overflowing with refugees, because the prefect had been given instructions to provide accommodation and a car. He advised us to avoid the roads through the Massif Central and to drive via Montpellier, Nîmes, the Rhone Valley and reach Vichy by way of Roanne and La Palice.

The only part of France Frank Norris knew was Paris and the châteaux of the Loire Valley. As for the photographer, he had never crossed the Atlantic. They were both amazed in Nîmes to see the arena and even more astounded to discover that it had been built by the Romans and was still standing. I told them that the one million German troops who occupied France were merely the remote successors of the Romans, the Vikings, the Arabs, the Spaniards, the Flemings, the English, and many other Germans who had invaded and occupied France. But she had always remained France, like those old stones that the Romans had brought down from the Alps to build temples, stadiums, and viaducts, after Julius Caesar had vanquished Vercingetorix, the Auvergnat leader, and conquered Gaul. Those two Americans could not believe that, over the last nineteen centuries, France had been occupied in whole or in part during sixteen of them, that is to say, over eight-tenths of her history.

As far as Lyon, a flood of returning French, Belgian, and Dutch refugees thronged the roads on foot, in cars, in carts, and on bicycles. Ed Riley, the keen photographer, kept on exclaiming, "I must shoot this!" It was almost as if we had been back at war. He wanted to "shoot" the refugees, the Belgian soldiers still wearing their bedraggled uniforms, for they had been unable to find other clothes. And we had to get to Vichy before the end of the day. One of his best shots was of the war memorial at Donzère, in the Rhone Valley. It was covered with fresh flowers, put there in memory of the "poilus" of the First World War, as if to thank them for affording their country twenty years of peace.

I accompanied Frank Norris and his colleague to a small hotel in Vichy. The town was bursting at the seams with a sudden influx of people and had suddenly turned into the capital of France. I did not want to disturb Pierre Laval, hard at work at the Hotel du Parc, where he had his office, and especially to run the risk of meeting people whom I might have known, as I was to be received by the marshal the day after.

I therefore got the prefect's chauffeur to take me to our house at Châteldon, twenty kilometers south. He would go on to Clermont-Ferrand for the night, where I had booked him a room for which I paid, adding a generous tip and thanking him profusely for his patience all along the route from Perpignan and the repeated stops for the "shooting" by the photographer.

It was more than a year since I had been back at Châteldon. Before the war, I used to spend the occasional happy weekend there with Josée. I was ill-prepared for the shock that awaited me at this first homecoming. I found Josée and my mother-in-law in the dining room, which led straight out into the pretty garden, lovingly cared for by Madame Laval. The shock was caused by the mass of postcards from prisoners of war. There must have been about one hundred, on a sideboard, arranged in separate stacks. Each bore the name of the sender, his ID number, the address of the "Stalag" or "Oflag," the prisoner of war camps. Josée had replied to personal friends and in particular to Lieutenant Billet, who informed me in the name of the trio of the Maginot Line that they were in captivity. It was to them my book was dedicated. Each officer was entitled to two postcards a month, which enabled him to give news of several comrades.

Billet, who worked in a small engineering firm before the war, explained that he had succeeded in making a set of chessmen out of breadcrumbs, thanks to a method of solidification that had been patented in his "Stalag." He added that each pawn was large enough to be seen without spectacles and that the morale of the officers, the former "boys of concrete," was firm as a rock.

I resolved then and there not to leave Châteldon before replying to each one of the cards. (I was to get a booking on the Yankee Clipper on August 29 for Josée and myself.)

Around ten o'clock—it had just become dark—the barking of the dogs warned us that Pierre Laval's car had begun to climb up the steep and stony drive to the château. I noted his first words after he had put down on the table, as was his habit, the heavy briefcase, standard issue to ministers of the Third Republic, "My little Bunny, I did everything to avoid this, and now, we must repair the damage."

It was the custom at Châteldon, after the evening meal, for the dining room, which led into the drawing room and the study of my father-in-law, to be used as a place of work by the last one to retire. Josée and I naturally remained there until early morning, for we had a thousand and one things to tell each other. Her account of her trip with her parents to Bordeaux, during the collapse of France, at the height of the exodus of the population from the North and a few days before the armistice, has remained graven in my memory, She said,

> We left at dawn, The drive through Clermont was shattering, for our car was stopped endlessly by long columns of refugees, Belgian and French, officers and men, unarmed. The same painful scene was repeated at Tulle, Brive, and Périgueux.
>
> I had, the day before, phoned the manager of the Splendide in Bordeaux, which you know well from our trips to Biarritz. The hotel was chockablock, but he promised to fix things up so that my father and mother could have a small room and myself a maid's room in the attic.
>
> We got there at last around eleven at night. The hall and the lobbies were full of ministers and members of Parliament whom Mama did not want to meet. Papa and I slipped into a corner of the dining room and sat down at a small table that had been reserved for us.
>
> I thought of you, far away, in America, and I pleaded with him that all three of us should go and join you. When I went to bed, I thought perhaps he would agree. But over coffee, at breakfast, Mama said to me, "You are mad to have tried to persuade your father to leave after what we saw yesterday on the way here. We have to stay. We have no right to leave. The little Bunny must return to you and his parents in France as soon as possible. He was lucky to escape from Dunkerque, but it will be the best way in which he can be useful to his comrades in prisoner-of-war camps."

I left with Pierre Laval for Vichy the following morning, at the crack of dawn. His office was on the second floor of the Hotel du Parc, and I went up to the third, which was occupied by the marshal and his staff. Dr. Bernard Ménétrel, his godson, physician, secretary, and general factotum, had an office next to his. When I walked in, he expressed surprise that I had not announced my arrival. At the same moment, Dumoulin de Labarthéte, the director of the Cabinet of the Head of State, emerged from the marshal's study. He caught sight of me and stopped short, utterly disconcerted. But Pétain had seen me and came forward with open arms:

"There you are! What fair wind has brought you here?" he asked.

"A Rooseveltian wind!" I replied.

My sudden appearance in this insulated, cocoonlike atmosphere seemed to cause a sensation. There was an irresistible urge to know what was going on in the world outside. I began by saying, with Dumoulin and Ménétrel looking on, that Roosevelt, with whom I had had several talks, had just entrusted me with a special mission and insisted that it should remain strictly confidential. The marshal, who carried his inclination for secrecy to extremes, was delighted, and ushered me into his study. When, on one or two occasions during our conversation, Ménétrel put his head through the door, Pétain told him sharply, "Leave us alone." And finally, raising his voice, he snapped, "I am available for no one."

During the best part of two hours, I summed up my travels since our sad parting on May 29 at the Invalides, my conversations with Roosevelt and Harry Hopkins, and the crucial meeting of August 1. I repeated Roosevelt's very words and his proposition. "Are you ready to go and see the marshal?"

I referred to my two talks the same day with Lothian, before and after Churchill's agreement to issue the necessary navicerts, Lothian's visit to Roosevelt to confirm Churchill's decision, and my second call on Roosevelt at the end of the afternoon, with his final exclamation, "René, it's a deal."

After a pause for reflection, on the stroke of eleven, the marshal called in Ménétrel to tell him to get Paul Baudouin, the foreign minister, to come over immediately. I suddenly had the feeling that Pétain, whom I was always used to seeing poker-faced, suddenly felt younger and was really happy.

A few minutes later, Ménétrel introduced the foreign minister, who bowed slightly. Without asking him to take a seat, the marshal said simply, "Monsieur de Chambrun is just back from America where he had talks with President Roosevelt. I am about to reach an agreement with him, and I ask you to put an end immediately to all your attacks against the British and publish no further communiqués or make any statements taking them to task."

"Very well, Monsieur le Maréchal." And Baudouin left the room as quietly as he had entered it.

The idea of talking to American journalists clearly delighted Pétain: "It will be my first press conference," he said. "Set it up with Ménétrel for five o'clock, to give me time to work out a statement with you and to prepare my answers to their questions." He called in Ménétrel once again and, explaining the scenario he had decided upon, ended by saying "I want them to be given champagne and Reims biscuits."

I phoned Ralph Heinzen,[3] the senior member of the American Press corps, and asked him, on the marshal's behalf, to invite his colleagues to

---

[3]He represented the United Press.

come to the Pavillon Sévigné at five P.M. All the reporters he had been able to contact were there on the dot, and the marshal appeared a few minutes later. He already knew a few of those present, including Heinzen, whom he greeted warmly, and began with the words "Gentlemen, I am happy to meet you." He then read out the following statement in a firm voice:

> It is a great joy for me to receive members of the American press and bid them welcome. I am happy to avail myself of this opportunity to express to you the sincere friendship of France for the two Americas.
>
> France will remain firmly attached to the ideals that she holds in common with the great American democracy, ideals based on respect for the rights of the individual, for the family and the fatherland, love of justice and humanity. She will make every effort to develop in the old and the new world cultural and economic ties designed to create a climate of understanding and friendship between their peoples.

His statement was followed by a flood of questions, many of which he prompted himself. He spoke of his friendship for General Pershing, from whom René de Chambrun had brought a message of affectionate regard, and answered very directly every point raised by the reporters.

The following day, August 21, the *Herald Tribune* published a summary of the press conference over three columns (see exhibit 6). As Roosevelt had wished, the report was headlined "Pétain Bids U.S. Arm With Help Of Technicians. Tells American reporters France Will Be 'highly disciplined democracy.'"

On the same day, the *New York Times* splashed over four columns: "Pétain Denies End Of French Liberty: In Chat With U.S. Newsmen, He Cautions Us That Unity Is Vital to Defense."

It was late when the three of us, the marshal, Ménétrel, and I, returned on foot to the Hotel du Parc. Pierre Laval was still in his office, hard at work. The marshal called him in. The three-cornered conversation was friendly and relaxed. Pétain showed his satisfaction. My father-in-law unfortunately had a cigarette stuck, as usual, between his lips—the marshal disliked the smell of smoke. Before taking leave, Laval gave him the latest news from Paris. As we were about to depart, Pétain said to me, "I invite you and Josée to dine tomorrow night. Général Brécard, who is at Lyon, will join us, and the maréchale will be glad to see you both."

The following day, I got a reassuring phone call from Ralph Heinzen, a good friend of Roy Howard's. He had on occasion interviewed Laval before the war. He did not know the purpose of my mission to Vichy, but he was keen to inform me that the reporters had been favorably impressed by what the marshal had said and that they had sent "good" stories to their respective newspapers.

Petain Bids U.S. Arm With Help Of Technicians

Tells American Reporters France Will Be 'Highly Disciplined Democracy'

By John Elliott

By Wireless to the Herald Tribune
Copyright, 1940, New York Tribune Inc.

VICHY, Aug. 20.—Marshal Henri Petain expressed lively sympathy with the American people in their drive for rearmament in his first talk with American newspaper men here this afternoon. At the same time he said he hoped they would have the advice of competent technicians before plunging into war.

"Each nation has not only the right but the duty to prepare itself," the marshal said. "A nation must be able to defend itself against invasion and must have the means to do so. But I hope your people before going to war will have the advice of technicians competent to give counsel on your preparedness."

The eighty-four-year-old head of the new French state said that the "new France," of which he is now the chief architect, would continue to be a democracy but that the people would decide whether it was to remain a republic. He indicated that the France of the future would be a "highly disciplined democracy," entirely different from the Third Republic which collapsed after military defeat in June.

Marshal Petain chatted informally with American reporters in the yellow-paneled living room of the Pavillon Sevigne, his official residence here. He gave out a prepared statement, and then each newspaper man was allowed to ask one question. The reporters were introduced to the marshal by Rene de Chambrun, former Assistant Military Attache of the French Embassy in Washington.

Touched by Pershing's Letter

After the armistice, Marshal Petain said, he received a letter from Gen. John J. Pershing expressing the wish that in that hour of crisis for France he could be by Petain's side, as he was during the World War. "I was very much touched by this letter," the marshal said, "and I, too, wish it could have been so."

Petain said it became impossible for France to go on fighting. "We had only the debris of an army, and not many troops in north Africa," he said. "The English had virtually withdrawn after the collapse of our army on the Somme. I do not wish to criticize our former ally, but I feel that France was left to fight the war alone too soon. England felt it was necessary to recall her troops to defend her soil, so France cannot be blamed for looking after her own interests."

The world, Petain predicted, would be as astonished by the rapidity of France's recovery as it was after 1870.

Questioned concerning accusations that France had at present neither a free nor a regular government, Petain replied that it was regretfully true the government was not fixed since the Germans were occupying two-thirds of its territory, but he denied that the government was not regular. It had been consecrated by all the appropriate sacraments, he declared smilingly, even by a two-thirds vote of the French National Assembly.

Text of Statement

The text of Marshal Petain's prepared statement follows:

"It is a real pleasure for me to receive representatives of the American press and to bid them welcome. I am happy to take this occasion to tell them of the sincere friendship France holds for America, for both Americas, Anglo-Saxon and Latin.

"We piously preserve the memory of the brotherhood in arms of our Lafayettes, our Rochambeaus, with the heroes of your War of Independence. The friendship linked at that time has enjoyed the rare privilege of remaining unchanged through all the vicissitudes of fortune. Recently you have again given us a new token in your magnificent generosity toward our refugees and evacuees. Precious in itself, this aid was even more precious for the testimony it brought of the fidelity of your sentiments toward us.

"With Argentina and Brazil, we feel united by the community of our Latin culture. Therein lies a bond the strength of which I was able to test during my embassy in Spain. We know the extent to which Latin America shares our trials, and her fidelity, too, touches us deeply.

"You have shown, gentlemen, a great and cordial interest in what France will be tomorrow. I am no prophet, yet there are certain things I may say, if not with certainty at least with absolute conviction.

Has "Faith in Recovery"

"First, I have faith in the recovery of France, and in a recovery which will once more astonish the world. France has ever been a land of 'luminous and surprising awakenings'—to quote our great Bossuet. Her past is pledge for her future.

"The France of tomorrow will be at once very new and very ancient. She will become again what she should never have ceased to be—essentially an agricultural nation. Like the giant in the fable, she will recover all her strength by renewed contact with the earth.

"She will restore those old traditions of craftsmanship which in the past made her fortune and glory. The classic land of quality, she will know how to import again to all her production that finish, that delicacy, that elegance, in which she was for long without a rival. It goes without saying that France will remain a land of arts, of high culture, of disinterested research.

"France will cultivate the virtues which make strong peoples; she will know how to temper by vigorous discipline an individualism which at times became excessive: she will honor anew those great truths of Christian morality which were the former solid basis of our civilization.

"France will remain firmly attached to the ideal which she professes in common with the great American democracies an ideal founded on respect for the human individual, on the cult of family, community and country, on the love of justice and humanity. She will strive more than ever to develop between the old world and the new those relations and those exchanges, cultural as well as economic, which create between peoples the very atmosphere of comprehension and amity."

Exhibit 6. *Herald Tribune* of August 21, 1940, comments on the press conference held by Marshal Pétain at Vichy attended by U.S. newspapermen.

I phoned Major Bonhomme, the marshal's ADC, to tell him that Josée would not be at the dinner because she had decided to come with me to New York and wished to spend her last evenings in France with her parents. I said I would knock on his door half an hour before the dinner for a brief chat with him. In the course of the three years before the war during which I would call on the marshal in late afternoon on my way home at least three times a week to work with him on the creation of the French Information Center in the United States, I had often chatted with Bonhomme. He must have been the only army officer of lesser rank whom the marshal addressed with the familiar *tu,* and he had, for his chief, a filial devotion and respect.

We had always talked quite freely to one another. From the outset, Bonhomme asked, "Why does the prime minister smoke in the marshal's study?" "Because he smokes much as the marshal breathes." "What a pity! And why does he see so many parliamentarians, Jews, and Freemasons?" "Because he has always worked with them, and many are his friends." "What a pity!" This was enough to give me a foretaste of the atmosphere of the Hotel du Parc and of the overall climate prevailing in Vichy.

I had the strange impression that evening of being the guest of a sovereign and his consort, surrounded by their retainers. General Brécard, the grand master of the Legion of Honor under the Third Republic, confirmed in the post by the French State of Pétain, was late. He was coming from Lyon along a crowded and winding road and only arrived for the cheese course. His journey to Vichy was of some importance: he submitted to the "sovereign" models of the future Francisque (the decoration created by the marshal's government) and the first specimens of Sèvres vases adorned with it (the vases were traditionally the gift of French heads of state to foreign dignitaries). The marshal gave me two, one for Madame Laval and one for Josée, and a model of the Francisque, which I was never to be awarded officially.

I returned to Châteldon with the decoration in my buttonhole and had to submit to a good deal of teasing from my in-laws. I could not help thinking that evening, before dropping off to sleep, that a breach would perhaps occur one day between the marshal and Pierre Laval, by reason of the presence, in the old soldier's entourage, of so many archconservatives, including two members of the monarchist Action Française, not one of whose members, to say the least, had a liking for parliamentarians. The only exception was Louis-Dominique Girard, a member of the marshal's cabinet who understood Laval and was to write a book after the war very much in his favor.

Major Bonhomme gave me a piece of good news: Colonel de Cardes, the head of the French liaison team with the British army during the "phony war," to whom I may have owed my life, was in Vichy. He had been retained on active service as part of the small army of the armistice that France had been allowed to retain by the Germans. Told that I was in town, he wished to see me.

I called Bonhomme the following day and invited him to lunch at Châteldon with Norris, the photographer, and Ambassador Henry-Haye, the senator and mayor of Versailles who had just been given the Washington post. The lunch was fixed for the eve of our departure.

During the remaining few days, I had my last two conversations with the marshal on August 23 and 24. On the second occasion, I spent the first hours of the morning exchanging with him recollections of the First World War, of his long visit to Morocco in 1926 at the time of the revolt of Abd-el-Krim in the Rif, of the creation of the French Information Center. We put the finishing touches to his letter to Roosevelt, on which he wrote the date of my departure the following day. Here it is, word for word:

Vichy, August 27, 1940.

Mr. President,

France today is living through the most tragic hour of her long history: three-fifths of her soil are occupied; there are few homes where the return of one of the two million prisoners of war held by Germany is not anxiously awaited; millions of refugees, from the most fertile regions of the country, with, as sole baggage, their burden of weariness and woe, are looking to the hour of deliverance when they can return to their abandoned fields. Today, they share with Belgian, Austrian, Czech, Spanish, and Polish refugees who have sought haven on our territory the sufferings and privations of the French people.

It is a fact without precedent in the annals of our history that the war, in the space of a few weeks, has ravaged half our land, bearing in its train the destruction of our roads, our bridges, our railways, and most of our factories.

Our country, cradle of a civilization that has stirred the admiration of the world, is today bruised and bereaved.

After the blandishments of those who, even yesterday, fed Frenchmen with words, illusions, and false promises, today they hear the sad message of the man who can only speak to each one of them of his woes and his privations, without, for all that, despairing of the future.

The main concern of my government, its daily quest, is to help all Frenchmen to endure their burden of misfortune. I know that our task will be hard; but we shall only consider that we have, to a modest degree, succeeded when we can give each man, each woman, and each child, rich or poor, a better life than before.

I also know that in this duty of help and assistance to the people of France, your generous country, which is bound to mine by a centuries-old friendship and has already made a tremendous effort, is also anxious to play its part today.

Problems over the purchase of supplies, their control and shipment to their final destination, their transport and distribution, and the coordination of individual efforts will arise both in France and in America.

I have come to the conclusion that a disinterested person could cooperate closely in this task of assistance with our embassy in Washington and with the American and French Red Cross organizations.

I have therefore called upon M. René de Chambrun, a citizen of both our countries, to devote his time and energy benevolently to this task, should you yourself and the American voluntary organizations consider that his assistance could be useful.

I remain, Mr. President, with profound esteem and warm expressions of friendship,

> Yours very sincerely,
> Ph. Pétain.

When the time came for me to take my leave, the marshal rose from his seat, looked me straight in the eye silently for a few seconds, and said, "What you are doing is good. We are going to live through very harsh times." And, after another pause, "Come, let me kiss you." And after embracing me, he kept on holding my hand.

I hesitated to speak my innermost thoughts. Then, returning his gaze, I told him, "It is not the first time you have kissed me." "When did I do so before?" "Oh, long ago. It was in early December, in 1918, at the Metz Arsenal, after the great victory parade of the Allies. The little Warren Pershing and I were given by the American commander in chief's ADC khaki uniforms of the 'Yankees' he had bought for us at the Bon Marché store in Paris. You teased us by putting on our heads the heavy helmets of German infantrymen, which fell about our ears, and pointing to us before the assembled dignitaries, who included President Poincaré and Georges Clémenceau, you remarked, 'They are little Boches. We got them!' And General Pétain, as he then was, kissed us on both cheeks."

I noticed that there was a lump in the old marshal's throat. "Go," he added, in a strained, slightly trembling voice.

I dropped in on Ménétrel to say good-bye. "How did you find him?" he asked. "A little changed, affectionate," was my reply.

CHAPTER 23

My return to New York: To my amazement de Gaulle says no

Before Harry Hopkins's Betrayal

Back at Châteldon, after taking leave of the marshal, we were waiting for the guests to arrive for this last meal before our departure. Pierre Laval usually had lunch every day with his assistants in Vichy; he made an exception on this occasion.

Fred Norris and Ed Riley gave me a few weeks later in New York a souvenir photograph of those present at the luncheon; they had destroyed the negative. I have since then kept in my office the only existing print in a small frame (see photo 1).

Pierre Laval had to return to his desk before the other guests, who left late, had all departed. When they were gone, I finished writing the last remaining cards to the prisoners of war. As we still had a little time left, Josée, my mother-in-law, and I went for a final walk through the village and along the little road that runs past the famous Châteldon mineral water springs, and winds uphill in the direction of Lachaux. We stopped at a vantage point from which we could see the old village, its medieval church, the château, and its ramparts. Along the way, my mother-in-law stopped to talk to passersby, most of them women whose husbands were prisoners in Germany.

In 1815, when Prussian and Russian troops were encamped in Paris and in the north of France, Châteldon must have looked much the same as it did in August 1940, likewise in 1871, when the Germans occupied France as far south as the Loire. On September 3, 1939, when the men of Châteldon, many of whom would later be held prisoners in Germany, had left their village to go and fight, something occurred the like of which had not happened in France since the Napoleonic wars. She had not been invaded, and the peasants of Châteldon were being mobilized for a war that their

Photo 1. Last lunch at Châteldon before Josée and I leave for the United States. Madame Laval has her back to the camera; on her left is Colonel de Cardes, head of the Franco-British liaison; myself; Fred Norris; Pierre Laval; the empty seat belongs to Ed Riley, the *Life* photographer taking the picture; Josée Laval de Chambrun; and Henry-Haye, who had just been nominated French ambassador to Washington by Marshal Pétain.

own country had declared. They had never met any Poles or Czechs; they had no idea where Dantzig was. The vast majority of them had never even seen the sea, and out of the blue sky, one of the greatest disasters in its history was about to engulf them, their native Auvergne, and the whole of France.

On the occasion of our last evening at home, Laval returned earlier than usual from Vichy. Josée had decided that she could not bring herself to see France under German occupation, and in order to avoid driving into Spain along the Atlantic coast, which was in the occupied zone, we decided to cross the frontier at Canfranc, in the Pyrénées. Early in the morning, we left Madame Laval, Châteldon, and our faithful dogs and followed Pierre Laval's car along the Street of the United States, which led out of the village to the point where it joined the main road from Vichy to Thiers. There Laval headed north, while we turned south.

We were spared the detour by Madrid and got onto a plane that flew us direct from Barcelona to Lisbon. At the Hotel Aviz, where we spent the night, I was greeted once again by the friendly porter who had fought in World War I and who had tried to boost my morale when I was there two months before.

Thirty-six hours later, just as the huge Pan Am Clipper was descending to land in Long Island Bay, Miss LeHand, by a radio message, asked me to call her direct line at the White House as soon as we had settled down at the Ritz. I can remember to this day the little two-room suite, Nos. 410–411, where we lived for six weeks until Josée, of her own will, decided to return to France to be at her father's side.

After we had sorted ourselves out a bit, I called Miss LeHand. Her cheerful voice seemed unchanged: "How was the flight? Did Madame de Chambrun enjoy it? I wanted to tell you that Harry, as soon as he heard of your arrival, took the train for New York that gets in at 6:30. He will go directly to the Ritz and invites both of you to dine with him in the Crystal Room." With a smile, I put down the receiver and was surprised to hear Josée remark, "I don't think this is good news." She is rarely mistaken in her forebodings, but, being fundamentally an optimist—she often reproaches me for it—I replied, "On the contrary, his coming means the first cargo of food for France will leave one day sooner."

Josée said nothing and began to unpack. She called the headwaiter to have him set the table for three in the living room of our little suite and ordered a white burgundy in case we had oysters, as this was the first of the months with an *r*.

Treachery

Around half past seven, Harry Hopkins rang from the reception desk: "René, Josée and you are dining with me downstairs in the Crystal Room." He had never met Josée. I had got to know him during my bachelor days in New York, before I met her. "No," I replied, "You are dining with us. It will be much easier to talk in our salon." Shortly after, he knocked at the door. After greeting me with both hands and bowing to Josée, he sat down in one of the three comfortable chairs beside the fireplace. Looking Josée straight in the eye for the first time—and, I believe, the last—he said one or two polite things and expressed his sympathy for the state of France. I noted down very precisely at the time the key phrases in the long discussion that was about to begin. This, word for word, was his preamble:

"René, I am afraid I am going to cause you great disappointment [silence]. The Chief, who is very fond of you and who is very grateful for the magnificent job you did and the very important results you obtained, has had to go back on his promise to you."

Dumbfounded, I exclaimed, "But Harry, it's impossible, quite impossible. The president didn't make a promise to me, he made it to France. It's the president of the United States who concluded an agreement, a treaty, with Marshal Pétain. I was merely the instrument. I acted at President Roosevelt's request. What on earth has happened?"

"Last week, Lothian came to see us, the Chief and me. He had just spoken on the phone to Churchill, who had received a visit from General de Gaulle. The latter came to protest against the sending of food supplies by the United States to unoccupied France." I replied, "General de Gaulle has nothing to do with this affair. He has chosen to go on fighting against Germany. That is up to him. But he has no right to oppose the execution of an agreement concluded between the president of the United States and Marshal Pétain."

I reminded him of the precise terms of the president's initiative, of the conditions he asked the marshal to meet, of the suspension of all the attacks against Britain by Paul Baudouin, the foreign minister, and the French State Radio, after the Mers-el-Kebir affair; of the press conference in Vichy; and of the statement by the marshal that Roosevelt himself had suggested. I showed him, thanks to all the press clippings I had carefully set aside, that Pétain had gone far beyond what Roosevelt had asked for, that he had written the letter that Roosevelt had wanted him to write and that he intended to publish on the occasion of the first press conference he would give after my return from France.

And then I quoted Roosevelt's spontaneous undertaking: "I will see to it that the free zone receives regular food shipments, particularly condensed milk, for the duration of hostilities." I showed him how easy it would be for the United States, by virtue of their dominant position, to make part of their aid to Britain conditional on the implementation of the promise made to France. As I went on, I had the impression of battling against a brick wall and felt more and more tired and dispirited as I went on.

Throughout this interminable discussion, which certainly lasted more than an hour, Josée remained silent. Her gaze rarely met Harry Hopkins's, for he avoided hers and stared at the carpet. Then she broke in on the conversation, in a deliberate, precise manner, "I understand. I think I understand only too well. We are going to order dinner and will talk about something else."

After he had gone, shortly before midnight, Josée said to me, "I find him revolting. He certainly told his boss, 'Chief, leave it to me. I will take the matter in hand and you will hear no more about it.'" Her hunch once again proved right: Harry Hopkins was to carry out his task to perfection.

One of the most effective means of getting Roosevelt to forget an unkept promise would, for Hopkins, be to cast a slur on the reputation of a friend who had suddenly become an embarrassment. He availed himself of the opportunity provided by the arrival in New York of the new French ambassador, Henry-Haye, to kill two birds with one stone. He entrusted the task to two of his journalist friends of the liberal left, Drew Pearson and Herbert Agar, and the latter's literary agent, Ulric Bell, whose offices were located at 2 West Forty-second Street, in New York.[1]

The trio, through a few phone calls and personal contacts, suggested to fourteen authors and playwrights that they should issue in their own names a statement to all the papers that appeared on Sunday, October 27, warning the United States "against two Vichy agents who have just arrived but who in fact are German agents intent upon running the British blockade against France for the sole benefit of Hitler's Reich."

Here is the first part of this unbelievable libel, which appears in full in appendix D:

---

[1] I learned, a few days before publication of the libelous document in most of the newspapers dated 27 October, that the brains behind the monstrous attack that was about to be launched was none other than Harry Hopkins.

I had a moving meeting with Drew Pearson at the Hotel George V in Paris shortly after the "Prague Spring" of 1968. In the course of a luncheon party given by an American woman judge, Florence Shientag, he not only apologized publicly for his role in the affair but invited me to appear on his radio program during my next trip to the United States in order, as he said, to "put the record straight."

October 24, 1940.

To the News Editor:

The attached is for release in the Sunday morning newspapers of October 27th. . . .

   A group of leading American authors, poets and playwrights today implored their countrymen "to beware of the men of Vichy, who now spread the virus of totalitarianism in America."

   Classifying themselves as citizens of "what was once the world-wide free republic of letters," fourteen of these literary figures asserted that many French propagandists now in this country are here as the "agents of the German government," some of them forming what amounts to a new offshoot of the Nazi gestapo in the United States.

   French Ambassador Henry-Haye and Count Rene de Chambrun, the latter the author of a volume just issued to American readers, were singled out as the principal pleaders over here for the Vichy regime. They were described as "pathetic wooden manikins" for the Nazis.

   Besides asking their own readers and followers to "view the words and gestures of the men of Vichy with the suspicion they deserve," the American writers asserted that the French spokesmen here "would aid the Germans by breaking the British food blockade."

   I distrusted the vague expression of "a volume released to the public" without any mention of the title of the work or the dedication to prisoners of war: "I saw France fall—she will rise again." I immediately got my publisher, Thayer Hobson, to find out the addresses of the fourteen signatories of the statement and sent them the book, with a polite covering note.

   I was not surprised to get in return half a dozen apologetic letters and telephone calls from people telling me that their good faith had been abused, and I asked Hobson to get the newspapers that had published the libel in whole or in part to carry a statement setting the record straight (see exhibit 7).

   Who was this French ambassador, my "Nazi accomplice," who had come to the United States to run the British blockade for the benefit of the Reich? It was impossible for him, about to take possession of a key post in Washington, to reply to this monstrous fabrication. Today, over half a century later, I feel it a posthumous duty to tell the reader of these recollections what kind of a man Gaston Henry-Haye really was.

   Born in the early 1880s, he served the last few months of the long term of national service of that time—two years!—in one of the finest French colonial regiments, the First Zouave. Starting off as a simple soldier, he rose successively to corporal, sergeant, master sergeant and became senior

DE CHAMBRUN DENIES NAZI CONNECTIONS

Brands Charges Made By 14 U.S. Writers As "Ridiculous"

New York, Nov. 9—(AP)—Count Rene De Chambrun, a statutory citizen of the United States by reason of his direct descendency from General Lafayette, declared tonight that he was "neither a stooge for the Nazis, an agent for the Gestapo nor an agent for the German government."

The former military attache and soldier of France asserted that charges made against him in a publicly issued pamphlet by 14 American writers and authors were "ridiculous."

De Chambrun said that the group last month signed a statement declaring that a book he had just written—"I Saw France Fall" —was "spreading the virus of totalitarianism" in the United States.

Made Public Prediction

The statement, he said, was signed among others by playwrights Robert Sherwood and Maxwell Anderson, Edna St. Vincent Millay, poet, and Vincent Sheean, foreign correspondent.

"Before making such a charge," said the former Maginot Line captain who escaped with the British forces from Dunkirque at the height of the German invasion of France, "these persons might have read a public statement which came out in the newspapers, radio and newsreels in this country, at a time when, just after the collapse of France, confidence in Great Britain was somewhat impaired."

De Chambrun said that at that time he predicted publicly that Great Britain would not bow to the Germans and that despite the capitulation of France, the British army and fleet would continue to fight.

Was Liaison Officer

An international lawyer, with offices in New York and Paris, De Chambrun declared that he was "not a representative of the Vichy government, but a private citizen of the French and American bars, just about to resume his law practice which was interrupted by the war."

Explaining that as a captain in the army of the French republic he had acted as liaison officer between the British and French, De Chambrun added:

"It is bad enough for France to have lost the war. It can only add to my sorrow after the defeat of my country to read such utter nonsense as that which has been printed about me."

Exhibit 7. An answer to the below-the-belt attack launched against me by Harry Hopkins.

master sergeant a few weeks after the general mobilization that preceded the First World War.

He was wounded the first time and mentioned in dispatches at the Battle of the Marne, on September 7, 1914. Altogether, he was wounded five times and mentioned five times before being so badly injured during the winter of 1916–1917 that he was invalided out. He was awarded the Legion of Honor with a citation to the Order of the Army, and his regiment was given a red lanyard. After his last injury, the most serious one, he volunteered in June 1917, with the rank of captain, to train an infantry regiment for combat in a big military camp in Kentucky. He came over to France with this unit a few months before the Allied victory in 1918.

After the war, he worked in a Franco-American firm, became a deputy, then a senator of Seine-et-Oise, and mayor of Versailles, a post he still held when Marshal Pétain appointed him ambassador to Washington. His unshakable friendship for the United States was the starting point of intimate relations with Ambassador Bullitt. When I met the latter after his return to the State Department, he told me how delighted he was at the prospect that Henry-Haye would arrive a few weeks later in Washington.

Henry-Haye was viscerally anti-German. But, contrary to the man who had engineered the shameful plot of October 27, 1940, he was also anticommunist.

This war hero was also a skilled diplomat, and I cannot resist the temptation of relating an anecdote about his relations with Britain, as on the occasion he was made a commander of the Order of the British Empire by King George V. The incident took place exactly one year before the outbreak of the last war.

Until that time, and from the beginnings of the Third Republic, the protocol for the reception of sovereigns on state visits was the following: they arrived by train at Versailles, where they were met at the station by the president of the republic, who escorted them to Paris first in a horse-drawn carriage and latterly in an automobile. The procession entered Paris through the Bois de Boulogne and the Arc de Triomphe.

Since the abdication of King Edward VIII, who later became duke of Windsor, the mayor of Versailles, Henry-Haye, together with the French government, had arranged for the duchess and him to live in a house in the grounds of the palace of Louis XIV. When, in July 1938, the visit of the British sovereigns to France was officially announced, the head of protocol at the presidency of the republic called on the mayor to ask him whether he could arrange things in such a way that when George VI arrived, his predecessor would not be in town.

The problem was a delicate one, and Henry-Haye got the great industrialist and inventor of Taylorism (assembly line production), who was a close friend of the Windsors and owner of a fine château at Candé, in Touraine, to invite them to stay for a few days.

In the large official Renault, one of the first armor-plated vehicles to be produced, President Lebrun sat between the king and queen and Henry-Haye opposite them on a jump seat. As they left the station, George VI put a question to Henry-Haye in English, in a tone of doubt, and with the slight stammer that afflicted him, especially in the early years of his reign: "I believe that my brother lives in your constituency?" He stumbled a little on the last word. "Yes, sir," the senator replied.

"Does he speak French as well as I do?" The senator, who had not yet heard the king speak a single word of French, answered diplomatically, "Nearly as well as you do, sir." When President Lebrun, who did not understand English, asked the interpreter what was going on, Henry-Haye replied, "Mr. President, I will tell you later."[2]

The state visit was the occasion of a big Bastille Day parade, in the presence of the king and queen, of the whole diplomatic corps and of the military attachés of all the countries accredited to France. The one representing the Third Reich was able, in the report to his government, to draw attention to the fact that the flypast by the French air force included not one modern bomber. When, a year later, France declared war against Germany, which had just signed the pact with Stalin, she had only seven modern bomber aircraft to pit against the thousands of German Heinkels. Eight months later, she suffered her most crushing defeat since Agincourt in 1415.

After the Betrayal

I had to try to get a grip on myself after the unexpectedly dramatic evening at the old Ritz Hotel, which was torn down a few years later. My good fortune in my misfortune was the presence of Josée until the beginning of November, when she left me to go back to her parents in France. And another comfort was the exceptionally speedy delivery, three weeks later, of a parcel containing the first twenty copies of the book, which would be in the stores on October 1.

The jacket of the book pleased me a great deal. The title stood out in gold letters on a sky blue background with, in the center, a reproduction of the old "Gate of the Germans" at Metz, the precursor of the Maginot Line.

---

[2]The king had Henry-Haye invested with the Order of the British Empire to thank him for what he had done for his brother.

I dedicated the first two copies to the American directors of the French Information Center, Clarence Dillon and Frank Polk, and popped the question at Josée, "And what about Roosevelt?" He knew, and Miss LeHand did too, that I had dictated a bit of the manuscript each day. Deep down, I had not forgiven his weakness, his failure to stand up to de Gaulle's refusal when approached by Churchill. Josée only allowed him one extenuating circumstance: Hopkins had certainly told him, "Trust me. I will settle the matter with René." After thinking the matter over, I decided to send two copies to Miss LeHand, one for the president and the other for herself.

Last year, I wrote about the book (entitled *My Battles for Pierre Laval*) that it was the outcome of a number of portents that occurred before my decision to take up my pen. The portents have continued to manifest themselves.

An American friend from Ohio, my mother's native state, and a benefactor, like many others, of Cleveland State University, recently had the strange idea of writing my biography. His research brought him to Hyde Park, Roosevelt's former home, now turned into a museum. In the library, he caught sight of *I Saw France Fall* and asked the curator for permission to photocopy the flyleaf with my dedication, the gist of which, naturally, I had completely forgotten. Under my signature, Roosevelt had written his own, with the year: 1940 (see exhibit 8).

During the weeks and months that preceded my return to France, my thoughts and actions were increasingly centered on the dispatch of food parcels to French prisoners of war. Neither General de Gaulle nor Harry Hopkins could obstruct the magnificent work of the International Red Cross (American and French) and of two great francophile ladies: Anne Morgan, a member of the Legion of Honor, also decorated with the croix de guerre, who ran a military hospital during the First World War in the combat area, and Mrs. Seton Porter. Mrs. Porter was married first to the founder of Morgan's Bank in Paris. After the death of her husband, she remarried Seton Porter, the founder of National Distillers. She had launched in France a charity called Parcels for the Poilus, which we in New York turned into the Gifts for French Prisoners of War. Thanks to the two digests of the book in the *Ladies' Home Journal* and a second and third reprint, I was able, before my return to France in February 1941, to ensure the shipment of more than fifty thousand parcels of food for unoccupied France. They were sent through the Strait of Gibraltar, unloaded at Marseilles, and posted on through the remarkably efficient French military distribution center in Lyon to the different "Stalag" and "Oflag" camps in Germany.

In the last days of October, there were reports that the flights of the Yankee Clipper were about to be suspended and that it would only be

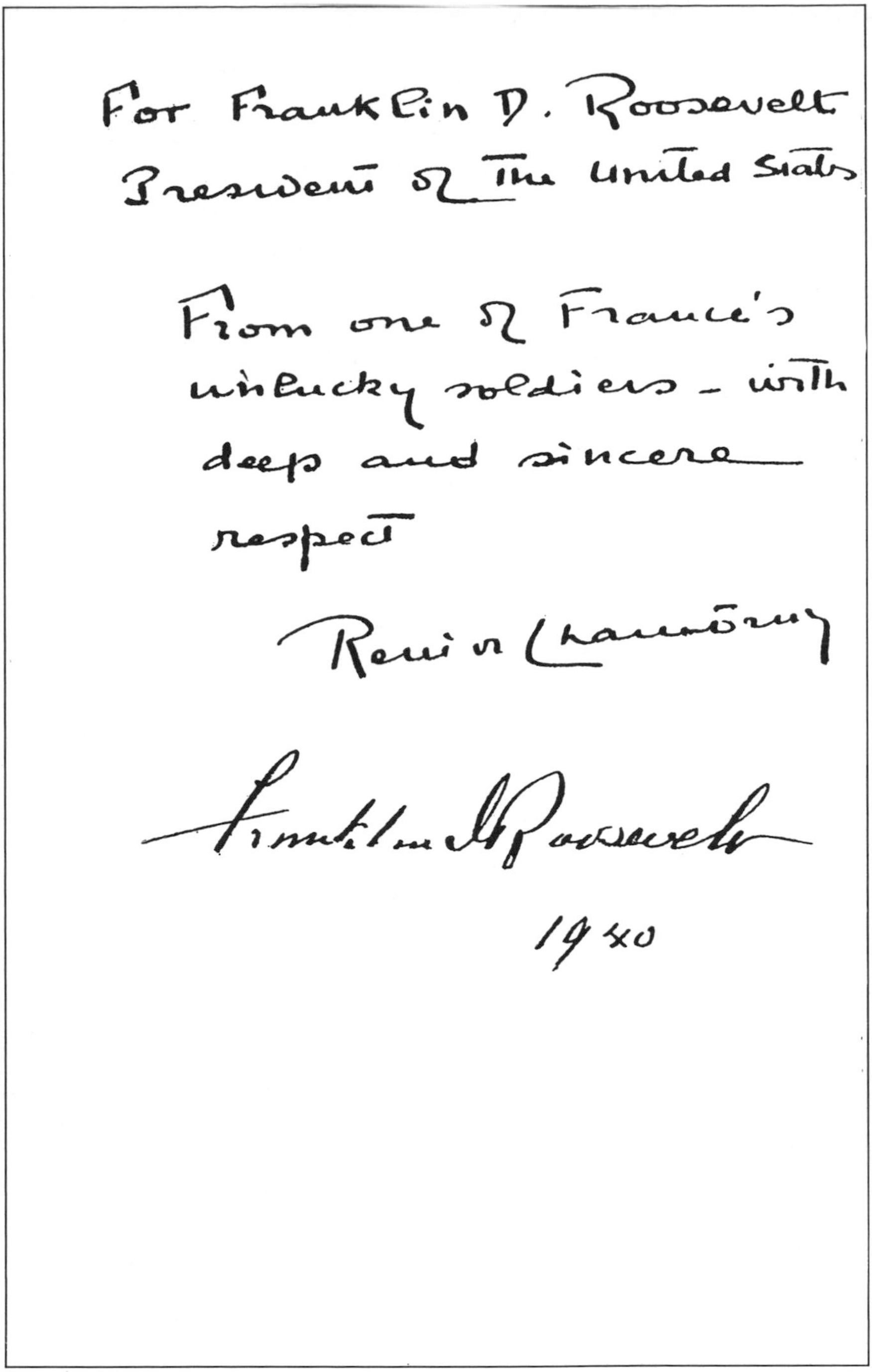

For Franklin D. Roosevelt
President of The United States

From one of France's
unlucky soldiers — with
deep and sincere
respect

Rein n Chammõrun

Franklin D Roosevelt

1940

Exhibit 8. I had sent the first inscribed copy of my book to President Roosevelt and was surprised to learn many years later that a privileged visitor to his library at Hyde Park was given a photocopy of our two signatures, dated 1940.

possible to reach France by sea in small boats that would sail irregularly between New York and Lisbon. Josée therefore decided to return to her parents and Châteldon. She took the Clipper that left on November 9.

She had come to the conclusion that, owing to the hostility of the marshal's entourage toward all parliamentarians, her duty was to be at her father's side. She had also understood that my "crusade" for Britain had come to an end with the mission Roosevelt had entrusted me on the *Potomac* but that the obligation I had assumed toward my friends of the Maginot Line now in prison camps endured. In this respect, I could only be really useful in New York, turning my royalties into parcels for French prisoners.

A Secret Harry Hopkins Begged Me to Keep

Before writing chapter 24, which is a brief survey of what I did before my final return to France in February 1941, and the epilogue to this book, where Harry Hopkins reappears, I feel compelled to revert to this unconditional admirer of Stalin's, as five years later he was to become my most deadly opponent, closely involved in the "judicial purges" of the liberation of France.

Our first private evening *en tête-à-tête* dated back to June 23, 1940, seven days after the weekend on the *Potomac*. I already referred in chapter 20 to the jolly celebration we had together, five weeks later, in the dining room of the Mayflower, that famous evening of August 1, after Roosevelt and Churchill had said yes to the proposal that I was to submit to Marshal Pétain on behalf of the president.

I will now attempt to describe this first "private" dinner of June 23, 1940, It was late afternoon at the White House in Harry Hopkins's office, and we had been working on a number of phone calls, preparing my appointments of the following week. To his question, "With whom are you dining this evening?" I replied, "With nobody." "No, you are dining with me," he insisted.

He drove me himself to Connecticut Avenue, and we went to a small restaurant with about a dozen tables run by a French chef, his wife, and one woman servant. By mutual agreement, we brushed to one side the subject of my "crusade for Britain" in order to exchange reminiscences of our years in New York between 1930 and my return to France in 1934.

I had met Harry Hopkins at the beginning of 1930 through a mutual friend of Italian origin. He was sixteen years my senior, but because of his youthful and dynamic character, he always gave me the impression of being a contemporary of mine. On one occasion, he had asked the "lone" bachelor in New York to celebrate his birthday in the "village."

That evening (in Washington, June 23, 1940), the conversation drifted to Josée and her father. Harry Hopkins was both an odd and an attractive individual. A political animal with convictions far to the left, he hated President Hoover and the archconservative Senator Borah and had, at that time, paid tribute to Pierre Laval for having held his own in the affair of the Hoover moratorium. But more especially, this man, whose destiny it was to become an arch-Stalinist friend, had a grudge against the Republican governments that had preceded Roosevelt's because they refused to give official recognition to the Soviet Union.

"When did you become engaged?" Harry asked me. "Between the time of Laval's visit to Rome where she had accompanied her father for the conclusion of the alliance with Mussolini, which was designed to prevent the 'Anschluss' of Austria by Hitler, and his journey to Moscow in May to meet Stalin and close the ring around the German Reich. Our engagement was only announced after Josée's return from Moscow." Did she meet Stalin?" "Yes, several times." "What did you make of him?" "She found him a disconcerting, quick-witted man. He agreed to do what her father had asked him. He was even ready to order the French Communist party to put an end to its violent campaign against two-year national service."

I added that Josée believed, as she had herself told me, that an apparently trivial incident, which she witnessed, had brought the two men, both of peasant origin, closer to each other. They had together visited the largest state farm in the Moscow area, and as they stopped to look at a herd of the finest milch cows, Laval had asked the Soviet minister for agriculture, who was with them, "I am going to put a question to you. Do you know how one can spot the best butter producer?" The interpreter's translation was immediate, but the minister remained silent. Laval said, "By the wax inside the animal's ear." Adding the deed to the word, he put his forefinger in the ear of the cow and withdrew it covered with a fatty substance. Stalin looked at Laval in silence. On the following day, the minister for agriculture was dismissed.

As I told him the story, I felt Harry Hopkins's eyes light up with interest. And I proceeded to relate certain details of this trip, as Josée had reported them to me: the evening at the opera, the grand ball at the Kremlin, the visit to Mounina Camp, where a huge air display had been staged. The planes deployed in the sky in the pattern of a huge R.F. (République Française). Then there was a drop of several hundred paratroopers, who landed impeccably. Much to Josée's amazement, three of them were women. They ran up to her, bearing a blue, white, and red bouquet of flowers, studded with small tricolor flags. Everywhere she went, Josée told me with a laugh, she was accompanied by her Russian "boyfriend," who stuck close to her the whole time: Anastas Mikoyan, the Georgian "number two" of the Communist party of the USSR.

I told Harry about the great ball. Josée complimented Mikoyan on his boots and his buttoned-up, Georgian-style jacket, which she found very handsome. Mikoyan replied that the same would be made to her measurements, and there they were among the gifts she brought back from Moscow. Stalin's presents, which also ended up at Châteldon, consisted of two large frames with enlargements of photographs of himself and Pierre Laval.

Everything I said seemed to do much more than entertain Harry Hopkins: it provoked a deep interest on his part. I was emboldened, after a moment's reflection, to reveal to him something that, at the time, Josée and I had agreed never to talk about, in order to have a quiet life and begin my legal career in Paris under favorable auspices.

This is what I told him: It was during the second half of October 1936. France was plunged in the turmoil of the Popular Front. Roosevelt was standing for a second term on the second Tuesday in November. The SS *Normandy,* which brought us back to France after our customary autumn visit to the United States, was about to leave New York at four P.M., on schedule. We had reserved on board the small Chantilly suite, and went down to the splendid dining room.

Henri Villar, the star purser of the French line, came over to our table to welcome us on board. Shortly after he had left us, and just as we were about to retire for the night, we saw five men coming down the grand staircase in Indian file behind a head waiter. They walked past our table and went through to one of the private dining rooms of which the frosted glass doors were the work of Lalique, like the rest of the decoration. Josée, dumbfounded, gazed at the new arrivals and turning to me just as the door closed behind them exclaimed, "It's incredible! The smallest one of the five, who is very dark, is none other than Mikoyan." "It can't be possible," I replied. "I am sure of it, absolutely sure," she insisted.

We remained seated, and Josée, calling over the maître d'hôtel, put the question to him, "Who are those five persons in the little private dining room next to us?" "They are Russians," he said. "There is an interpreter who speaks French fluently and probably an important personality with his bodyguard."

Slowly, Josée wrote Mikoyan's name on a piece of paper. She asked the maître d'hôtel to tell the interpreter that Josée Laval had just recognized Mr. Mikoyan, who entertained her so lavishly during her visit to Moscow with her father, and would be very happy to receive him for a cup of tea during the crossing in the Chantilly suite.

After a relatively long time, which amounted to some minutes, the reply came that Mr. Mikoyan would be very happy to call on Madame "Josée Laval de Chambrun" during the crossing. Still overcome with surprise, we decided before going for a last walk on deck to knock on the door of Henri Villar.

I had known him for years, and Josée had made the crossing there and back on the *Ile de France* in 1931, when she had accompanied her father on his official visit to the United States and rekindled for the first time the torch of the Statue of Liberty.

"Do you know, Monsieur le Commissaire, who is having a private party in the Lalique dining room?"

"Ah, Madame de Chambrun," was the reply. "You cannot imagine what we are asked to do since the coming to power of the Popular Front! They are Russians who do not appear on the ship's manifest. They embarked at Le Havre, disembarked and reembarked in New York by the staff door, next to the engine room."

"It's Stalin's number two, Anastas Mikoyan," Josée went on. "I got to know him well during my father's four-day visit to Moscow last year. I have just invited him to come and have a cup of tea with us during the crossing. But I think you had better forget the whole story." "You are certainly right," Villar concluded thoughtfully.

The tea party, arranged through the interpreter, took place on the day before we reached Le Havre. Mikoyan came alone with him. Josée shrewdly avoided any indiscreet questions and merely brought up a few reminiscences. He, for his part, talked about the impression "the president," her father, had made on Stalin and on Molotov, the Soviet foreign minister.

As he was about to leave, Josée mentioned the pleasure it would give her father to see him again in Paris. He expressed regret and said that he was being met at Le Havre and would drive directly "East."

At the gala traditionally given for sea charities, we were the objects of a little operation of "psychological deterrence." The interpreter of the Soviet party had asked the head waiter to arrange a table for five next to ours for the floor show. A bottle of champagne was waiting for them, and they sat down when the main cabaret act began. Mikoyan gave a friendly wave to Josée and came over to kiss her hand. The party left, after drinking their champagne, as soon as the lights went on again in the dining room. The purpose of this performance was to indicate that the Soviet "number two" was not traveling strictly incognito but that discretion was advisable.

The following morning, when we docked at Le Havre, I was keen to observe, from the upper deck, what was going to happen down below at the staff entrance to the ship. As soon as the gangway had been run out, Thorez, the leader of the French Communist party, Ramette, Duclos, and two or three others surrounded the five Russians and escorted them quickly to half a dozen waiting limousines, which drove off immediately, as Mikoyan had said, "for the East."

Even when I put my case for the Royal Air Force to Roosevelt on board the *Potomac,* Harry Hopkins had not stared at me as intently as he did on this occasion. I still remember how we were seated side by side on the small sofa in this narrow rectangular room with three or four couples facing us. When I finished my narration, Harry grabbed my left hand and pressing it on the table, he said, "René, you know how I feel toward you. We are real friends, and I am going to ask you something: please don't tell that story to anyone over here."

I respected his wish until the end of the war, but long before the events I will attempt to sum up in the epilogue of this, my last book, I acquired the conviction that Hopkins knew about the secret meeting in New York of Anastas Mikoyan with Earl Browder, the head of the American Communist party, if he had not, in fact, organized it. The meeting took place exactly two weeks before Roosevelt's reelection, and Harry Hopkins wanted to make certain his "boss" got as many votes as possible.

CHAPTER 24

New York without Josée.
My return to occupied Paris

AFTER JOSÉE'S DEPARTURE, I COULD NOT BRING MYSELF TO REMAIN IN THE little suite at the Ritz, which reminded me too much of her disgust at the attitude of Harry Hopkins. I took a large room, where I could receive callers in the afternoon if necessary.

The book-launching operation was very successful, in spite of the below-the-belt blow of Harry Hopkins and his accomplices of the "liberal" press a few days before publication. The annual autumn book fair in Boston also went well. In addition to Bruce Lancaster, the prominent American author, the organizing committee had earmarked for the speeches the English writer Jan Struther (author of *Mrs. Miniver,* a best-seller at the time), André Maurois, and myself, both representatives of the Entente Cordiale (see photo 2).

The publisher gave the leading newspapers, including the *Herald* and *New York Times,* for New York City, and the big provincial dailies a well-concocted press release (see a reduced facsimile in exhibit 9). In the week that followed publication, the *New York Times* and *Time* magazine carried very favorable reviews of the book.

General James Harbord, the chief of staff of the American expeditionary corps in 1917–1918 and a man of strong personality, got the Radio Corporation of America, of which he was president, to broadcast a fifteen-minute analysis of the book. This enabled my publisher friend, Thayer Hobson, to quote on the jacket of the second and third printings the following phrase: "Ought to be read by every intelligent American as a lesson in advance for his own country." Similarly, on the inside flap, the appreciation of *Time* was reproduced: "the first full-length account of how France's 33rd invasion looked to a front-line soldier, *I Saw France Fall* is a document of first importance."

Lowell Thomas, the celebrated writer and radio commentator, devoted half an hour of his regular program on NBC to a question-and-answer session with me on the contents of the book.

All the work involved in ensuring success of publication did not prevent

NOTED GUESTS OF BOSTON HERALD BOOK FAIR—These literary figures were guests at last night's session. They are (left to right): David McCord, chairman; Bruce Lancaster, Jan Struther, Capt. Rene de Chambrun and Andre Maurois.

Photo 2. From the *Boston Traveler*, October 28, 1940.

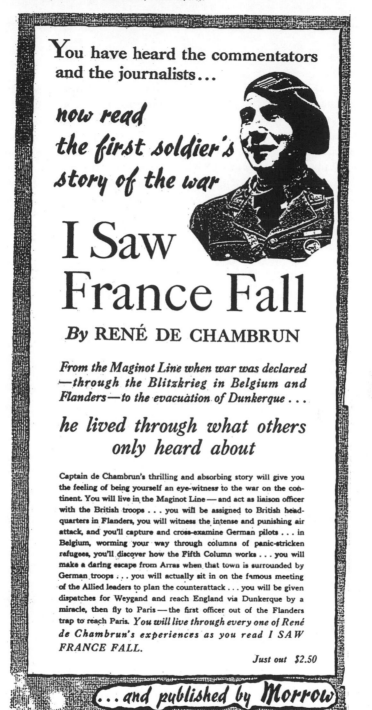

Exhibit 9. Publisher's press release for *I Saw France Fall*.

me from taking time off frequently to see Mrs. Eugene Meyer and her family. The weekend after Josée's departure for France was spent with her, her husband, the owner of the *Washington Post,* and their daughters. She repeatedly drew my attention to German-Jewish intellectuals who had fled to France from persecution in Nazi Germany, and Pierre Laval's office was kept busy procuring them exit visas. I continued to maintain close contacts with Mrs. Shipley, head of the Passport Division at the State Department, over the refugees arriving in Lisbon, in order to obtain for them long-term entry permits to the United States.

The palace revolution that led to Laval's dismissal on December 13 was announced the following day by the New York dailies. It was no surprise to me because, when in Vichy, I had sensed the animosity between the extreme right-wing group around the marshal and all parliamentarians and Pierre Laval, in particular, who had been one throughout his career, first as a deputy then as a senator. I was getting more anxious as the hours went by, waiting for a cable from Josée to give me the inside story. It came at last. It read, "Stay in America and do not worry—except for the country."

Those last three words haunted me as New York was preparing for the year-end festivities and a Christmas that was the saddest in my life, in contrast with the relatively happy one the year before, on the Maginot Line, with the Scottish "Black Watch," in an atmosphere of jollification characteristic of the "phony war."

A few days before that Christmas, Frances Perkins called me. She was coming to New York for her season's shopping, and I invited her to dine with me in the Japanese garden of the Ritz. She arrived in good time, loaded with parcels.

I have extremely fond memories of those few hours spent with this exceptional woman. Born in 1882, she was fifty-eight in 1940, when we first met. Full of life, energy, and intelligence, she showed lingering traces of the beauty that had driven Sinclair Lewis to declare his passion for her. She turned him down, and he later wrote a portrait of her in *Ann Vickers.* Even later, she married an invalid.

In the course of our first conversation at her office, on the day following the cruise on the *Potomac* with Roosevelt, she asked me, "How old was your ancestor Lafayette in 1761?" "Four," I replied. "He was an orphan. His father had been killed in battle by the English two years before, and his mother had just died. Fifteen years later, Washington was to become his adopted father and best friend." "Your ancestor would have got on well with mine, James Otis," she added. I knew he had been the first to speak out against British rule in America.

I also knew that she had been the brains behind the social insurance legislation of the United States, which was voted on August 14, 1935. She turned up well in advance for the dinner she had organized for me at the Mayflower with trade union leaders the preceding July. During our private talk before the guests arrived, she surprised me by making a startling pro-Laval statement. "I was working in New York," she said, "when Pierre Laval came on a visit with his daughter, your future wife, to meet President Hoover. I had thoroughly studied the law on social insurance, which he inspired and got through Parliament in April 1930, and I regard him as my mentor."

It was impossible for the subject of Harry Hopkins not to crop up at some point in the course of this long evening. I had the clear impression that she had no great liking for him and was concerned about his growing influence on Roosevelt. "It was obviously his duty," she insisted, "to use his credit with the president to get him to tell Lothian that de Gaulle had no business meddling in this affair and that, de Gaulle or no de Gaulle, Roosevelt should make the supply of arms and food to Britain conditional on some shipments to France. Roosevelt demonstrated great weakness over this," she went on, "and it was typical of Harry to tell him, 'Leave it to me; I will fix the matter up with René de Chambrun.' His fixing the matter through a press campaign against you and Henry-Haye was ignoble."

I naturally accompanied her to Pennsylvania Station to put her on board the midnight train, and we affectionately kissed each other good-bye.

In the first few days of the New Year, France was increasingly on my mind, and deep down in my heart, I began to feel a bit of a stranger in my second homeland, which had eyes only for Britain. She had had no stauncher supporter than I, and I felt that my conviction, proclaimed everywhere in the dark days of June and July 1940, had now proved right. Britain had become invulnerable in her island, bristling with antiaircraft guns and defended from air attack by fighters that were coming off the assembly lines at an accelerated rate.

In spite of Josée's advice to the contrary, I felt it my duty to return to France. The regular Clipper service to Lisbon had been suspended, and all that was left were two old liners, the *Excambion* and the *Excalibur,* which sailed between New York and Lisbon, packed to the gunwales, in ten to eleven days. I was able to obtain on the black market a berth in a cabin for four on the ship sailing in mid-February.

As soon as they learned of my decision, a number of wealthy American friends, the Strassburgers, Mrs. Seton Porter, John Jay, and others, pressed letters, messages, dollar bills, and gold coins on me for the faithful servants they had left behind in the homes they owned in France.

I had set aside my last lunch for the Maurois, firm friends in their hours of trial and mine. My dinner and my last few hours in New York were for Herbert Hoover, Roosevelt's immediate predecessor. Swept out of office by the New Deal, Hoover had taken refuge in an apartment on the thirty-first floor of the Waldorf Towers, which was to become his permanent home in the city. He was to live and work there until his death in 1964.

We had dinner served in his suite. I knew that he was one of the loyal supporters of food shipments to France. Sixteen years before he entered the White House, in 1929, he had agreed to undertake, along with Brand Whitlock, the minister to Belgium, the tremendous task of ensuring the shipment of food to seven million Belgians and nearly one million Frenchmen living in the Nord–Pas de Calais region occupied by the Germans. In August 1914, they had violated the neutrality of Belgium, which was to be held a prisoner of war, so to speak, for over four years.

Our long conversation took place more than six years before the many others we were to have during each of my biannual visits to New York. On every occasion, Herbert Hoover talked about the task he had undertaken of collecting all the documents and evidence concerning France under German occupation, which have been stored in the tower bearing his name at Stanford University. He always gave me the impression that those years in which he tried to save the Belgian people from starvation had left more of a mark on his life than even his years at the White House battling against the world economic crisis.

It was past midnight when I left him. During that evening, I had appreciated his thorough understanding of the tragedy that had struck down France and of the problem of food supplies. His friendliness was such that I was on the point of telling him what I had just been through and the depth of my disappointment over the weakness of Roosevelt in failing to keep a promise, which was sacred in my eyes, and Harry Hopkins's betrayal. But I resolved to remain silent on the subject and did so until February 19, 1946, when I told the whole truth to the senior investigating magistrate of the High Court of Justice in Paris (see in appendix C the most important document included in this book, the written evidence I gave to Judge Marchat on that day).

Submarine warfare was at its height when I left New York, and neutral ships sailing between the United States and the Iberian Peninsula described increasingly wide circles to the south in order to avoid U-boat attacks. I arrived in Lisbon after a crossing lasting thirteen days, just in time to jump into the night train to Madrid. The sleepers were full. I ended up in a corner seat in a second-class carriage and slept fitfully. On arrival at the French embassy in Madrid, I sent off three telegrams to each of the three places where Josée was likely to be found: Châteldon in Auvergne, our home in Place du Palais-Bourbon in Paris, and her parents' home in Villa Said in Paris, giving my address of the following day: Grand Hotel Tivolier in Toulouse.

On the previous return journey, there was no question of crossing the frontier at Hendaye and of entering occupied France. I did not have the necessary German "Ausweis," or permit. François Piétri, the French ambassador to Spain, lent me a car and driver to get to the frontier post of Canfranc. I was going to try to enter France at this post with my pockets full of gold and dollars, like a real smuggler, and I did not feel very reassured.

Happily, the diplomatic passport that ambassador Henry-Haye had given me in Washington smoothed over all difficulties, and when I reached the Grand Hotel Tivolier, I was overjoyed to hear the receptionist inform me with a broad smile, "Madame de Chambrun is waiting for you in your room, and here is the key."

We had dinner in the vast dining room adorned with large 1900-style mirrors in chocolate-colored frames. The hotel reminded me of the happy days when my rugby fifteen of the Stade Français would come to play against the Stade Toulousain. We enjoyed our cassoulet served in earthenware pots, while Josée told me in minute detail about the "coup" of December 13. How far away all that seems now!

The following day, "on the spot" at Châteldon, I relived every episode of the "coup." Laval was absent, but there were three important witnesses to the event: Nanouk, the husky, and his three pups. More than three months had gone by since I had left, and the joy of being back in the family outweighed any feelings of anger. Josée joked readily, "Those four wretched animals suffered most from those two interminable days we spent under a kind of house arrest. Their little bladders were bursting, as they were not allowed to go outside to lift a leg!"

The day after, we left for Paris to join our respective parents. As we approached the demarcation line, a strange thought crossed my mind: all the Germans I had met until then were prisoners of war, airmen shot down by the British antiaircraft batteries. They were "our" prisoners, and I attended their interrogation, suggesting the questions to be put to them. And now, in turn, I was to become a prisoner of the Wehrmacht, camping in the land of France. For how many months or perhaps years?

Fortunately, Boudot, the driver my father-in-law had lent us along with his car, was not lacking in cheek and panache. He saluted the German lieutenant at the control post, handed over to him Josée's, my own, and his papers in a batch: "Ausweis," passports, car papers, the lot. In a few seconds, I was "free" to enter enemy-occupied territory.

Epilogue

D Day (June 6, 1944)—
the "Blitz" in Reverse

Four years before D day, June 6, 1944, I was driving along the roads of northern France, trying to dodge the bombs and machine gun bullets of thousands of Stuka bombers. A similar deluge of bombs and shells was to strike the Normandy coast four years later a few hours before the successful Allied landings.

As the sequence of events reported in this book is frequently punctuated by anecdotes, here is a very precise one about an event historians have ignored or forgotten: on that same morning of June 6, a little before five, while the assault troops were setting foot on the Normandy beaches, Gauleiter Fritz Sauckel, the Nazi slave driver and Laval's most determined opponent, was sound asleep in a luxury suite of the Ritz, on Place Vendôme.

He was awoken suddenly by a telephone call informing him of the Allied assault and dashed to his writing table to send off the following emergency order to Otto Abetz, the German ambassador to the French government.

Dear Ambassador and Comrade Abetz:

The long-expected invasion has at last begun. This ends the period of procrastination over our labor demands, a procrastination used to justify openly or tacitly the alleged impossibility of transferring manpower to Germany because of the supposed political disturbances it might cause.

Now that the German soldier must again fight and shed his blood in Normandy, and that the battle can at any time spread to many other parts of France, all the pleas and all the arguments of Laval can no longer carry any weight. . . .

. . . I demand that you request President Laval to comply with this necessary act even though it will be manifestly painful to him. He must sign the order of mobilization of the class of 1944. I will accept dilatory tactics under no circumstances.

All technical details are ready to handle the quotas of workers to be provided by each French department, and the means of transport are available as a result of our meetings. Heil Hitler - Fritz Sauckel.[1]

A dispatch rider took the letter to the German embassy in Rue de Lille shortly before six A.M. Abetz, who disliked Sauckel and his brutal methods, took it upon himself not to phone Pierre Laval at Châteldon. He wanted to be certain first that the Gauleiter had taken off from Villacoublay, near Paris, in the plane that was flying him to Hitler's headquarters in East Prussia; and only then did he call the Hotel du Parc in Vichy.

Laval turned down the request without a moment's hesitation. This did not surprise Abetz. At the same time, he sent off Bichelonne, his minister for industry, to Paris with written confirmation of his refusal; right through that day, telegram 555 containing an imperative order to oppose all collective or individual requisitioning of French workers for service in Germany went out to each one of the regional and departmental prefects and to Generals André Martin and Jean Perré, commanders of the Gendarmerie and the Garde Républicaine, respectively. It was the concluding episode of the long two-year struggle that opposed Laval to Sauckel.

I have often said to myself that if, through some twist of fate, the Allied landings had failed, it is more than likely that, on the orders of Hitler, Laval would have been shot long before the ghastly miscarriage of justice of October 1945 in Paris.

The following day, our little Simca car took us to Normandy, a few kilometers from Lisieux, to the stud farm of our old American friends, Mr. and Mrs. Strassburger, one of the finest in the world. By some fluke, those old Norman half-timbered houses with their fine Chippendale furniture, their brood mares and foals, were to remain unscathed, protected from malignant curiosity by thick privet hedges and by an astute manager. The owners recovered their properties intact in Paris, Chantilly, Deauville, along with the stud; after their death, their son gave the municipality of Deauville the Ferme du Coteau, which stands on the cliff like a lighthouse above the fashionable resort. An avenue of the town was named after those two most loyal friends of France.

---

[1]Sauckel's handwritten note on the stationery of the Ritz was produced by the French prosecutor, Herzog, at his trial in Nuremberg.

Pierre Laval's Return to Paris.
His Arrest by the SS.
My First Spell in Hiding

Journalists and historians of the Resistance have completely distorted the
course of events at the Hotel Matignon, traditionally the prime minister's
office, after the return of Laval to Paris, his conversations with Edouard
Herriot,[2] the president of the Chamber of Deputies, and his arrest by the
Germans. I therefore feel duty-bound to relate exactly what happened.

At that particular time, three concerns were uppermost in Laval's mind:

1. To ensure food supplies for Paris and its suburbs

2. To negotiate through the support of the Swedish consul general,
Raoul Nördling, a convention with the local commander in chief of
the Wehrmacht, von Choltitz, to save Paris from destruction

3. To call an emergency session of the National Assembly

An exceptional situation had caused it to be convened on July 10, 1940,
to vote special powers to Marshal Pétain. Laval felt that it should, through
the normal procedures, resume the powers it had surrendered then to the
head of state. That was why he remained in permanent contact with
Edouard Herriot through one of his friends, André Enfière, and through
the prefect of Nancy, André Jean-Faure.

Early in the morning, he summoned to Matignon the steering committees of the Paris Municipal Council and of the Departmental Council of
the Seine. He informed their members, most of whom were former members of Parliament, senators, or deputies, of his plans, and on the day after,
August 10, he issued the following press release:

> Upon his arrival yesterday from Vichy, President Laval received M. Pierre
> Taittinger, chairman of the Paris Municipal Council, and M. Victor Con-
> stant, chairman of the Departmental Council of the Seine, along with
> members of the steering committees. He told them why he had returned
> to Paris and his wish to share the fate of the Paris population.

During the whole of that day, I stayed at the Hotel Matignon, on which
dozens of members of Parliament converged. To a man, they endorsed the

---

[2]Edouard Herriot, during the fifteen years preceding the war, was the president of
the Parti Radical Socialiste, the leading political party of France. He served several
times as prime minister and was president of the Chamber of Deputies when the
war broke out.

plan for an emergency session of both Houses sitting as the National Assembly. I do not believe that, throughout the many crises that marked the tumultuous history of the Third Republic, so many parliamentarians ever responded so spontaneously to the call of a prime minister. They came in small groups, some of them straight out of hiding, like William Thorp, Eugène Frot, and Lucien Lamoureux. I can still remember Anatole de Monzie looking at me with his big round eyes and saying, "It is the Pierrot [Laval] of the great days."

In the evening, Laval received the eighty-seven mayors of Paris and of the suburbs of the capital. Most of them were Radical Socialists or Socialists—some Communists. He spoke to them for one hour and a half. The only others present were the secretary for his constituency of Aubervilliers and myself, standing discreetly in a corner of the room. Laval explained what he had done and what he had tried to do to alleviate the sufferings of his fellow countrymen and disclosed his secret plan of attempting to bring President Edouard Herriot back to Paris from Lorraine. "It's the first time," he quipped, "that I earnestly ask eighty-seven persons to be as tight as clams!"

Ambassador Abetz arrived a few minutes before the end of the meeting, which was taking place in the room next to Laval's study.

Here is the motion voted unanimously by the eight-seven mayors once Laval had departed, less than two hours after he had spoken to them:

> The Union of Mayors of the Seine send Pierre Laval, the head of the government, their affectionate and loyal greetings. They express their entire confidence in his policy, convinced as they are that, through love for his stricken country, he will find the ways of salvation that lead to its resurrection. With deep attachment to his person, they are pleased to be able to give, through their cohesion, an example of discipline and unity, and their sole ambition is to serve their country.

Laval greeted Abetz[3] and, with apologies for keeping him waiting a few minutes, put forward his arguments in favor of allowing Herriot to return to Paris. He added curtly, "You are defeated. The Reich bears a heavy responsibility for all that has happened in France during the last four years. At least, leave us alone now, since you yourselves are pulling out. Only the convening of the National Assembly will make it possible for all Frenchmen to unite and avoid a bloodbath."

Abetz concurred and phoned Ribbentrop in Berlin then and there. The

---

[3]Laval in his talks with his wife and his daughter would refer to Abetz as the least anti-French of all Germans.

foreign minister, overwhelmed by the turn of events, allowed matters to take their course. A few moments later, Abetz told Laval that he could go to Edouard Herriot and inform him that he was free.

On August 12, 1944, four years after the meeting of the National Assembly in Vichy, Pierre Laval and Edouard Herriot met in a suburb of Nancy, in Lorraine. Laval announced his intention of reconvening Parliament; Herriot agreed, and they returned together in the same car, arriving at the Préfecture of the Seine in Paris on the morning of the following day. Both called on the German officers and staff occupying the Hotel de Lassay, the residence of the president of the Chamber of Deputies, to leave the premises immediately. The order, suggested by Abetz to General von Choltitz, was sent out then and there.

Meanwhile, Herriot telephoned my father-in-law and advised him to get in touch as soon as possible with the president of the Senate, Jules Jeanneney, who was in Grenoble. Laval summoned the head of his personal staff and asked him to make posthaste for Grenoble, as all telephone links between that town and Paris had broken down.

On August 15, Abetz came to tell Laval that the Wehrmacht would order its forces not to stand and defend Paris. Already thanks to his strong protests, the prime minister had prevented them from blowing up all the power stations and telephone exchanges in the Paris area.

The following day, events took a dramatic turn. Amédée Bussière, the prefect of police, who was keeping an eye on Brinon, Déat, and Darnand, three advocates of unconditional collaboration with the Nazis, came to inform Laval that they had just fled to Germany. They had been received by General Oberg, Himmler's personal representative in France, and condemned the Laval-Herriot plan as high treason against Germany. They got Oberg to telephone Himmler, who gave orders for the arrest of Herriot, Laval, and the whole French government.

This betrayal, which had such doleful consequences for the future, was the ultimate revenge of the "ultracollaborators" against Pierre Laval. They had never forgiven him for rejecting the alliance Hitler had proposed to France at the time of the Allied landings in North Africa, in November 1942.

Around eleven P.M., a French police inspector detailed to ensure Herriot's security and M. René Bouffet, the prefect of the Seine, called on the prime minister to inform him that the German police had just arrived at the offices of the Prefecture of the Seine with an order to take Herriot back to Lorraine.

Laval immediately went to the Hôtel de Ville, where he found SS Captain Nosek, who was entrusted with Herriot's arrest. He immediately expressed his firm opposition to the order and telephoned Abetz, who arrived on the spot twenty minutes later. In the ambassador's presence, Herriot and Laval solemnly protested against this breach of faith. The ambassador was shattered. To give him the possibility of playing for time and of persuading Berlin to rescind the order, Laval handed him a letter, which he wrote there and then. It ran as follows:

Mr. Ambassador,

You informed me that I could advise President Herriot that he was free. I went to Nancy and brought him back to Paris.

The news that he has been rearrested and is about to be taken back to Nancy is deeply distressing to me. Should it prove true, I would regard it as 'a most serious personal offense. It would certainly lay me open to the charge of duplicity, which, as you well know, has never been in my character.

I would have to ask you to regard me your prisoner on the same basis as President Herriot, and, whatever the outcome, I would be compelled to resign my office forthwith.

With highest regard, I remain, Mr. Ambassador, Yours Truly,

(signed) Pierre Laval.

Edouard Herriot, with the agreement of Pierre Laval, wrote the following letter at the same time:

To his Excellency
The German Ambassador in Paris:

After being informed in Nancy by President Pierre Laval that I was free, without my taking any initiative to that effect, and following my return to Paris where, for reasons of caution and in the general interest, I (had) deliberately foregone that freedom of which I had been notified. I am once again removed to an unknown place, along with my wife, who has voluntarily and courageously shared my fate, although I have not committed any act that could be held against me.

I have no means of resisting force when it prevails over the given word. But I hand over this solemn protest to President Laval, head of the government, with a request that he transmit it to the German ambassador in Paris.

(signed) Edouard Herriot.

Abetz then agreed that the Herriots could spend the night at the prefecture and come to lunch on the following day at the Hotel Matignon, pending a reply from Berlin. When Abetz turned up with the Herriots at

Matignon for lunch, he was crestfallen; the two orders he had received were confirmed: Herriot must be arrested, and the whole government sent prisoner to Germany.

This lunch, at which I saw my father-in-law for the last time, was attended by Abetz, M. and Mme Herriot, M. and Mme Laval, my wife, and myself. It was related by my wife in a document deposited in the archives of the Hoover Institution on May 2, 1947, under no. 25 (vol. II, p. 1078).

The meeting of the Council of Ministers had been called for that afternoon at six. Pierre Laval was able to warn his two best friends, Pierre Cathala, the minister of finance, and Dr. Grasset, the minister for health, that they should go into hiding. The ministers, to a man, refused to comply with the German order and leave Paris. Cars of the Gestapo were waiting outside the Hotel Matignon to take them away. That was how Pierre Laval was arrested and deported to Germany.

After the Matignon lunch, M. and Mme Herriot were taken back, under SS escort, to the Hôtel de Ville. I myself arrived at the Préfecture of the Seine in the evening. Captain Nosek was on duty outside the door of President Herriot's apartment. I made my way in and brought him some books and my last cigars. With the agreement of Prefect Bouffet, I suggested to Herriot that he escape through the sewers, as the side door to the apartment was not guarded. My wife and I had arranged a hiding place for him in the district of Passy. Herriot hesitated for a long time, then said that he wished to allow things to take their course. We embraced one another.

Sadly, I returned to Josée, and we both decided to go into hiding the very next day in the flat I had proposed to the Herriots, located in a small building at 18, Rue d'Andigné, which still exists today. It was only four floors high, with a single staircase and no porter. It was rented by Seymour Weller, the nephew of the Clarence Dillons, who ran their vineyard at Haut Brion. Weller was an intimate friend of mine, and as he lived in the château on the estate near Bordeaux, he had put his pied-à-terre in Paris at our entire disposal because the situation was so critical. Subsequently, I asked him to join the board of the Baccarat Crystal Company, of which I was chairman, and he remained a member of it until his death.

The First Phase of My Semiclandestine Existence until Laval's Return to France

Equipped with three keys, a big one to open the gate in the railings around the small apartment block, a medium-sized one to open the door to the stairs, and a little one to the door on the first floor that let us into our hiding place, a comfortable home with high ceilings, we began our semi-clandestine existence on the morning of August 18.

My first outing was to the Préfecture of Police, to obtain two false identity cards in the name of Jacqueline and René Gosset. The friendly stationer of my law office on the Champs-Elysées, Belleville-Reneaux, produced visiting cards with our new names in twenty-four hours. They were not a complete deception since the initials of our first names were the same!

We made the acquaintance of the couple living on the ground floor; for them, we were the owners of a small farm in the region of Avranches, in Normandy, practically destroyed in the first raids preceding D day, who had taken refuge in Paris.

Only our faithful servant, Elie Ruet, and a couple from Auvergne who lived nearby in Rue Raynouard were in the know. For the first three or four weeks after our move, Josée went out very seldom and Ruet did the shopping. We were still at Rue d' Andigné on the day of de Gaulle's triumphal walk down the Champs-Elysées, after the liberation of Paris by the troops of General Leclerc's Second Division. And I went out to mingle with the ecstatic crowd.

On two occasions before the war, I think, Josée had met Madeleine Porthault, whose Paris shop was a byword in fine table linen. She sent her one or two rich American friends on their way through Paris for shopping. And she had commissioned Elie Ruet to go and purchase two or three dozen napkins, which she could embroider in order to kill time. Madame Porthault spontaneously came up with the proposal of a delightful house at Emancé, near Rambouillet, about thirty miles southwest of Paris. She told Elie Ruet that it would give her the greatest pleasure to place this home at the disposal of "Norman refugees." We gratefully accepted the offer. Our stay at Emancé was to last several weeks, during which I rode several times into Paris on my bicycle, as there was no way of obtaining petrol to go there by car.

In this way, I was able to renew contact with an Auvergnat police inspector, Louis Vert, whom I had known a long time and who was devoted to me. Later he was able to give me valuable information about Madame Laval when she was imprisoned at Fresnes, outside Paris along with common criminals, and about my own personal case before the new legal authorities of liberated France.

During our stay at Emancé, we acquired a little dog, Siki, whom we took with us to our next hideout—a charming house at Houilles, an outlying suburb of Paris on the Seine, which belonged to a friend of the Eugène Vincents, intimates of Josée's, who did not use it. My wife taught me how to grow radishes, cabbage, green peas, and tomatoes, while she went on with her needlework and with her reading of Saint-Simon's interminable memoirs.

My cycle trips to Paris became an almost daily event, and in the very last days of July, we learned of the incarceration of Laval and his wife at Fresnes. This decided us to return immediately to our home on the Place du Palais-Bourbon. Then I learned through Police Inspector Vert that judicial proceedings, under the heading "René de Chambrun, collaboration and intelligence with the enemy," were being contemplated by the High Court of Justice, including an investigation into all my tax returns, my bank statements, etc. But no summons was issued and no formal charge leveled against me, and I continued to go regularly to my office in order to work with Baraduc and Jaffré on the transcription of the pages written by Pierre Laval in his own defense from his prison cell.

A Dramatic Twist of Fortune: My Traitor Reappears, and I Must Disappear

In the early days of September 1945, there occurred a dramatic twist in my fortunes: Hugh Fullerton, the American consul general in Paris and an intimate friend of my parents, called my father and asked to see him urgently. He was very agitated and told him what follows: "I was in the office of Douglas MacArthur, the first secretary at the American embassy, a few moments ago when he received a call from Harry Hopkins at the White House, who said, 'We must see to it that René de Chambrun is put out of action. He knows too much.'

This message was confirmed shortly afterward by Robert Pell, a former attaché at the embassy, who called on my parents. He was also an intimate friend especially of my mother's because he had taken over from her as chairman of the American Library in Paris, which she had saved from destruction during the German occupation. He said to them, "René is in danger. Douglas MacArthur has been given the task of putting him out of action. He is getting in touch with his friends in the French administration to see how this can be done."

The family were consulted. Their advice was unequivocal: I must not spend the night at the Place du Palais-Bourbon. I was therefore to sleep almost every night from October to January 1946 in a large apartment on Boulevard de Courcelles, in front of the Parc Monceau, belonging to a friend of Josée's and of her parents.

At the end of January 1946, I received at long last by registered post a summons of the senior investigating magistrate of the High Court to appear before him on February 18, at two o'clock, to answer charges of criminal intelligence with the enemies of France. I then decided, as my mother-in-law had done before me, not to have a lawyer but to conduct my own defense. I seem to remember that at about the same time Marcel Poignard, the chairman of the Paris Bar, informed me that an action against me had been brought before the Bar Council. The chief public prosecutor, acting on instructions of Pierre-Henri Teitgen, the minister of justice, had demanded that I be immediately disbarred. I really felt, during that month of February 1946, that my fate as a free man was in the balance.

A second dramatic turn of events during this decisive month brought on a feeling of enormous relief. That morning, before going out, I glanced out of the window to make sure there was no suspicious policeman outside my front door and went to the newsstand to buy my daily *Figaro* and *Herald Tribune*. To my amazement, I saw on the front page a photograph of Harry Hopkins—he had died the day before! Yes, the number two in the White House during the whole of Roosevelt's "reign," the number one friend of Stalin in the United States, the man who betrayed me three times, had just passed away. My astonishment turned to boundless joy, for now I felt a free man!

It was therefore with a song in my heart that on February 18, a few minutes before the appointed time, I knocked at the door of Judge Marchat, with two heavy files under my arms. The first contained original documents and notes on my activities with the British troops during the "phony war" and on the mission that Prime Minister Paul Reynaud and President Roosevelt had entrusted to me; the second, evidence of everything that I had been able to accomplish with Josée and my parents in defense of American interests in France during the German occupation (the American Hospital in Neuilly, the American Library, the American Cathedral, interned American citizens, etc.). I came determined to reveal for the first time the truth about all I had done in the United States and afterward, in France, until the deportation of Pierre Laval to Germany.

The judge's manner was polite but distinctly aloof. He asked me whether Madame Laval, whose case he had investigated, and who had been discharged without trial, was living at my home since she had come out of prison. He added, "She is a lady." To this I replied, "A great lady, Your Honor." "That is what I meant," he added, correcting himself with apparent sincerity.

During the six hours of interrogation that followed, the atmosphere became gradually more relaxed, to the point of becoming surprisingly warm. I noticed that the clerk, on a sign from the judge, stopped typing. He listened.

For the first time in five years, I produced the documents relating to my mission to the United States: my report, annotated by Roosevelt and dated June 17, 1940, which I had commented at the Cabinet meeting on the following day, the list written in his own hand on a radiogram form of the twenty-three persons whom I should meet and convince that Britain was invulnerable. My account seemed to cause the judge increasing surprise as it progressed.

When it came to the point of relating what Josée and I had been able to do during the German occupation in response to endless calls for help that converged from all sides at my home and my office, he interrupted me at one point to ask, "Maître, you really did all that?" I replied, "But, Your Honor, I am sure you would have done the same in my place." He was surprised that there had been so many appeals for help. I told him that Pierre Laval had only one daughter and one son-in-law. Had he had two, we would have had half the number of calls for assistance and could perhaps have taken three or four days off during those endless and terrible years.

On two or three occasions during the interrogation, the judge got a phone call and went out of his room. During the first interruption, the clerk of the court smiled at me and said, "Captain, you remember me, I was Sergeant Bitsch of the 164th Fortress Infantry Regiment, in the Rotherberg, and I met you before you were posted to the British." He added, "Perhaps I should not show it to you, but here is a curious document, dated September 6, which was sent to the judge by the Quai d'Orsay [the French Foreign Ministry]." And he produced the note, of which he gave me a copy when the judge went out of the room the second time. (It bore the date of September 6, 1945, and is reproduced in exhibit 10.) "A secretary of the American embassy is pursuing the matter and saw Mr. Tixier at the Ministry of the Interior, who spoke to the chief public prosecutor, expressing astonishment that you had not yet been put under arrest."

When Judge Marchat returned after his fourth absence, the atmosphere was palpably less tense. The "interrogation-conversation" had certainly gone on for more than five hours, when the judge, looking me straight in the eye, said point-blank,

> Maître, I know now that France owes you a considerable debt. It is in any case a rare thing to be awarded the Legion of Honor at the age of thirty, and in peacetime, without having applied for it. You can see that I know a lot of things about you, and I am compelled by my conscience to tell you the following:
>
> At the end of September, I was obliged, against my will, to summon President Laval before me for interrogation. The decision had just been taken at the highest level to put an end to the investigation into his case and to eliminate him before the elections due to take place in the third

Lettre N° 748 adressée au Ministre des Affaires Etrangères par
l'Ambassadeur des Etats-Unis à Paris,le 6 Septembre 1945

-:-:-:-:-:-

L'Ambassade des Etats-Unis présente ses compliments au Ministre d
Affaires Etrangères et à l'honneur de l'informer qu'une instruction a é
reçue du département d'Etat donnant à l'Ambassade l'instruction d'info:
le gouvernement français que l'attention du Gouvernement des Etats Uni:
a été attiré sur le fait que l'opinion est largement répandue parmi le:
personnalités françaises que René DE CHAMB-UN et sa femme née José LAV.
n'avaient pas été arrêtés par les autorités françaises comme collabora-
tionniste en raison d'une intervention d'officiels américains, motivéer
par les relations de la famille de CHAMBUN aux Etats-Unis, son statut
citoyen honoraire de l'Etat de MARYLAND, que René de CHAMB-UN porte en
r y de sa descendance du marquis e LAFAYETTE.

Ainsi que M.le Ministre des Affaires Etrangères ne l'ignore pas il
n'y a rien de vrai dans la croyance que ces personnes sont de quelques
manières protégées par le Gouvernement des Etats Unis. Avant tout René
de CHAMB-UN est un citoyen français et il ne peut jouir à aucun titre d
la protection desEtats-Unis.

Croyant que, c'est dans l'intérêt des relations franco-américaines
dissiper la rumeur erronée que ces personnes sont de quelques manières
protégées par le Gouvernement des Etats-Unis. L'Ambassade a reçu des in
tructions pour dire clairement au Gouvernement français que ce n'est pas
le cas et que le Gouvernement des Etats-Unis ne désire pas empêcher tel
le action que le Gouvernement français peut désirer entreprendre contre
ces personnes, contre leurs actes et leur lignes de conduite durant la
période entre la conclusion de l'armistice franco-allemand de .940 et
la Libération de lé France.

-:-:-:-:-:-

Exhibit 10.

Letter No. 748 addressed on September 6, 1945, to the minister of foreign affairs of France by the U.S. ambassador in Paris (translated from the French).

The American Embassy presents its compliments to the Minister of Foreign Affairs and begs to inform him that it had been instructed to call the attention of the French government upon the following facts: there are rumors that René de Chambrun and his wife, Josée Laval, have not been arrested by the French authorities as "collaborators" by reason of the intervention in their favor of American authorities motivated by the fact that the Chambrun family benefits from their honorary American citizenship as citizens of Maryland, because of René de Chambrun's descent from the Marquis de Lafayette.

The Minister of Foreign Affairs of France must know that those two persons do not in any way benefit of the protection of the United States. René de Chambrun is a citizen of France and cannot, we repeat, benefit in any way of a U.S. protection.

We believe that it is in the interest of Franco–American relationship to clarify this situation and the government of the United States does not want in the slightest way to interfere with whatever action the French government wishes to take against those two persons for their acts and conduct during the period running between the Franco-German armistice of 1940 and the liberation of France.

Exhibit 10. Translated from the French.

week of October. Since his death, I have postponed as much as I could this first summons to you, at a time when the official investigation was switched to your case, at the instigation of the first secretary of the embassy of the United States.

Your personal account with Morgan's, the account of your law office with the National City Bank, and your tax returns have been gone through with a fine-tooth comb. Not the slightest trace of irregularity has been discovered. The investigation will continue. In a case of this kind, as you can easily guess, my powers are limited. But I want you to know my personal opinion. This is what I recommend: take away all the documents you have submitted to me. Some of them, like the testimonials of the chief of staff of the French Forces of the Interior, of members of the Resistance, of the vicar of the American Pro-Cathedral, the letter of the British ambassador in Washington and others, are extremely important. Have them all photographed. Spend the next twenty-four hours drawing up a very detailed memorandum for me about your case. Bring it tomorrow evening around seven. I have an appointment the following day with the public prosecutor to discuss your affair. I can give you the only promise that is in my power: I will authorize you to remain at your home with Madame Laval and Madame de Chambrun who need your presence.

When I came out of the building in the Rue Boissy d'Anglas, where this "special" Court of Justice was located, I made a dash for home, Place du Palais-Bourbon, and telephoned the two secretaries at my law office, Madame André Verlé, who lived at Aubervilliers, a near suburb of Paris— she is still of this world—and Mademoiselle Georgette Clark, who died a few years ago. Both agreed to come to my office as quickly as possible and worked, in fact, right through the night until the end of the following afternoon. In the meantime, I phoned the clerk of the court that I would be at his office late with the memorandum that I had been asked to produce.[4]

When I called on the judge at the appointed time, I found him alone and handed to him the twenty-nine typewritten pages and all the documents. He asked me whether I could stay on while he read them all carefully, which took nearly two hours.

"This contains revelations that will give persons in high places cause for reflection," he remarked when he had finished. I took leave of him and

---

[4]At the press conference that followed publication of the French edition of this book, I gave all those present a photocopy of the signed carbon copy of this twenty-nine-page document dated February 19, 1946. This exhibit, translated verbatim by Charles Hargrove, covers the most important points of this document. I feel that it has a historic value that can place the events of that period in the right perspective (see appendix C).

he said he did not think that in view of all the information in the memorandum and the attached documents, he would summon me again before the end of March or the beginning of April.

A few months later, he disappeared without a trace, and I was informed some time after that his name had been struck off the list of examining magistrates. I only saw him again eight years later, in surprising circumstances, which I have described in chapter 12 of my book on *Mes combats pour Pierre Laval*.

I heard later that the note of September 6, 1945, which had been passed on to me surreptitiously by the clerk of the court, was written by the same Douglas MacArthur, the nephew of the famous general and a son-in-law of Senator Alben Barkley, then vice-president of the United States. He had brought pressure to bear on officials of the Ministries for Foreign Affairs, Justice, and the Interior to have me put out of the way.

The court order dismissing the case was a document thirty-five pages long that ended with the following words: "The defense put up by René de Chambrun makes it possible to maintain not only that his conduct was beyond reproach from the national point of view, but also that his devotion to the cause of France and of the Allies was notorious and unflinching, and his patriotism unquestionable."

As for the request that I be immediately struck off the roll of attorneys, which was filed by the chief public prosecutor on instructions from Pierre-Henri Teitgen, the Bar Council[5] devoted the whole of its afternoon session at the Palace of Justice on February 26 to examining it. The hearing was impressive. The judges in such a case are all the past and present chairmen of the Bar Council, flanked by every one of its eighteen members, sitting in a half-circle in front of the culprit, who feels rather like a country parson charged with some grievous offense appearing before a court of archbishops and bishops. It was nearly seven P.M. when the chairman, after consulting his two neighbors in a whisper, told me that the council would deliberate on the verdict then and there—which meant that I could expect to have it before leaving the law court.

Jacques Baraduc, who had become something of a brother to me, was counseling me as, in such cases, the presence of a colleague is almost mandatory. He had more experience of these matters than I and said in a low voice, "We have won!" An hour later, the chairman of the Bar Council congratulated me on the outcome, and a day later, he gave me two original copies of the closely argued decision, so that I could pass one on to the

---

[5]Conseil de l'Ordre

High Court of Justice, charged with trying crimes of "collaboration" with the enemy.

A few days later, in early March, Hugh Fullerton, the U.S. consul general, a strong francophile with a big heart, came to see me. The purpose of his visit was to compliment me on the decision of the Bar Council. He gave me a very sad piece of news: soon after the liberation of Paris, the U.S. State Department notified the embassy that any request for a visa by René de Chambrun should be turned down and that this decision was final.[6]

Faced with this "ukase," which prevented me from seeing America again, my parents immediately got in touch with Senator Robert Taft.

Three weeks later, he sent my father a letter enclosing one he had received from Dean Acheson, acting secretary of state (see exhibit 11).

Senator Taft immediately got in touch with General Marshall who ordered the door of my second country, which Harry Hopkins had closed, to be opened to me again.

My Reasons for My Publishing These Recollections So Long after the Event

In 1989, I met John Horton, a benefactor of the Archives of Contemporary History of Cleveland State University, in Ohio. For several years, he had been studying the life of my mother, Clara Longworth de Chambrun, and had read all that she had written on Shakespeare. The idea struck him of writing her biography, along with mine.

But it was only at the beginning of last year that Horton was authorized to pass on to me a number of secret documents concerning myself of which the FBI and the National Archives in Washington had allowed him to have copies. I have selected five, which appear at the end of this book in appendix E. Naturally, all those documents are related to the instructions of Harry Hopkins to the American ambassador in Paris to have me eliminated.

I was on a visit to the United States in October 1990 when Harper Collins in the United States and Britain and, a little later, Fayard in France published a large volume by Christopher Andrew and Oleg Gordievsky entitled *KGB—The Inside Story*. I must emphasize that Andrew is one of the greatest authorities on the subject and produced this monumental work together with Gordievsky, a senior official of the KGB, who defected to Britain in 1983.

In the book, the authors insist that Harry Hopkins was "the most

---

[6]After his retirement, Hugh Fullerton decided to continue to live in France, where he died.

May 8, 1946

Dear Bob:

I have your letter concerning Rene de Chambrun. I am informed that no affirmative action is contemplated by the Department concerning him. I might add, however, that the Department and our Embassy in Paris would oppose strenuously any attempt on his part to obtain a visa to visit this country.

Sincerely yours,

Dean

~~Acting Secretary~~

The Honorable
    Robert A. Taft
        United States Senate

Exhibit 11. Letter from Dean Acheson, acting secretary of state, to Senator Robert Taft.

important of all Soviet wartime agents in the United States." I was not unduly taken aback by this surprising description. However, I am convinced that Hopkins did not "betray" his country for any material advantage, but that, as an unconditional admirer of Stalin and Stalinism, he acted persistently with unconscious naivety during the last six years of his life in the interests of Moscow.

By reason of his exceptional position as the closest permanent adviser to the president, his activities proved valuable to Stalin, all the more since Roosevelt and his secretaries of state were utterly ignorant of the fact that very senior officials like Harry Dexter White, Alger Hiss, and others were professional spies, under orders of a chief who sat permanently in Washington and transmitted all the information they provided directly to Moscow via Canada.

The "disinterested" role of Hopkins and his unbelievable dedication to the Soviet leader and his regime incited me also to recall some of the events in which he was involved and which I followed closely at the time.

This commitment began with the visit of Harry Hopkins to Moscow at the end of July 1941—five months before Pearl Harbor—when the United States was not yet at war. After dealing with the lend-lease operations with Britain in London, and in spite of his poor state of health, he went up to Scapa Flow, in the far north of Scotland, from where a U.S. Air Force bomber, which had been flown in from the United States and refitted with a huge fuel tank, took him nonstop to the Soviet base of Arkhangelsk on the Arctic Circle. There, he was welcomed by the head of Stalin's personal staff, who brought him on to Moscow in a Soviet air force plane.

On the following day, he handed over to Stalin the note of introduction, which he had got Roosevelt to write out in his own hand and which ended with these words: "I ask you to treat Mr. Hopkins with the same confidence as if you were talking directly to me."

Almost from the outset, complete agreement was reached on a promise of unconditional and unlimited American aid to Russia in both arms and food. There was never the remotest suggestion then or afterward that after the defeat of Germany, which both sides anticipated, the Soviet Union should respect the frontiers of its neighbors.

In the course of this first meeting, when Hopkins promised everything without demanding anything in return, he fell under the spell of Stalin. He was deeply impressed by his intelligence as a military leader and a statesman and by the efficiency of his advisers. The Soviet leader succeeded in persuading him that Russia was a strong, disciplined, and egalitarian democracy. Hopkins called him "Uncle Joe," and this nickname stuck until the Allied victory. From his point of view, the only real danger for the United

States and the rest of the world would be the death of Stalin—he said so many times.

The role of Harry Hopkins three years later at the incredible "summit" conference in September 1944 between Roosevelt and Churchill on Canadian soil, which bore the code name Quebec II, is known to very few people in France or elsewhere. The object of the conference was crucial: to decide, after the liberation of France and just before the Allied victory on all fronts, on the creation of a Germany purged of all traces of nazism. This key problem had already been studied by the staffs of the two secretaries directly concerned, Cordell Hull at the State Department and Henry Stimson at the Pentagon.

Harry Hopkins had obtained from Roosevelt that Hull and Stimson, along with their closest advisers, should not make the journey to Quebec. On board the presidential aircraft, U.S. *One,* there were only present, in addition to Roosevelt, Henry Morgenthau, the secretary of state for the Treasury, and his personal assistant, Harry Dexter White, who brought along a seven-page plan for the "pastoralization" of Germany, which he had drawn up and to which Roosevelt had given his approval by signing it with his usual formula, "OK FDR." Before even this plan was submitted to Churchill on a take-it-or-leave-it basis, Harry Dexter White's text had been transmitted to Stalin via Canada.

The plan stipulated the total destruction of German industry, the flooding of all the mines, and the transformation of the whole country into an agricultural state. It also called for the execution without trial of all Nazis who had held important posts under the Third Reich.

Churchill was horrified by this plan, which he described as barbarous, and began by rejecting it out of hand. But he was finally compelled to agree to it when Morgenthau threw into the scales the famous $6.5 billion loan, which Britain needed desperately for survival and the repayment of her war debts.

I think few modern historians in France know of the determined battle waged by two great American statesmen, Henry Stimson and Cordell Hull, after Roosevelt's return from his extravagant journey to Canada to get him to go back on the plan. After three weeks' struggle, in a final meeting with Cordell Hull, Roosevelt agreed to put away this dangerous document and consign it to the limbo of history. To both these great Americans, our country, France, owes her salvation from the deadly prospect of becoming, on the morrow of the German capitulation in May 1945, a neighbor of a Soviet Union dominant from the Urals to Alsace-Lorraine.

Henry Stimson was a great personality. He had a long and brilliant political career. Secretary for war before the United States joined the struggle against Imperial Germany in 1917, then secretary of state under Herbert

Hoover (1929–1933),[7] he was asked in 1940 by Roosevelt, owing to his great prestige, to return to office. He had the habit of noting all important data in his personal agenda. Thus, on September 9 and 11, 1944, he made the following entry: "I have been much troubled by the President's physical condition. He was distinctly not himself Saturday. He has a cold and seemed tired out." (Sept. 9.)

"I am particularly troubled that he is going up there [to Quebec] without any real preparation for the solution and the underlying and fundamental problem of how to treat Germany." (Sept. 11.)

The conclusion of the two thick volumes of memoirs written by Cordell Hull is fascinating. He relates the tough battle he had with the president at their last dramatic meeting on October 1, 1944. It was to be his farewell meeting with Franklin Roosevelt. Worn out by the struggle, he handed in his resignation.

Here is the final sentence of his memoirs, which confirms how deeply shaken he was by the whole episode: "My conversation with the President on October 1 was the last I had in his office. At that time, I was on the verge of collapse, and had to resign."

Cordell Hull's closing chapter is revealing of the tragedy that nearly struck France, Europe, and the world.

I would like to conclude this record of facts corroborated by official documents with a last thought:

Josée had only needed four hours, during that sinister evening at the Ritz in the spring of 1940, to discover the real personality of Harry Hopkins, while I myself had had no inkling of the kind of man he really was during my relations with him over four years in New York before the war.

She took no part in writing these recollections, and it is to Her, who never let me down, that I dedicate them.

---

[7] I got to know him personally during that period.

Appendixes

ROOSEVELT'S OWN LIST
OF 23 LEADING AMERICANS

He wrote it on a cablegram blank and handed it to
René de Chambrun, saying, "These are the people
to see." A wartime episode told for the first time

(Copyright, 1948)

ON A *Friday night eight
years ago, aboard the
yacht* Potomac, *the President of the United States
tore off a cable blank.
He wrote, hurriedly, the
names of the 23 Ameri-
cans who jumped first to
his mind as the most im-
portant figures . in this
country. The story behind that cable blank,
reproduced here for the first time, is told below.
The words, taken from official records now in
Paris, are those of René de Chambrun, who was
rushed to Washington from Paris by Ambassador William Bullitt in the eventful days during
the fall of France.*

WHEN the "blitzkrieg" began on May 10,
1940, I was appointed Liaison Officer
to the 10 divisions of the British Expeditionary Corps. During the Flanders campaign
most of my time was spent examining the
crews of German bombers brought down by
the British anti-aircraft guns.

Numerous interrogations led me to form
the following conclusion: "German aviation,
strong enough to overwhelm France, was no
longer able to mount a mass attack against
Great Britain whose pursuit force was growing stronger and stronger."

From Dunkirk I was evacuated to London,
then to Paris, arriving at the end of May.
The first person I saw there was U. S. Ambassador William Bullitt. I told him that
although it was impossible not to foresee the
defeat of France, I felt certain that Great
Britain would hold out until final victory.

Flight to the U. S.

MR. BULLITT asked whether I would be willing to go at once to Washington to explain
this situation to President Roosevelt. Within
an hour, at Ambassador Bullitt's request, I
was appointed by the French Government as
Special Military Attaché to Washington, and
instructed to leave immediately for the
United States. My Clipper, delayed by bad
weather and engine trouble, arrived in New
York on June 13.

President Roosevelt's secretary, Miss
Le Hand, summoned me to Washington where,

The text of an article by René de Chambrun in the June 20, 1948, *Los Angeles Times*
"This Week" magazine section. The original layout of the article had photographs
of the 23 persons named on the list surrounding the text on the second page. A
photo of Franklin Roosevelt's list appears as exhibit 2 on page 71..

CHAMBRUN, descendant of Lafayette, honorary citizen of U.S., husband of Laval's daughter Josée, member of Paris and N. Y. bars.

she said, the President was waiting to take me with him for a week-end cruise on his yacht, the *Potomac*, so we could talk in an atmosphere of tranquillity. Those who attended this week-end cruise were Harry Hopkins, Secretary of Commerce and adviser of the President; Mr. and Mrs. W. Averell Harriman; Miss Le Hand and myself. The cruise, which began Friday afternoon, was to end on Sunday evening.

As long as I live I will never forget the hours which followed. The weather was very warm. As dusk fell and we were seated on the after deck of the boat, radiograms kept coming in, informing the President of the situation in France.

Shortly after dinner, a dispatch was brought informing the President that German forces had already crossed the Seine and were marching toward the Loire. He seemed very depressed and his arms fell along the sides of his swivel chair, as he said, "René, the show is over," adding with a deep sigh, "I don't think' that Great Britain can hold out."

Thereupon I answered that, unhappily for us I believed he was right about France but that I was unable to share his opinion about Great Britain. "That is what Bill Bullitt says you're going to tell me about," he said. "Tell me what you have in mind."

Immediately I started on my long tale, which I later condensed in a memorandum I wrote for the President, at the White House, during the nights of June 16 and 17. As I went on with my story it became more and more obvious that the President was beginning to agree with my reasoning and this in turn made me more confident.

Finally, the President said, "René, do you know you have convinced me," and after a moment's reflection he added: "I am going to ask you to undertake a big job, and that is to convince this country."

To this I replied: "This job seems practically impossible, as there are 130,000,000 Americans and they all seem to have decided in the past few days that Germany has won the war."

The President smiled and said: "What I am going to ask you to do is not so difficult as what you have just done." He then sent for the ship's Captain and told him he wished to get back to Washington the next day instead of Sunday.

Truman's Not Listed

THEN he explained to Hopkins and Miss Le Hand that he wanted a list of the most influential people in the United States — Congressmen, industrialists, labor leaders, publishers, etc. He himself started it by reaching for one of the ship's cable blanks. Rapidly, he wrote the 23 names that leaped first into his mind.

Later that evening and early next morning, the list was expanded. The President asked me if I was ready to hold out for three days and nights. He asked me to see these persons one by one.

"Harry Hopkins and Miss Le Hand will organize the meetings for you," he added, "and I want you to tell each person exactly what you have just told me, no more, no less."

He then told me why it was essential that this job be accomplished at the earliest possible moment because there were at that time, in the port of New York, 450 fighter planes, 500,000 rifles, several thousand antiaircraft and antitank guns which had previously been ordered by France and Great Britain.

Isolationism Was Spreading

BUT the German victory on French soil had caused a wave of pessimism and isolationism throughout the United States and the Government had decided to retain in the country this war material, which constituted about all the available supply. It was thought in official circles that this material would not reach Great Britain in time to help, and that America might find herself wholly disarmed following a German invasion of the British Isles.

Said the President: "I want you to convince the political leaders and the Cabinet
members that this war material must be
sent at once to Great Britain without any
delay."

We reached Washington at about four
o'clock on Saturday afternoon, and I went
straight to work.

At the Mayflower Hotel and at the White
House, day and night, I held interviews
with 87 persons and told each one the same
facts I had told the President. Every hour
and every meal was disposed of by Miss
Le Hand and Harry Hopkins. On Monday
the seventeenth, I was invited to luncheon
by the Foreign Relations Committee of the
U. S. Senate. I also spoke individually to
each member of the Cabinet which was to
meet the next day.

Confidential Report

DURING the same evening I prepared for
the President a strictly confidential report
of which only two originals were typed at
the White House. I have kept one, which
bears President Roosevelt's pencil marks.
He made only one correction: where I had
written "to prevent Germany from dominating the world," the President scratched
out the word "Germany" and wrote "the
Nazis."

This report was read to the members of
the Cabinet and it was decided by the
United States Government that all available war material would be sent to Great
Britain.

(Editor's note: The list reproduced
on page four is exactly as FDR wrote it.
He misspelled General Knudsen's name
— with a "t" instead of a "d." He
checked the names he wanted either
Miss Le Hand or Harry Hopkins to contact. Hopkins wrote the "Joe" after
Patterson to indicate that it was the
publisher, not the government official.

It's ironic that the name of Harry
Truman, then a Senator, does not
appear. The list contains four Cabinet
members, three other high government
officials, one Supreme Court Justice,
seven members of Congress, two labor
leaders, one publisher, two businessmen, one mayor, FDR's military aide
— "Pa" Watson, and one woman —
"Mrs. F.D.R.")

Duplicate of Report for
President Roosevelt[1]

CONFIDENTIAL

Washington, June 17th, 1940.

—:—:—:—:—:—:—:—:—

The following impressions are based upon observations which I was able to make between the day when the German attack began on May 10, 1940, and the fifth of June. I acted as liaison officer between the group of French armies (Seventh, First and Ninth) and the divisions of the British Expeditionary Force which were placed under the command of General Blanchard.

During the campaign of Flanders I spent most of my time attempting to establish liaison between General Blanchard and the British divisions, hampered as I was, owing to all roads in Belgium being blocked by the fleeing refugees. (Incidentally, this exodus was "organized" methodically in every village by agents of the German Fifth Column). I was able to examine many members of the crews of German bombers brought down either in Belgium or in France in the sectors of these British divisions. Owing to the impracticability of communicating between units, I informed only General Weygand of the result of the following investigations when I was in Paris just before taking the Clipper to fly to the United States.

On May 10th the German bombing force (i.e. excluding fighting and reconnaissance planes) was comprised of nine thousand planes, all of which were placed before the attack on innumerable fields throughout German territory. To explain the importance of the initial air attack and its subsequent repercussions, I will quote from the testimony given by one of the lieutenants acting as aircraft commander, who was brought down on the morning of May 10th. His testimony was corroborated by two or three other prisoners.

Question: Where were you during the evening of May 9th?
Answer: I was at airport No.127a, a few miles south of Charlottenburg..

---

[1]Photographs of the first and last pages of this document appear following the transcript.

Question: How many planes were there on that particular field?
Answer: Eighteen bombers, that is to say, two squadrons.

Question: Who commanded the squadrons?
Answer: Either captains or majors.

Question: When did you receive your orders?
Answer: At midnight (ninth-tenth of May) our captain received
           the orders to fly my squadron, that is to say, nine
           bombers, to airport No.65b.

Question: Did you know where this airport was situated?
Answer: No.

Question: How did you learn where it was situated?
Answer: A few minutes before we took off an itinerary of the
           flight was given to each pilot.

Question: When did you reach airport No.65b.?
Answer: At three o'clock in the morning, May 10th.

Question: What happened there?
Answer: Thirty-six small calibre bombs were loaded on each
           plane. Each plane was refueled, and we received orders
           to go and bomb the railroad stations of La Bassee and
           the airport of Lille.

Question: Did you know that Belgium and Holland were being
           invaded at that time?
Answer: No.

Question: Did you know that other raids were taking place?
Answer: No.

The other interrogations and the information received by the Royal Air
Force and the French military command went to show that five thousand
bombers had been put into the air on that particular morning in order to
bomb Holland, Belgium and France. The total losses sustained by the
German Air Force during those raids, which according to the German
expectations—as subsequently disclosed by officers captured after May
10th—should not have exceeded some fifty to eighty planes, were 342 ships
officially brought down. These five thousand planes represented the first-
line planes with the best trained crews; there were at that time four thousand bombers in reserve, but there were not four thousand reserve crews
in Germany sufficiently trained to be used.

Ever since this first huge onslaught, the number of objectives to be attacked became progressively fewer as the toll of German aircraft brought down by the French and British air forces increased. Starting on the 20th of May, I found that the Germans had begun to use their reserve planes, which were not as modern as the first-line planes; some of them even lacked certain equipment, such as watches and flight instruments, etc. . . The morale of the reserve crews was far from good, and their training had obviously been very scanty. Some of these men had only from fifty to eighty hours of actual flight. As the Germans were forced to use 1936–1937 model bombers with inadequately prepared crews, and as the first line crews became fatigued by their constant raids, the effectiveness of the Allied fighters became greater and greater. At the beginning of the campaign they were able to bring down an average of two German planes to every one British plane lost. During the last days, when they began to make use of the Defiant planes, that average increased in the favor of the British to four and five planes to one. When German bombers made a formidable effort on Calais, Boulogne, Dunkirk, it was interesting to observe that they did not have enough bombers to complete the task on the other side of the Channel at Dover and Folkestone.

The effectiveness of the action of British fighters is getting greater and greater as an increasing number of Spitfires and Defiants are being produced. The last aerial encounter which I saw before leaving the French coast was between three squadrons of Heinkels (27 planes) and six Defiant planes. Twenty Heinkels were brought down without one single British loss.

A few days later the Germans put into the first line all of their available aircraft, and they were only able to organize one raid of 155 bombers over Paris, of which twenty-seven were brought down. Losses sustained were well over three thousand when I left France. The official figure of German losses for the first twelve days of the campaign, communicated to me confidentially by the Royal Air Force when I was in London, was 1,487 bombers brought down by the Royal Air Force *behind* the Allied lines. This figure did not take into account French figures, nor enemy planes brought down behind German lines. We do not know, of course, the figures for bombers destroyed on the ground in Germany and occupied Belgium and Holland. To these figures one should, of course, add the wear and tear, ships partly destroyed, etc. When I left Paris, I was informed at the French headquarters by General Weygand that a message had been captured by the French second bureau, sent by Goering to the superior officers, not to be communicated to noncommissioned officers or men, of the German Air Force, urging them to hold out for a few more days despite the severe losses they had suffered.

All the above and many other details which I observed point to the conclusion that the German bombing force, while not destroyed, is no longer, on account of the scarcity of trained crews, in a position to deliver a decisive blow to the British Empire.

As far as large scale attacks on Great Britain are concerned, the following observations should be made:

1. The morale of the Royal Air Force fighters is extraordinary. While certain reservations can be made with reference to the ability of the British infantry and artillery to fight the Germans on land, the pilots are far superior to the German pilots. They like their jobs, and they know they have the best equipment.

2. While it was difficult for Great Britain to use many fighters to protect France (the number of fighters of the advance striking force under the orders of the French command was about 25% of the total of the number of fighters retained in England), today all the fighters which can only stay in the air for one-half to one and one-half hours because of the weight of armament and consumption of fuel, are protecting in a most efficacious way the vital objectives in Great Britain.

3. The output of fighters is increasing every day in Great Britain.

4. The Dunkirk experience, where practically all the German strength was employed to prevent traffic in one single small port, shows that it will be very difficult, if not impossible, for the German air force to bottle up all the British sea ports. One must remember that in Dunkirk during five days and five nights, despite continuous raids, ships came with food and munitions and left with 335,000 men. Moreover, the British fighters which were based on airports on the British side of the Channel brought down an average of some seventy-five to one hundred bombers a day over Dunkirk.

5. As against the British Isles and the British Empire, the objectives of the German bombers are innumerable (all the ports and industrial centers, Leeds, Glasgow, Sheffield, Birmingham, London, Canada, Australia, South Africa, etc.) whereas the Ruhr, comprised of over twenty million inhabitants engaged in making war materials, concentrated in an area seventy miles square, is the greatest target for bombing in the world. Moreover, the people of the Ruhr, who are mostly Rhinelanders and not Prussians, do not possess the warlike morale of the latter, and we know in France that the small raids made over this district have already produced a very great moral effect and caused material damage, which explains one of the reasons why Hitler has to win this war very quickly. Before I sailed, the local German radio stations were constantly sending appeals to the civil population of the Ruhr for calm and confidence, stating that although the people

of Germany were suffering, their hardships were far less than those of the British and French peoples.

Were Great Britain to have at her disposal an ever increasing number of bombers, and destroyers, for her convoys of food supplies, I believe that the effect of continuous raids on the Ruhr (while the German Government would have to explain the reasons for not attaining the immediate victory over Great Britain which they have announced), might well prove decisive.

I do not envisage the possibility of a direct attack by the German forces against the British Isles because

a) of the decreased power of the German air striking force and the effectiveness of Great Britain's air defense;

b) of the weakness of the German fleet as compared to the British Home Fleet;

c) of the power of the action of coastal batteries which was shown in Norway where four old Norwegian guns destroyed two German cruisers before the Home Fleet entered into action.

The British Empire is, in my mind, very far from being beaten for the following reasons:

1. Historical—Hitler controls today one-half of Europe and has not yet reached the British Isles; Napoleon controlled the whole of Europe and was incapable of defeating Great Britain, which, then, did not have the power she has today;

2. Preparedness—Great Britain is now just beginning to feel the possibility of defeat. All her industries which were not ready for war on September 3rd are just now swinging into production. She is not tired like Germany by a campaign of several years of production on a severe wartime basis.

3. While France was fighting *for* Great Britain and fatiguing the German war machine, Great Britain was getting ready, and today, after France's Army's defeat and nine months of war, Great Britain, whose empire is comprised of 400,000,000 men, has sustained only extremely minor losses, to wit: 35,000 men, that is to say a total of only two divisions (prisoners, wounded, or killed). These losses are less than those of the Dutch. (It is not known in this country that the British Expeditionary Force lost only 1,200 men in Norway). On the other hand, the Home Fleet has only lost two airplane carriers, one battleship, a few cruisers, and about thirty destroyers, and ten sub-

marines. (Incidentally the British must replace those thirty destroyers). To attack the British Empire successfully, the Germans would
have to employ a great air force, which they no longer have, and a
considerable fleet. In this connection, it is my opinion that the Italian
Fleet will not help Germany in the Atlantic. The fleet was built in
order to operate in the Mediterranean (bases, equipment, etc. . .).
Moreover, the Mediterranean is the "Mare Nostrum" of Italy, and I
do not believe that Italy's dictator, who needs his fleet to control the
Mediterranean, will place it at Hitler's disposal in the Atlantic. One
must not lose sight of the fact that the war is not won for the Axis in
the Mediterranean, where Great Britain can offer a great resistance to
Italy. The Arabs, who are all sympathetic to France and hate the
Italians, constitute a considerable strength along the African coast
where Italy has her colonial problem. Moreover, she will have to take
into account the strength and ambitions of Russia, which will doubtless move into action before long, and even Turkey, etc.

Should the European people, particularly the French, acquire the feeling
that, given adequate assistance from the United States, Great Britain will
not yield to Germany, they will, by their active or passive resistance to the
sixty million Germans be able to play their part in the struggle of all the
forces which today, as in 1918, are consciously or unconsciously fighting
to prevent Germany from dominating the world.

Washington June 17th
[signed]
René de Chambrun.

Washington, June 17th, 1940.

DUPLICATE OF REPORT FOR PRESIDENT ROOSEVELT.

-:-:-:-:-:-:-:-:-:-:-

The following impressions are based upon observations which I was able to make between the day when the German attack began on May 10, 1940, and the fifth of June. I acted as liaison officer between the group of French armies (Seventh, First and Ninth) and the divisions of the British Expeditionary Force which were placed under the command of General Blanchard.

During the campaign of Flanders I spent most of my time attempting to establish liaison between General Blanchard and the British divisions, hampered as I was, owing to all roads in Belgium being blocked by the fleeing refugees. (Incidentally, this exodus was "organized" methodically in every village by agents of the German Fifth Column). I was able to examine many members of the crews of German bombers brought down either in Belgium or in France in the sectors of these British divisions. Owing to the impracticability of communicating between units, I informed only General Weygand of the result of the following investigations when I was in Paris just before taking the Clipper to fly to the United States.

On May 10th the German bombing force (i.e. excluding fighting and reconnaissance planes) was comprised of nine thousand planes, all of which were placed before the attack on innumerable fields throughout German territory. To explain the importance of the initial air attack and its subsequent repercussions, I will quote from the testimony given by one of the lieutenants acting as aircraft commander, who was brought down on the morning of May 10th. His testimony was corroborated by two or three other prisoners.

Question : Where were you during the evening of May 9th ?

Answer   : I was at airport No.127a, a few miles south of Charlottenburg.

Question : How many planes were there on that particular field ?

Answer   : Eighteen bombers, that is to say, two squadrons.

Question : Who commanded the squadrons ?

Answer   : Either captains or majors.

Question : When did you receive your orders ?

Answer   : At midnight (ninth-tenth of May) our captain received the orders to fly my squadron, that is to say, nine bombers, to airport No.65b.

Question : Did you know where this airport was situated ?

Answer   : No.

Question : How did you learn where it was situated ?

......./

(5)

Empire successfully, the Germans would have to employ a
great air force, which they no longer have, and a considerable
fleet. In this connection, it is my opinion that the Italian
Fleet will not help Germany in the Atlantic. The fleet was
built in order to operate in the Mediterranean (bases, equipment, etc...). Moreover, the Mediterranean is the "Mare Nostrum"
of Italy, and I do not believe that Italy's dictator, who needs
his fleet to control the Mediterranean, will place it at Hitler's
disposal in the Atlantic. One must not lose sight of the fact
that the war is not won for the Axis in the Mediterranean, where
Great Britain can offer a great resistance to Italy. The Arabs,
who are all sympathetic to France and hate the Italians, constitute a considerable strength along the African coast where Italy
has her colonial problem. Moreover, she will have to take into
account the strength and ambitions of Russia, which will doubtless move into action before long, and even Turkey, etc.

Should the European people, particularly the French, acquire
the feeling that, given adequate assistance from the United States,
Great Britain will not yield to Germany, they will, by their active
or passive resistance to the sixty million Germans be able to play
their part in the struggle of all the forces which today, as in
1918, are consciously or unconsciously fighting to prevent Germany
from dominating the world.

                                   Washington June 17th

                                   René de Chambrun.

Excerpts from René de Chambrun's Twenty-nine-page Statement to Judge Marchat made on February 19, 1946

Your Honor,

You have asked me for an account of my activities during the years which preceded and followed France's entry into the war (September 3rd, 1939). This account will deal with four periods:

I From 1930 to September 3rd, 1939, during which time I practised as an international lawyer both in New York and in Paris, and founded the French Information Center in New York.

II From September 3rd, 1939 to June 1940: the beginning of the war until the defeat of France.

III From June 1940 to March 1941, when I made trips to the United States and carried out two tasks requested of me by President Roosevelt.

IV From March 1941: my return to France and my activities during the German occupation.

PART I

After graduating from the Ecole Libre des Sciences Politiques, the University of Paris and the Paris Law School with a doctor's degree, I became a member of the Paris Bar and went to the United States, where I worked from 1930 to 1934–1935.

As an honorary citizen of Maryland, I passed my New York State Bar

---

My twenty-nine-page report to the Chief Investigating Magistrate of the "Cour de Justice", which I drew up with the help of two stenographers in twenty-four hours, in order to be placed under house arrest instead of going to jail, appears in full in the French edition of this book, in the shape of a photograph of the signed carbon copy of the original handed over to the Judge and now deposited in the National Archives.

Mr. Hargove has translated verbatim the portions dealing with my activities immediately preceding World War II (Part I) and after my return to France in March 1941 to protect American institutions in Paris (Part IV). Between Part I and Part IV, he has chosen a few excerpts from the narration I made for the first time to the judge after four years of silence.

Examinations and was admitted to practice law in the State of New York . . . (Page 1 of the original)

. . . While in America, I lived the ordinary life of any American citizen, remaining passionately attached to France, my native land. In those days, our country was often criticized in the United States. We had huge gold reserves. Many thought that we were overarmed and expressed the view that we acted too harshly with Germany. Practically alone among the French citizens residing in the United States, I publicly denounced German underground activities and constantly warned Americans of them in personal conversations, press interviews and radio talks. I am attaching to this statement the printed text of a radio broadcast which I delivered in New York on March 22, 1933, explaining France's military position and denouncing Hitler's policy of wholesale and clandestine rearmament. (See Exhibit No. 1).

I carried on my law practice with the firm of Davis, Polk, Wardwell, Gardiner & Reed, whose senior partner, John W. Davis, former democratic nominee for President in the 1924 election, is today President of the American Bar Association.

My experience during those years convinced me that there was a great need in the United States for an institution which could supply the American public and press with true and accurate information about France. So when I returned to Paris, I founded the French Information Center. By creating this organization, I hoped to neutralize the influence of German propaganda in the United States. The French Information Center which was a strictly private institution without any political ties either in France or in the United States, was approved and sponsored by the highest authorities in all walks of life on both sides of the Atlantic. (Page 2 of the original)

It was granted a charter by the Board of Regents of the State of New York and it proved a success from the start. As a result of this work, I was awarded the Legion of Honor for "exceptional services rendered to the cause of France in the United States" . . . (First 5 lines of Page 3 of the original)

PART II

. . . On August 24, 1939, I was called up with the rank of Lieutenant to join the 162nd Regiment of Infantry, then garrisoned at Metz. During the first few months of the war, I was stationed in the Maginot Line; and in January 1940, was appointed liaison officer to the British Army. I asked to remain at the front rather than be sent to headquarters at Arras. I remained in Lorraine and volunteered as instructor of the British Brigades each of which was sent to the front for a period of one or two weeks in the Sierck-Bouzonville sector. My appointment to the rank of captain came at a time when promotion was rare. . .

. . . When the "Blitzkrieg" began, on May 10, I was appointed liaison officer between General Blanchard's army and the ten divisions of the British Expeditionary Corps. During the Flanders campaign, most of my time was spent interrogating crew members of the German bombers brought down by the British anti-aircraft guns over the sectors of these British divisions. The numerous interrogations I supervised led me to form the following conclusions:

> The German Air Force which had been strong enough to overwhelm France was no longer powerful enough to sustain a mass attack against Great Britain, which had kept at home a strong combat force growing stronger as the war continued.

I was evacuated from Dunkirk to London and flown from London to Paris where I arrived in the last days of May. The first person I saw upon my arrival was the U.S. Ambassador William Bullitt. I told him that although I foresaw a French defeat, I felt absolutely certain that Britain would hold out until final victory. Mr. Bullitt asked whether it would be possible for me to go to Washington at once in order to explain this situation to President Roosevelt, who, he said, was extremely preoccupied by the evolution of the war. I replied I would be glad to go. He talked with President Paul Reynaud and General Weygand, and at the Ambassador's request, I was appointed by the French Government Assistant Military Attaché to the United States, and instructed to leave immediately for Washington, bearing a private message from the President of the Republic, Albert Lebrun, to President Roosevelt. After calling upon General Weygand, I left Paris . . . (Page 4 of the original)

PART III

After describing the beginning of the weekend cruise on the "Potomac" with President Roosevelt and his decision to turn back immediately to Washington:

. . . We reached Washington at about 4.00 o'clock on Saturday afternoon, and I went straight to work. Never before in my life did I work so hard at one stretch practically without interruption. At the White House and at the Mayflower Hotel, I talked with 87 persons during the day . . . and part of the night and next day, telling each one the same story.

The mornings often began with an early breakfast with Lord Lothian, the British Ambassador, or with Casey, the Australian Minister. Every hour and every meal was taken up with appointments arranged by Miss LeHand and Harry Hopkins. On Monday the 17th, I was invited to luncheon by the Foreign Affairs Committee of the United States Senate. I also spoke individually to each member of the Cabinet which was to meet the next day.

A press conference had been arranged by the White House Press Secretary, when I made a statement which appeared in the leading American newspapers, denouncing German methods of warfare and expressing absolute confidence in a British victory. (I am attaching a photocopy of the New York Times of June 18th, quoting my words and marked Exhibit V) . . . (Page 8 . . .)

After my long trip in the Prairies and back to Washington:
 . . . When reading this account of the events about which I am writing for the first time after years of silence, a question may arise in your Honor's mind: why after the defeat of France did I enlist with such enthusiasm in the cause of Britain? My motive was simple: a few weeks before leaving France, I had witnessed the rush of millions of Dutch, Belgian and French people desperately fleeing south into what was known as the "free zone". I wondered with anxiety how these millions of refugees would be kept from starvation if the Government failed to obtain from the Germans their mass repatriation before the winter. Even in normal times, the southern part of France was not rich enough to feed its indigenous population without outside help. I had one obsession: to get America to ship food to southern France in order to relieve the distress of these people. Alas! The fate of France did not, at that time, seem to be of much concern to American public opinion. News from our country had suddenly disappeared from news headlines. The eyes of a small pro-German minority were focused on the victories of the Wehrmacht and those of the great majority of the American people were turned towards the British Isles. It was difficult to interest Americans in the problems of France. André Tardieu, who knew America well, wrote in 1925: "Before attempting to negotiate an alliance with America, one must prove oneself". How prophetic these words seemed to me in the dark days of June 1940! I thought at that time that if I were able to carry out successfully the task which Franklin Roosevelt had assigned to me, I might interest him in sending food to France the problem that was uppermost on my mind. And that is why I did what I could to help the cause of Britain . . . (End of Page 11 and Page 12 . . .)

After summing up my conversations with Roosevelt and Lothian of August 1 and

*Roosevelt's request for me to go immediately back to France to propose to Marshal
Pétain the conditions for the shipments of food supplies to the unoccupied zone:*

. . . I had already spoken several times to Ambassador Lothian and to
Casey about my idea. The Ambassador had approved my plan. He told me
one day that, in his opinion, a gesture by Britain in granting *navicerts* for
such a humanitarian objective would favorably impress American opinion.
When I saw him again that same evening with Harry Hopkins, both told
me I could inform the Marshal that the shipments would be authorized,
provided the amounts were reasonable and the ships which were to carry
these supplies were of light tonnage. I sincerely believe that day was the
happiest in my whole life.

Before taking leave of the Ambassador, I asked him for an introduction
to the authorities in Bermuda in order to avoid delay or difficulties on my
way to or from France. He sent me a diplomatic visa and also a handwritten
letter. Following is the text of this letter:

Washington, August 9, 1940.

Dear Captain de Chambrun,

I take pleasure in sending you a diplomatic visa for your safe return to
your country together with a letter of introduction to the Governor of
Bermuda.

I am pleased to report to you that it has been my privilege in the past
weeks to inform His Majesty's Government of the splendid work you
accomplished in Washington and throughout the United States to support
the cause for which the British Empire is fighting. Practically single-
handed, you were able to sway official opinion over here in favor of my
country. Your amazingly energetic action in the dark days of June was
providential and inspiring to us all. You were able to find at the right time
the arguments and words which convinced the highest authorities of
America and the Committee of Foreign Affairs of the United States
Senate.

For all this, I want you to rest assured that Great Britain will never
forget what you did for her in her days of plight and distress.

Wishing you a happy and successful voyage, I beg to remain,

Faithfully yours,
Lothian.

. . . I gave your Honor yesterday, for the first time, details of my conversation with Marshal Pétain which lasted the whole morning. He accepted at once President Roosevelt's suggestions. He summoned Baudouin and
ordered him to refrain from any criticism of Britain. He asked me to invite
American newspaper correspondents at 4.00 o'clock that afternoon to the

Pavillon Sévigné. He told me to order champagne and Reims biscuits for them and added jokingly: "This is the first time in my life that I have ever held a press conference". Together, we wrote a statement along the lines of the one which had been prepared by President Roosevelt. He read out the statement to the American correspondents. I am attaching as Exhibits VII and VIII photocopies of the "New York Herald" and "New York Times" of August 21st, commenting upon the Marshal's statement. (Pages 16, 17 and 18 . . .)

After my return to New York, I reported to the Judge as follows:
    . . . Upon my arrival at the Ritz Hotel in New York, accompanied this time by my wife, I at once phoned the White House to find out whether I was to go down immediately to Washington. Miss LeHand told me that Harry Hopkins, upon learning of my arrival, had flown to New York to see me and would be at the Ritz in an hour or two. The three of us dined together.
    I was to experience a tragic disappointment. After a few opening words, Hopkins informed me that the President had been obliged to give up his plan of shipping supplies to France: Winston Churchill, upon General de Gaulle's insistence that the blockade should be enforced, had changed his mind. I argued, in vain, that the President had made a treaty with Marshal Pétain, of which I had been the instrument, and that it seemed only natural to me that the shipment of food to France should be made a condition of the supply of arms to Britain. Our conversation lasted several hours, but it seemed to me as though I were battering against a brick wall. Harry Hopkins made it clear that the President's decision was final and that there was no point in my seeing him. I therefore sent Marshal Pétain's letter to the President by registered mail with a request for a receipt. I was never to see President Roosevelt again. I am attaching to this memorandum a photocopy of the New York post office receipt for this letter. . . .
    . . . On October 17th, I was one of the first to volunteer for the selective draft which was to constitute the nucleus of the future American army.
    Thanks to the splendid work carried out by the Red Cross, the Quakers, and the "Paquet au Front" ("Parcels to the Front"), and to the appeals of President Hoover and other Republican leaders, a limited amount of food was sent to our country. I made speeches in and around New York and confess that with deep sadness I found my action was undermined by French citizens in America who had failed to enlist, when their year was called up on September 1, 1939, and who out of the blue began, with Harry Hopkins and others, to spread the slogan: "No food for Europe. Enforce the blockade". Some even went so far as to demand without success that the constitutional law of the State of Maryland granting American citizen-

ship to General de Lafayette and all his descendants be abolished because of my activities.

It was then that I resolved that my duty was to be in France. Before I sailed, I was asked on every side to do all in my power to safeguard American institutions in Paris in the event of the United States going to war.

My last meal was dinner at the Waldorf in the company of former President Hoover. His sympathy and understanding for the misfortunes of France and his personal kindness touched me so deeply that I was strongly tempted to reveal to him what I am now disclosing for the first time. I resisted the temptation and remained silent.

Should your Honor wish to have my personal opinion on these events, I would say this: President Roosevelt is dead. I respect his memory. I am convinced his good faith was abused in this whole affair. Of Harry Hopkins, I cannot say the same. I have proof that he instigated a press campaign against me in the United States alleging that I, who had worked all my life for France and America, and in the dark days of June 1940 for Britain also, "had sold myself to the Nazis". I demonstrated to your Honor how he did everything in his power to harm me through an agent in France who, as your Honor knows, instigated a judicial investigation which was carried out a few months ago. (From Pages 21, 22, 23 and 1st Par. of Page 24 . . .)

PART IV

Pages 24, 25, 26, 27, 28 and 29 corresponding to PART IV are quoted in full.

I returned to my office in Paris on March 1, 1941, and worked there unremittingly until the Liberation of France. I had gladly volunteered to defend the American institutions and, in addition, the interests of many of my French and American clients who were soon in trouble. My first visit upon arriving in Paris was to the President of the Bar Association, Jacques Charpentier who, I understand, informed your Honor that he had specifically instructed me to have whatever contacts were necessary with the German authorities, in order to defend those American interests. He also authorized me (which was against the old rules of our Bar) to conceal in my office and my home private papers and valuables belonging to French and American friends and fellow lawyers.

Among my preoccupations was the safeguard of the American Hospital at Neuilly. My father, General de Chambrun, was President of this institution, one of the most modern and best equipped in Paris. It would be too long to relate all the difficulties we met with, time and again, to prevent the requisition of the buildings, beds, sheets, bandages, medical supplies, etc. The hospital took care of all the Americans remaining in Paris and of the American and British citizens released from the internment camps of

Vittel and Compiègne because of ill health. Thousands of repatriated French prisoners of war were also given treatment at the hospital. (I am attaching as Exhibit X a letter from the Marquis de Mun, President of the French Red Cross, describing what I did for the American Hospital and the Red Cross).

The safeguarding of the American Library in Paris proved more difficult. My mother, a Charter member of the Board and by birth an American citizen, was obliged to remain alone in charge of this institution where she went every day in spite of transport difficulties. The Library contained over one hundred thousand books in English which were *in principle* banned by Goebbels' edicts. Had the Library been closed, its valuable books would have been removed to Germany and its male staff would have been deported. The book circulation increased month by month between June 1943 and June 1944. Every week, a secret session of the Acting Committee of the French Information Center, composed solely of friends of the United States, took place at my office or at my home. We were able to finance the library until the Liberation. (I am attaching as Exhibit XI a letter signed by the members of the Acting Committee of the Center showing how we were able to save the American Library).

I also took charge of the American Protestant Churches and of the Cathedral in the crypt of which were bodies of the Americans who died during the Occupation. I made arrangements for the American flag to be placed upon each coffin at funeral services. (I am attaching as Exhibit XII Dean Beekman's letter confirming these points).

I arranged to have supplies sent to Compiègne where French and American civilians were interned. These supplies were purchased by my wife who visited the managers of the three or four Paris department stores who were friends of hers. She personally bought a large amount of supplies which had been hidden from the French and the Germans and arranged to have these delivered periodically to the Camp of Compiègne through the Red Cross and the "Assistance Sanitaire Automobile." It seems superfluous to dwell upon the help I was able to give to all the prisoners who had escaped from Germany and whose testimony is before your Honor. (I am attaching as Exhibit XIII a letter from the Chief of Staff of the Francs-Tireurs Partisans for the Region of Paris, which shows all I was able to do for members of the Resistance).

Every time I travelled into the Unoccupied Zone, I carried two suitcases, one of which was full of papers, letters and messages which I had been asked to send over to America at my own risk. When crossing the demarcation line, the German non-commissioned officer in charge would open the door of my compartment and enquire whether I had any papers and I would answer: "Nicht Papiers." (I am attaching as Exhibit XIV a letter from John B. Robinson, Dean of the American Lawyers, who remained in Paris and who centralised the documents which it was my job to send over to America at my own risk).

Thanks to my old comradeship with René Bousquet, Secretary General at the Ministry of the Interior, (we were members of the same rugby team in our boyhood), I was able, as your Honor knows, to organize the escape of all the prisoners of my Army Corps in Lorraine who quite naturally knocked at my door after reaching Paris on their way to the Unoccupied Zone. Every one of them was given false identity papers to cross the demarcation line. But why continue to dwell upon the services which it was my privilege to render? It is true, of course, that every day, I risked my own freedom and perhaps my life, but was it not my elementary duty to do so under the circumstances? If I were to claim credit for one thing only, I would say this: under no circumstances whatever since my marriage (after 1935, my father-in-law was three times Prime Minister of France) did I take the slightest advantage of my family links with the head of Government. I believe I was one of the few members of the Paris Bar to observe, during the Occupation, the following self-imposed code of ethics.

— I never acted on behalf of a so-called "aryanized" company.
— I never counselled any person or corporation accused of engaging in the black market.
— I never acted for any firm or corporation in which there was a German minority stock interest.
— I never defended any official or semi-official organization.

In defending the French and American interests which had been entrusted to me, I never had any dealings with the German armed forces or with the German police. My contacts in the defense of the above interests were, as your Honor knows, strictly limited to the staff of the German Embassy and of Dr. Michel, whose organization controlled the so-called "Aliens Property Custody". With the exception of Ernst Achenbach and von Bose, whom I had known in Paris before the war, no German ever entered my office, as I made it a policy always to call myself at the Embassy, rue de Lille, or at the Hotel Majestic. For the purpose of defending the interests of the American Hospital, I also attended four or five official meetings organized at the Ritz by Prince de Beauvau Craon in 1942.

My activities provoked the suspicion of the German police and I was periodically attacked by collaborationist newspapers such as "Le Pilori", "Je suis Partout" and "Le Cri du Peuple" which contained, as your Honor knows, many allusions to the pro-American sentiments of the son-in-law of "a certain French political leader". (I am attaching as Exhibit XV a selection of articles which appeared against me in the collaborationist press of Paris). Yesterday, your Honor asked me to describe quite objectively the nature of my relations with my father-in-law. Nothing is easier. I admire him more than I do any other living person. He knew and approved all that I had done. He used to tell us that in the interest of France, two policies must be followed simultaneously: resistance abroad and negotiation at home. The Government in France had to sacrifice itself to defend the country and the people day in and day out against the harshness of the occupying power which was bound to grow as its military position weakens. He never wished me to have any relation with his government since 1935.

Day and night, people would knock at my door to ask for help. I never refused during the entire occupation to receive anyone, and in every serious case, I would take to my bicycle (I never possessed a circulation permit) and dash off to see whoever might be of assistance.

Since your Honor's request for a statement at very short notice, I have tried, during several hours of dictation, to give a summary of my activities during four long years. I believe it is not an overstatement to claim that during this period, I did more than my share to help Britain and used whatever ability and influence I had to protect the French and American interests which had been entrusted to me.

[Signed] René de Chambrun
February 19, 1946.

Release to Sunday Morning
Newspapers, October 27, 1940

ROOM 2940
11 WEST 42ND STREET
NEW YORK CITY
-:-
Telephone CHickering 4-6747

October 24, 1940

To the News Editor:

    The attached is for release in the Sunday
morning newspapers of October 27th.

    The text of the statement is enclosed in
full and the news story is sent only as a quick means
of acquainting editors with the nature of the material.

    Any further information may be had from
ULRIC BELL, at the above address.

PHILIP WYLIE	MARC CONNELLY
ROBERT SHERWOOD	CHRISTIAN GAUSS
VINCENT SHEEAN	STRUTHERS BURT
ELMER RICE	VAN WYCK BROOKS
HENRY PRINGLE	MAXWELL ANDERSON
EDNA ST.VINCENT MILLAY	FREDERICK·LEWIS ALLEN
LEWIS MUMFORD	HERBERT AGAR

The cover letter that was sent with the release to Sunday newspapers is shown above. The text of the release is on the following pages.

Release to:
Sunday morning newspapers,
October 27, 1940.

A group of leading American authors, poets and playwrights today implored their countrymen "to beware of the men of Vichy, who now spread the virus of totalitarianism in America."

Classifying themselves as citizens of "what was once the world-wide free republic of letters," fourteen of these literary figures asserted that many French propagandists now in this country are here as the "agents of the German government," some of them forming what amounts to a new off-shoot of the Nazi gestapo in the United States.

French Ambassador Henry-Haye and Count Rene de Chambrun, the latter the author of a volume just issued to American readers, were singled out as the principal pleaders over here for the Vichy regime. They were described as "pathetic wooden manikins" for the Nazis.

Besides asking their own readers and followers to "view the words and gestures of the men of Vichy with the suspicion they deserve," the American writers asserted that the French spokesmen here "would aid the Germans by breaking the British food blockade."

They warned the American people to reject the pleas of the French agents as pleas for steps on the path of appeasement.

The signers are: Philip Wylie: Noted novelist and author of "Fennelly Wren"; Robert Sherwood: "There Shall Be No Night," etc.; Vincent Sheean: "Personal History"; Elmer Rice: "Street Scene"; Henry Pringle: Biographer of Taft, and Pulitzer Prize Winner; Edna St. Vincent Millay: Poet; Louis Mumford: "Faith for Living"; Marc Connelly: The play "Green Pastures"; Christian Gauss: Dean of Princeton University, possessor of the French Legion of Honor and outstanding authority on French literature; Struthers Burt: Novelist, author of "Festival"; Van Wyck Brooks: "The Flowering of New England"; Maxwell Anderson: Playwright and dramatic poet, author of "Winterset"; Frederick Lewis Allen: Author of "Only Yesterday," and Associate Editor of Harper's Magazine; Herbert Agar: Author of "The People's Choice" and Pulitzer Prize Winner.

Action by the group signing this manifesto follows a demand made this week by Senator Ernest W. Gibson of Vermont calling for expulsion from this country of all diplomatic representatives of Germany, Italy, Vichy "and all others that are German puppets." Senator Gibson referred to these agents as hirelings of the dictators and asserted they were using diplomatic immunity as a cloak for vast propaganda activities.

In an added statement Edna St. Vincent Millay said, "I am against sending support or comfort in any form designed to reach the betrayed and suffering people of Europe which would naturally and without doubt fall into the hands of the pillagers of the conquered territories." Miss Millay is the author of a new sonnet "The Old Men of Vichy" which appeared in last Sunday's New York Times Magazine.

We, the undersigned writers, come before our countrymen to implore them to beware of the men of Vichy who now spread the virus of totalitarianism in America.

We belong to what was once the worldwide free republic of letters, in which the writers of France were especially close to us, because we cherished and always shall cherish the France of Voltaire and Rousseau, of Stendhal and Hugo and Flaubert, a France no less dear to us than the England of Shakespeare and Dickens. Whenever Frenchmen speak and write in the spirit of that France, they are our compatriots.

As artisans who seek to use words as the sacred tools of thought, the only kind of word having meaning for us is that issued by free men, expressing their own true feeling, without any other scruple than respect for truth and without any fear other than the fear of betraying the truth.

But today a new kind of Frenchman has appeared in our midst to play upon our traditional loyalties and friendships. He possesses the charm, the skill, the subtlety, the finesse of his predecessors; but he no longer speaks for France. He speaks for his German masters and for those politicians who have sought to cover up their weakness, degradation and even disloyalty by accepting the doctrine and policy of their masters.

Whether here of their own free will or because of orders of the Nazi Gestapo, under the usual Nazi penalties for defiance, these servants of the Vichy Government are plainly performing a definite mission for the German tyrants. They are attempting to undermine our confidence in the British. They ask us to penalize the brave people who are still fighting superbly in behalf of civilization. Theirs is not the voice of the true France we shall always honor and respect but of a defeated and misguided France, led by some of the very traitors who contrived the defeat.

The voice of Ambassador Haye is the voice of Petain, who has bowed to the terror as Hindenburg did in Germany. The voice of Count Rene de Chambrun is the voice of his father-in-law, Laval, the old accomplice of Mussolini. Their words are French but they are only pathetic wooden manikins mouthing the words of the Nazi ventriloquists.

Because we love France and we pray for its restoration as a free nation, we ask our readers to view the words and gestures of the men of Vichy with the suspicion they deserve. They are over here now to plead a cause— that of breaking the British food blockade. They seek to persuade us to lighten the task of the frustrated Nazi "conquerors" and liberate fresh energies for their attack on our civilization. They are over here as the agents of the German government—or as voluntary scavengers in its behalf, hoping to earn a bone from their German masters.

They are asking the American people to be as faithless to democracy and freedom as were those French leaders whose complacency made Vichy the sombre fact it is.

We, the undersigned writers, view with compassion the sufferings of the innocent in Europe, but we know that only the defeat of Hitler will permanently bring hope to their lives. Dedicated as we are by the nature of our task to truth and freedom, we say there is more at stake than temporary physical relief and we urge our countrymen who share our love and respect for the true France to give no heed to the spokesmen of appeasement and betrayal, whether they be agents of a new gestapo or the thinned-out scions of the brave race that once shed its blood for American freedom.

Philip Wylie	Marc Connelly
Robert Sherwood	Christian Gauss
Vincent Sheean	Struthers Burt
Elmer Rice	Van Wyck Brooks
Henry Pringle	Maxwell Anderson
Edna St. Vincent Millay	Frederick Lewis Allen
Lewis Mumford	Herbert Agar

Correspondence between Woodruff Wallner at the State Department and Douglas MacArthur at the U.S. Embassy in Paris (and related letters)

DEPARTMENT OF STATE
WASHINGTON

September 4, 1945

AIR MAIL

CONFIDENTIAL

Dear Doug:

I have obtained the following information concerning René de Chambrun from a French businessman now in the United States on a mission for his Government: My informant states categorically that René de Chambrun is being protected by a "Colonel, Chef d'Etat Major des FFI à Paris" who is also "L'Administrateur Délégué de Coty". I did not press him to name the protector as I thought it would be easy for you to find out who he is. My informant spoke with apparent authority and sincerity. He indicated that René was living with his protector at Garches and that he moves about very little for fear of an act of private revenge. According to my informant this protection is based not on any cash payment made since the occupation but on gratitude for the services rendered in the past to Coty and to the protector personally of René in "Franco-American matters". My informant said that if the other directors of Coty knew how we felt about this matter they would require their colleague to abandon his protection of René.

Upon hearing this information, our good director instructed me to pass it on to you with a view to its being checked and if found correct the best use being made of it. This I do not doubt you will do.

Sincerely,

W. Wallner

Douglas MacArthur, 2nd, Esquire,

Secretary of Embassy,

American Embassy,

Paris.

Letter from Woodruff Wallner of the Department of State's Division of Western European Affairs to Douglas MacArthur, first secretary of the U.S. Embassy in Paris. A more legible transcription follows on next page.

DEPARTMENT OF STATE
WASHINGTON

September 4, 1945

AIR MAIL

CONFIDENTIAL

Dear Doug:

I have obtained the following information concerning René de Chambrun from a French businessman now in the United States on a mission for his Government: My informant states categorically that René de Chambrun is being protected by a "Colonel, Chef d'Etat Major des FTP à Paris" who is also "L'Administrateur Délégué de Coty". I did not press him to name the protector as I thought it would be easy for you to find out who he is. My informant spoke with apparent authority and sincerity. He indicated that René was living with his protector at Garches and that he moves about very little for fear of an act of private revenge. According to my informant this protection is based not on any cash payment made since the occupation but on gratitude for the services rendered in the past to Coty and to the protector personally by René in "Franco-American matters". My informant said that if the other directors of Coty knew how we felt about this matter they would require their colleague to abandon his protection of René.

Upon hearing this information, our good director instructed me to pass it on to you with a view to its being checked and if found correct the best use being made of it. This I do not doubt you will do.

Sincerely,
[signed] Woodie

Douglas MacArthur, 2nd, Esquire,
        Secretary of Embassy,
                American Embassy,
                        Paris.

DEPARTMENT OF STATE
DIVISION OF EUROPEAN AFFAIRS

Confidential

4. September

Dear Doug:

My "informant" in the Rene the Rat affair is Raymond de Balasi, General Manager of Cheris. You will remember him in Vichy, where he met you through the Rifés and the young Cheris couple. He was involved with them, in some of Tom Cassidy's cloak and dagger work. Naturally he does not want his name used, as I presume Coty is a heavy customer of Cheris. Therefore I suggest you disassociate the scrawl from the accompanying typed letter.

Incidentally Mancin is responsible for securing Balasi's willingness to talk about the Rat. Let his him

---

(Above and on next page) Handwritten confidential letter dated September 4, 1945 that was sent with preceding typewritten letter from Woodruff Wallner at the Department of State to Douglas MacArthur at the U.S. Embassy in Paris. A transcription follows.

grounds," he spoke with philosophical bitterness about this and other glaring miscarriages of justice.

The night your Uncle took the Japanese seventh Mania and I finished the Hennessy generously furnished by another MacArthur. We saw a lot of other things too and went shakily to bunk next day at [illegible] the Archbold place. Nichol was in form, but we were much intrigued by the stuffed head and neck of a giraffe which stands in a corner of their château. It is about seven feet tall. We want to have one on casters to wheel silently [illegible] beside the beds of sleeping alcoholic guests.

                        Best to you
                        [signature]

Department of State
DIVISION OF WESTERN EUROPEAN AFFAIRS

CONFIDENTIAL   4 September

Dear Doug:

My "informant" in the Rene the Rat affair is Raymond de Balasi, General Manager of Chiris. You will remember him in Vichy, where he met you through the Rijas and the young Chiris couple. He was involved, with them, in some of Tom Cassidy's cloak and dagger work. Naturally he does not want his name used, as I presume Coty is a heavy customer of Chiris. Therefore I suggest you disassociate this scrawl from the accompanying typed letter.

Incidentally, Monica is responsible for securing Balasi's willingness to talk about the Rat. We had him around, and he spoke with philosophical bitterness about this and other glaring miscarriages of justice.

The night your Uncle took the Japanese surrender, Monica and I finished the Hennessy generously furnished by another MacArthur. We drank a lot of other things too and went shakily to lunch next day at the Archbold place. Michael was in form, but we were much intrigued by the stuffed head and neck of a giraffe which stands in a corner of their château. It is about seven feet tall. We want to have one on casters to wheel silently beside the beds of sleeping alcoholic guests.

Best to you
[signed] Woodie

Paris, September 13, 1945

Dear Woody:

I have received your letter of September 4
and was interested to have further information
concerning "René the Rat". I have passed this
information on to our friend in the Interior and
I am also endeavoring through our CIC people to
obtain more information about the "Colonel, Chef
d'Etat Major des FTP à Paris" who is also "L'Administrateur Délégué de Coty". I am wondering if the
gentleman in question was not a member of the FFI
for as you know the FTP was the militant action arm
of the Communist Party and it occurred to me that
an administrateur délégué of Coty and Company might
possibly not have obtained such a position if he were
a comrade. In any event, please believe that I am
following this matter with great attention.

All the best to you, Jamie and Doc.

Yours ever,

Woodruff Wallner, Esquire,
    Department of State,
        Washington

Letter from Douglas MacArthur to Woodruff Wallner dated September 13, 1945.

Paris, September 13, 1945

MEMORANDUM FOR MR. GREY

Dear Charlie:

    I have received information, which I have not
been able to confirm, that René de Chambrun, son-in-
law of Laval and notorious collaborationist, is
being protected by a "Colonel, Chef d'Etat Major des
FTP à Paris" who is also "L'Administrateur Délégué
de Coty". As you know, our Government is concerned
by the numerous stories circulated in French circles
that de Chambrun is being protected because of the
intervention of the U.S. Government or its representatives in Paris. The Embassy, acting on
instructions from the Department, has informed the
Foreign Ministry that René de Chambrun is entitled
to no American protection, and that the U.S. does
not wish in any way to impede such action as the
French Government may wish to take against René de
Chambrun for his collaborationist activies between
the Armistice of 1940 and the liberation of France.

    Have you any means of ascertaining unofficially
who the "Administrateur Délégué of Coty" might be
who is said to be protecting him? Any other information
you may be able to obtain as to why such a pro-Nazi
and collaborationist individual as René de Chambrun
is going freely about his business in Paris will be
greatly appreciated.

                    DMacA

                        D MacA

Letter from Douglas MacArthur to the head of the Secret Services in France,
Charles Grey.

- copy -

NATIONAL CITY BANK.

January 2, 1947.

My dear Bunny,

This will confirm what I thought it my duty to tell your parents at the time.

Some time after the liberation I met Mr. Mc Arthur of our Embassy in Paris who criticized our Bank for having you in our building and suggested your lease should not be renewed.

My best to Josée and to you,

As always,

Bob.   *R.P.*

(Robert Pearce).

Testimony of Robert Pearce, the president of the National City Bank and owner of the premises of the Chambrun law firm, stating that he had received a visit from Douglas MacArthur of the U.S. Embassy in Paris who suggested that the lease should not be renewed.

Index